REGIONAL BUSINESSES IN A CHANGING GLOBAL ECONOMY

In a highly globalised trade and investment environment, businesses in regional areas must learn to take advantage of the benefits that stem from their geographical location. This book explains the immense value regional businesses bring to local communities and to Australia as a whole through case studies.

The case studies are diverse in nature and highlight how regional businesses utilise their competitive advantage to introduce innovative practices and use local expertise, knowledge, skills, and networks to benefit from local social capital in a synergetic manner.

The case studies in the book will help readers better understand the processes of industrial localisation. The examples of how innovative regional businesses have used innovative practices, local resource leverage, social and entrepreneurial skills and knowledge of international markets to develop and expand their businesses will provide insights into how regional businesses can achieve growth and secure jobs in an innovative and sustained manner.

Quamrul Alam, Professor of International Business and Strategy, School of Business and Law, Central Queensland University, Melbourne, Australia.

Robert Grose, Lecturer, Accounting, School of Business and Law, Central Queensland University, Melbourne, Australia.

'The editors have endeavoured to integrate incredibly interesting interdisciplinary novel concepts and ideas in this book… the book chapters delved into the complex theoretical concepts related to the contemporary business challenges. The cases from different industry sectors are analysed in a reflective manner. These exemplary works are certainly contributory not only to the business students but also to the business academics.'

M Abu Saleh, *Associate Professor of Marketing, Canberra Business School*

'This collection of assorted cases in regional businesses is intended to provide innovative material for the exploration of current business management challenges and trends. This case book will resonate and provides an excellent opportunity for students of business management to understand the complexity of international business on a truly global landscape.'

Professor Prem Yapa, *PhD Coordinator, RMIT University, Melbourne, Australia - Ernst & Young Endowed Professor in Accounting (USJP)*

'In this book, the authors have collected 12 case studies that analyse businesses from diverse sectors to shed light on how innovative strategies and practices have been effectively adopted by managers… I believe that this book provides considerable value for both undergraduate and postgraduate/research students in developing their strategic thinking relating to many of the emerging topics in the business management discipline.'

Professor Amrik Sohal, *Department of Management, Monash Business School, Monash University, Australia*

REGIONAL BUSINESSES IN A CHANGING GLOBAL ECONOMY

The Australian Experience

Edited by Quamrul Alam and Robert Grose

LONDON AND NEW YORK

Cover image: © Manfred Gottschalk / Getty Images

First published 2022
by Routledge
4 Park Square, Milton Park, Abingdon, Oxon OX14 4RN

and by Routledge
605 Third Avenue, New York, NY 10158

Routledge is an imprint of the Taylor & Francis Group, an informa business

© 2022 selection and editorial matter, Quamrul Alam, Robert Grose; individual chapters, the contributors

The right of Quamrul Alam, Robert Grose to be identified as the authors of the editorial material, and of the authors for their individual chapters, has been asserted in accordance with sections 77 and 78 of the Copyright, Designs and Patents Act 1988.

All rights reserved. No part of this book may be reprinted or reproduced or utilised in any form or by any electronic, mechanical, or other means, now known or hereafter invented, including photocopying and recording, or in any information storage or retrieval system, without permission in writing from the publishers.

Trademark notice: Product or corporate names may be trademarks or registered trademarks, and are used only for identification and explanation without intent to infringe.

British Library Cataloguing-in-Publication Data
A catalogue record for this book is available from the British Library

Library of Congress Cataloging-in-Publication Data
Names: Alam, Quamrul, editor. | Grose, Robert, editor.
Title: Regional businesses in a changing global economy: the Australian experience / edited by Quamrul Alam and Robert Grose.
Description: Abingdon, Oxon; New York, NY: Routledge, 2022. | Includes bibliographical references and index.
Identifiers: LCCN 2021048621 (print) | LCCN 2021048622 (ebook) | ISBN 9781032188720 (hardback) | ISBN 9781032188713 (paperback) | ISBN 9781003256717 (ebook)
Subjects: LCSH: Small business–Australia. | Regional planning–Australia. | Regional economics–Australia.
Classification: LCC HD2346.A85 R44 2022 (print) |
LCC HD2346.A85 (ebook) | DDC 338.6/420994–dc23/eng/20211019
LC record available at https://lccn.loc.gov/2021048621
LC ebook record available at https://lccn.loc.gov/2021048622

ISBN: 978-1-03-218872-0 (hbk)
ISBN: 978-1-03-218871-3 (pbk)
ISBN: 978-1-00-325671-7 (ebk)

DOI: 10.4324/9781003256717

Typeset in Bembo
by Newgen Publishing UK

CONTENTS

List of figures vii
List of tables viii
Preface xi
Acknowledgements xiii
List of abbreviations xiv

1 Shifting sands in the regional business environment
   in Australia 1
   Quamrul Alam and Robert Grose

2 Agricultural innovation in a remote setting: Natural
   Evolution company in Far North Queensland 11
   Elena Konovalov

3 Bundaberg Brewed Drinks: regional to global 25
   Quamrul Alam and Rumana Parveen

4 Revival of declining small businesses in Australia 41
   *Sardana Islam Khan, Ho Yin Wong, Tasmiha Tarafder
   and Parves Sultan*

5 Social innovation in health response: a rare case of social
   enterprise meeting rural health needs 59
   *Lisa A. Caffery, Olav T. Muurlink and
   Andrew W. Taylor-Robinson*

6 Return of the bushrangers? Technological determinism
   and the collapse and revival of independent Australian
   rural newspaper publishers   69
   Olav T. Muurlink

7 Mt Buller's snow business   79
   Michael Segon

8 Australia Post: a successful government business enterprise   92
   Quamrul Alam and Robert Grose

9 GBR Helicopters: surviving the downdraft of COVID-19   113
   Malcolm Johnson

10 Australian macadamia industry: a community-supported
   regional industry   118
   Quamrul Alam and Rumana Parveen

11 Harvey Norman: a competitive business model   133
   Quamrul Alam and Robert Grose

12 Human resource management innovation in
   regional Australia   148
   Linda Colley and Upamali Amarakoon

13 The tale of a failed small business   164
   Robert Grose and Tasadduq Imam

14 Conclusion   178
   Quamrul Alam and Robert Grose

Biography of contributors   *184*
Index   *189*

FIGURES

4.1	A flowchart of small business turnaround responses and outcomes	53
8.1	Postal service industry profit as share of revenue 2016–2021	95
8.2	The wage trend in the postal service in Australia	96
8.3	Australian Post's supply chain – end-to-end capability	106
10.1	Australian macadamia production	120
10.2	Australian macadamia export	121
11.1	Franchising model of Harvey Norman	138
11.2	Strategic group map of Harvey Norman competitors in Australia	141
11.3	Omni-channel strategy for Harvey Norman	142

TABLES

3.1	Popular Ginger Beer of UK	28
4.1	Respondent profiles and revival status of 25 declining Australian small businesses	42
4.2	The key concession entitlements of small businesses in Australia	43
4.3a	Factors influencing the turnaround decision of the key manager(s) and responses of a declining small business in Australia	46
4.3b	Summary of findings from the key managers/entrepreneurs of Australian small business	47
5.1	Company overview	61
5.2	Attributes of CHH social enterprise	62
7.1	Comparative information of Alpine resort areas	82
7.2	Economic significance of snow season in Victoria during 2016–2020	84
7.3	Visitor days to Victorian resorts 2011–2020	84
7.4	Summarises the upgrading of lifts, their estimated cost, and their impact on ski capacity	88
8.1	Major players in the industry	94
8.2	Diversity profile of Australia Post workforce	100
8.3	Five-year trend – Australia Post	101
8.4	Performance against targets 2020	108
9.1	Financial status of experience Co	114
10.1	Australian macadamia production and export trend	120
11.1	Harvey Norman's market positions in the retail industry	134

11.2	Differences between Harvey Norman and standard franchise models	138
11.3	Distinguishing features of Harvey Norman's broad differentiation strategy	140
14.1	Business size measured by employment	179
14.2	Businesses by annualised size range	179

PREFACE

In recent years, there have been major changes in the way global business and economic activities have evolved. As the emerging economies of the world assume a greater share of business activity and production relative to advanced economies, local and international businesses are poised to reposition their engagement portfolios. Globalisation and the shifting political and economic landscapes are contributing to significant changes in the mobility of people, urbanisation, resource utilisation, technology usage, and locations of production. In this highly globalised trade and investment environment, attention needs to be given to how businesses in regional areas can take advantage of the benefits that stem from their geographic location. The world and businesses are more connected through trade and movements in the capital, people, and information. With the evolution of communication networks, there is now greater connectivity. Trade and finance have long been part of the globalisation story, but in recent decades there has been a significant shift. Instead of a series of lines connecting major trading hubs in Europe and North America, the global trading systems have expanded into a complex, intricate, and sprawling web. Asia is becoming the world's largest trading region. "South-South" flows between emerging markets have doubled their share of global trade over the past decade. The challenges of the post-global financial crisis have forced businesses and countries to be innovative. The links forged by technology have ushered in a dynamic new phase of globalisation, creating unmatched opportunities and yet at the same time provoking unexpected volatility. The COVID-19 pandemic is an example of a phenomenon that has disrupted the global business value chain.

This case book aims to illustrate the immense value regional businesses bring to regional communities and to Australia as a whole. The cases in this book investigate how regional businesses in Australia have used their present competitive advantage to introduce innovative practices, develop networks, and use the skills of the local workforce to establish healthy local businesses that use local social capital.

An analysis of the success stories, challenges, and failures will assist academics and researchers to theorise how the development of regional businesses can achieve growth and secure jobs in an innovative and sustained manner.

In recently published management and international business texts, most studies focus on large US and European-based companies and their affiliates. The contextual relevance of these cases is different to that which exists in Australia. The disappearance of the unipolar global economy, the rise of BRICS economies, the post-global financial crisis, the signing of various free trade agreements, BREXIT, and the COVID-19 pandemic have significantly changed the international and domestic business environment. The mobility of people, skill shortages in Australia, the introduction of temporary workers in the agricultural sector in Australia, and the mobility of knowledge and capital have created new economic growth centres. Companies are now setting up their businesses in regional locations. The strategic importance of this trend and the need for a better understanding of the business challenges prompted us to develop a case book to examine this strategic change. This book will assist the reader to better understand the processes of industrial locations and the emergence of new value-adding activities. Authors from numerous disciplines have sought to explain how firms in regional Australia can foster and develop regional economic growth and grow local and export markets.

Another reason for putting together this case book is to offer students an opportunity to understand the impact of recent global financial and trade issues affecting regional businesses in different industry sectors. We believe that this book provides students with a critical analytical framework for examining the business and management issues confronting managers in regional Australia. The case study approach to business strategy analysis is an exercise in learning by doing, as this mode of learning provides students with detailed contextual information about changes and opportunities in different industries and companies. The cases have been selected to help students improve their analytical skills and expose them to real-world situations in which company managers perform their strategic responsibilities. This book will certainly introduce the innovative and unique features of Australian regional businesses to academics, researchers, and students and help them to understand that distance is not an issue. How you do business is important, not where you do it from.

Quamrul Alam
Robert Grose
September 2021, Melbourne, Australia

ACKNOWLEDGEMENTS

The compilation of a book like this is possible only due to the untiring efforts and sincere dedication of the authors and others who assisted me. Among many, persons who have been instrumental in seeing this book project through are Adjunct Professor Julian Teicher, CQUniversity, Associate Professor Michael Segon, Director MBA Program, College of Business, School of Business and Law, CQUniversity, and Dr Robert Grose (co-editor). Our sincere thanks go to our postgraduate students for their insight and enthusiasm in asking critical questions, providing information, participating in case discussions, and making suggestions. We would also like to express our sincere appreciation and thanks to Dr Margaret Ellis, Kasey Bion, Md Azad Khan, and AKM Fazlul Haque who have collected data and helped us – often at short notice. Last, but not least, we are indebted to Rumana (Annie) Parveen for her considerable help at various stages in preparing the manuscript for submission. We want to thank all the authors for telling stories of regional and rural Australian businesses from their individual perspectives.

My sincere thanks to Professor Lee Di Milia, Dean, School of Business and Law, Central Queensland University and Professor Peter Best, Head of College of Business, who have permitted me to take time and work on this book. I am grateful to Routledge (Taylor & Francis Group) for publishing this book. The publisher's contribution and support are even more important at this crucial time for the world.

Professor Quamrul Alam
College of Business
School of Business and Law
Central Queensland University, Australia
10 September 2021

ABBREVIATIONS

ABC	Australian Broadcasting Corporation
ABS	Australian Bureau of Statistics
ACCC	Australian Competition and Consumer Commission
AFR	Australian Financial Review
AIHW	Australian Institute of Health and Welfare
AMHA	Australian Macadamia Handlers Association
AMA	Australian Medical Association
ASIC	Australian Securities and Investment Commission
ATO	Australian Tax Office
ATMs	Automatic teller machines
BBD	Bundaberg Brewed Drinks
CHDC	Central Highlands Development Corporation
CHH	Central Highlands Healthcare
CEO	Chief executive officer
CSR	Colonial Sugar Refiners
CSO	Community Service Obligations
DPID	Delivery point identifier
DSITI	Department of Science, Information Technology and Innovation
EU	European Union
EIS	Extended identity services
FNQ	Far North Queensland
FY	Financial year
FDI	Foreign direct investment
FITs	Free and independent travellers
FTA	Free trade agreement
GP	General Practitioner
GST	Goods and Services Tax

GBE	Government Business Enterprise
GBR	*Great Barrier Reef*
GDP	Gross Domestic Product
HN	Harvey Norman
HIA	Horticulture Innovation Australia
HR	Human resource
IT	Information Technology
MFM	Macadamia Farm Management
MNEs	Multinational enterprises
NBN	National Broadband Network
NSW	New South Wales
NIS	Nut In Shell
PMG	Postmaster General's Department
R&D	Research and Development
RBA	Reserve Bank of Australia
RTA	Revival and Turnaround
SIP	pirit International Prestige
SDGs	Sustainable development goals
TFN	Tax File Number
AMS	The Australian Macadamia Society Limited
MCT	The Macadamia Conservation Trust
TMT	Top management team
TTIP	Transatlantic Trade and Investment Partnership
TPP	Trans-Pacific Partnership
UK	United Kingdom
UNCTAD	United Nations Conference on Trade and Development
USA	United States of America
WTO	World Trade Organization

1
SHIFTING SANDS IN THE REGIONAL BUSINESS ENVIRONMENT IN AUSTRALIA

Quamrul Alam and Robert Grose

Introduction

In recent years, there have been major changes in the global location of economic activity. As emerging economies assume a greater share of economic activity and production relative to the advanced economies of the world, local and international businesses are poised to reposition their engagement portfolios. Globalisation and shifting political and economic landscapes are contributing to significant changes in populations, urbanisation, resource utilisation, technology, the internationalisation of production locations, and stakeholder attitudes. The transformation of international production systems creates opportunities for development such as promoting resilience-seeking investment, building regional value chains, and entering new markets through digital platforms. To capture these opportunities a shift in business strategy development and adaptive and innovative management practices is required. Finding cost-effective factors of production, resources, and low-cost labour will remain important. But the pool of such investment is shrinking, and a degree of rebalancing towards growth based on domestic and regional demand and promoting investment in infrastructure and domestic services is paramount (United Nations Conference on Trade and Development, UNCTAD, 2020).

In such a highly globalised trade and investment environment, attention needs to be given to how businesses in regional areas can take advantage of the benefits that stem from their geographical location. The world and businesses are more connected through trade and movements in capital, people, and information. With the evolution of communication networks, there is now greater connectivity. The rise and role of non-profit organisations and civil society groups increase the pressure on business enterprises to comply with international standards of human rights and labour laws. Trade and finance have long been part of the globalisation story but, in recent decades, there has been a significant shift. Instead of a series of lines connecting major trading hubs in Europe and North America, the global trading systems have expanded into a complex, intricate, sprawling web. Asia is becoming the world's largest trading region. 'South-South' interactions between emerging markets have doubled their share of global trade over the past decade.

Business context

Australia, as a highly functional capitalist economy, is geographically very close to the Asian growing economies. This geographic proximity has offered opportunities to Australian businesses and created challenges too. The challenges of the post-global financial crisis have forced businesses to move out of Australia creating huge disruption in the local supply chain network. The links forged by technology have ushered in a dynamic new phase of globalisation, creating unmatched opportunities and, yet at the same time, provoking unexpected volatility. Businesses need to be proactive, resilient, and innovative and reposition themselves in such a constantly changing business environment.

The changes in the regional location of economic activity have occurred primarily through the growth of locally owned firms in emerging economies and through increased foreign direct investment (FDI) by multinational enterprises (MNEs) from advanced economies. The proliferation of outsourcing arrangements, coordinated by firms in advanced economies, has also influenced these changes. MNEs from emerging markets are using cross-border arrangements to acquire strategic and natural resources. Businesses from emerging economies like Asia are looking to penetrate the Australian market. In today's business environment firms reach across borders to fill capability gaps caused by limited access to strategic resources such as technology, management capabilities, raw material and other intangible assets not readily available in their home markets.

Economic integration through free trade agreements (FTAs) receives mixed responses from different industries because some sectors have gained a significant competitive advantage from these initiatives while other sectors have faced challenges. As different regions possess locational attractiveness for different business activities, economic integration will further accelerate the transformation of the Australian economic geography. According to the World Investment Report 2016, China will be home to more large companies than either the US or Europe by 2025. Companies with revenue of $1 billion or more will move to emerge markets as growth has moved to Asia, Latin America, and the Middle East.

New realities

It is noticeable that the locus of economic activity is shifting to emerging markets. The urban population has been rising globally by an average of 65 million people annually during the past three decades. Nearly half of global Gross Domestic Product (GDP) growth between 2010 and 2025 will come from 440 cities in emerging markets – 95% of them from small- and medium-sized cities (Dobbs,

Manyika, & Woetzel, 2015). Cities like Mumbai, Dubai, and Shanghai are familiar. New cities like Hsinchu, in northern Taiwan; Brazil's Santa Catarina state, halfway between São Paulo and the Uruguayan border; and Tianjin, a city that lies around 120 kilometres southeast of Beijing, have attracted international companies due to sourcing efficiency, opportunity, and resources. These changes have restructured the world economy and the locational advantages. As a result, businesses in regional locations need to reconfigure their resource capability so that ownership and locational advantages match the market conditions.

Technological development has become a disruptive force. The speed of change, scale, and economic impact of technology are enormous. The proliferation of technology-enabled business models, from online retail platforms like Alibaba to car-hailing apps like Uber, click-collect e-platform, has threatened the old business models. It took more than 50 years after the telephone was invented until half of the American homes had one. It took radio 38 years to attract 50 million listeners (Dobbs, Ramaswamy, Stephenson & Vigueri, 2014) . But Facebook attracted six million users in its first year, and that number multiplied 100 times over the next five years. China's mobile text and voice messaging service WeChat has 300 million users, more than the entire adult population of the US. Technology offers the promise of economic progress in all economies at a speed that would have been unimaginable without the mobile internet. Twenty years ago, less than 3% of the world's population had a mobile phone; now two-thirds of the world's population has one, and one-third of all humans can communicate on the internet. Technology allows businesses such as WhatsApp, Messenger, Zoom, and Microsoft Teams to start and gain scale with stunning speed while using little capital. Entrepreneurs and start-ups now frequently enjoy advantages over large, established businesses. The furious pace of technological adoption and innovation is shortening the life cycle of companies and forcing executives to make decisions and commit resources much more quickly. In Bangladesh, 120 million people have a mobile phone. Most of the areas of Bangladesh are now in mobile network coverage. Five international mobile operators are working in Bangladesh, and they have reached every corner of the country (Rahman, Abdullah, Haroon, & Tooheen, 2013).

There is an urgent imperative for businesses to adjust to these new realities. International knowledge sourcing has for a long period been a hot topic in the innovation studies literature. Scholars in this tradition initially debated on the magnitude of this phenomenon (Cantwell, 1995; Patel & Pavitt, 1991), while converging on the idea that international knowledge sourcing is a 'North-North' phenomenon with Research and Development (R&D) FDI departing from advanced countries and targeting other advanced countries (Arvanitis & Hollenstein, 2011; Cantwell & Piscitello, 2000). As a result, the hierarchy of foreign R&D locations concerns mainly advanced country locations (Cantwell & Janne, 1999; Patel & Vega, 1999), which are ranked on the ground of technology and R&D activity-specific advantages (Dunning & Narula, 1995; Florida, 1997; Pearce & Papanastassiou, 1999). Innovation studies research has also suggested that R&D internationalisation increasingly aims at sourcing knowledge abroad to complement and enhance knowledge production at home (Almeida, 1996; Cantwell & Santangelo, 2001). A significant change has occurred: emerging economies are now major host locations of R&D offshoring. R&D FDI departs from advanced countries and targets primarily emerging economies, which are now top-ranked in the hierarchy of foreign R&D locations (Contractor, Kumar, Kundu & Pedersen, 2010; D'Agostino, Laursen & Santangelo, 2013; UNCTAD, 2005). The offshoring of R&D by firms originating in emerging economies is increasing too. The target is advanced countries (UNCTAD, 2005; Von Zedtwitz & Gassmann, 2002). Thus, the emergence of new locations and players has transformed knowledge sourcing from a cross-border to a truly global phenomenon.

These recent developments raise questions related to the effective possibility of 'traditional' actors to source knowledge in 'non-traditional' locations as well as the effective capability of 'non-traditional' actors to source knowledge in 'traditional' locations (Athreye & Cantwell, 2007; Lewin, Massini & Peeters, 2009). Although emerging economies are experiencing an upgrading of technological capabilities and enjoy a large number of available talents, the ability of these new locations to develop state-of-the-art knowledge remains open to debate (Von Zedtwitz & Gassmann, 2002). Specifically, a critical issue concerns the type of knowledge and R&D activities that are more likely to be sourced and located in emerging economies. The new international division of labour in knowledge production and the global mobility of skills and capital have emerged as important determinants of business decision strategy (Fifarek & Veloso, 2010; Moncada-Paternò-Castello, Vivarelli & Voigt, 2011).

There is some evidence that firms located in fast-growing emerging economies invest in developed economies with the intent to seek technology (Athreye & Kapur, 2009). The mobility of capital from North to South, South to North, and South to South challenges the traditional view of the FDI phenomenon. The most recent FDI patterns reveal that emerging economies are now top-ranked in the hierarchy of foreign R&D locations. Businesses from developed countries need to be strategic in positioning themselves to effectively source knowledge in 'non-traditional' locations. Recent research points to a new international division of labour in knowledge production challenging the 'North-North' pattern. International businesses need to be very strategic to devise business development strategies to select the type of knowledge and R&D activities they should outsource and what type needs to be kept at home. How to develop interaction mechanisms between offshored and home-based R&D activities has become a business challenge.

The changing nature of the international economy suggests that speed and innovation are critical factors for business success. The ability to innovate quickly and cheaply, respond to customers' feedback, and reposition products and services regularly have become a necessity for businesses to remain competitive (Bhens, Lau & Markovitch, 2015). Business capabilities to continuously produce new products and integration of IT operations can reduce product-testing times from weeks to minutes and increase companies' speed to market. This practice can significantly reduce the cost of delivering new products and services.

The recent trend of FTAs between developed and emerging economies has become an opportunity and a challenge for businesses interested in global positioning. Due to globalisation, tariffs, and non-tariffs, barriers are dramatically reduced compared to decades ago, thus increasing the movement of goods, services, and capital globally. The World Trade Organization (WTO) promotes free trade and has played a crucial role in unifying the rules and setting up the multilateral regime (Krueger, 1999). However, preferential trade agreements are still possible and legitimate provided that protection against outside states is not increased. Due to the faltering negotiation at Doha in WTO, countries resort to alternatives like FTAs or regional integration rather than a unified multinational agreement for their business (Kawai & Wignaraja, 2011). FTAs aim to decrease trade barriers among the members involved, thus promoting international trade and economic development. Many FTAs are enforced, and there are mega-FTAs like Transatlantic Trade and Investment Partnership (TTIP) and Trans-Pacific Partnership (TPP) currently under negotiation. FTAs have become more complex than just two countries signing agreements. FTAs could happen between two (Japan and Australia) or more countries (NAFTA, EFTA, and ASEAN), one country and a region (EU-Korea Free Trade Agreement and ongoing TTIP), or one region and another region (the halted European Union and Mercosur FTA negotiation). FTAs have become something very desirable for a country for getting a favourable position in world trade activities.

Market access is a significant reason driving the increasing emergence of FTAs. FTAs provide a faster and more flexible tool for promoting trade among member states compared to the halted multilateral negotiations. Countries themselves could actively choose which country to negotiate and determine how far the negotiations should go. By reducing the tariff and non-tariff barriers, members within the agreement could attain a price advantage compared to the outside member states that are faced with higher tariffs or inhibited by regulations and policies. With better access to the market, trade gains are created between member states (Baier & Bergstrand, 2004). Also, the price advantage for foreign firms brings lower-priced and more diverse products for consumers. Baier and Bergstrand's (2004) empirical research related to the Heckscher-Ohlin endowment theory suggests that different factor endowment among the member states could be one of the factors that lead to a higher probability of FTAs. FTAs that reduce the barriers could assist member states in promoting further specialisation in goods, with comparative advantage brought by the factor endowment.

As for capital movement, the formation of FTAs increases the intra-flow and inter-flow of capital within the trading bloc, though sometimes the trade and investment divert from a lower-cost country outside the bloc to a country within it (Krueger, 1999). Internally, tariff reduction pushes business expansion, which attracts intra FDI either for the market itself or resources embedded in that market. FTAs provide some member states location advantage for attracting FDI due to their preferential market access to other member states in the bloc (the effect of trade deflection). Also, the trading bloc could work as a whole in attracting FDI, thanks to the low tariff in the transactions within the bloc. ASEAN, as a manufacturing hub (along with China), shows a significant increase in trade of intermediate products within the bloc (Baldwin, 2011). FTAs are crucial in paving the way for production networks and supply chain coordination in this region (Kawai & Wignaraja, 2011). The interconnectedness of the production and business activities becomes an incentive for investment in the bloc.

These advantages between members, however, may result in welfare loss to non-member states, which lose their trade to the acceded states. As the FTAs incorporate more members, the outsiders are cornered into a more uncompetitive situation. The discrimination by FTAs against outsiders prompts more countries to join or negotiate their own FTAs, forming a domino effect in world trade (Baldwin & Jaimovich, 2012). The effects of FTAs on world trade, in the long run, are ambiguous. Some argue that the broadening of FTAs promotes trade liberalisation, while others fear that the trading blocs may entail protectionism and fragmentation keeping discriminative external tariffs high for the rest of the world (Krueger, 1999). The rise of FTAs will significantly change the trade and investment regime, industry structure, labour relationship, labour market practices, and tariff structure.

Tax avoidance practices by MNES have become an important global issue. G20 countries are in discussion to find a solution. Tax avoidance and profit shifting can have a negative impact on sustainable business development. Developing countries are not equipped to deal with tax avoidance practices. This is a business ethics issue that needs to be seriously considered by global businesses, as tax avoidance practices by MNEs lead to loss of government revenue in both developed and developing countries. In anti-tax avoidance discussions, investment policies are considered as a part of a problem. The role of investment in building the corporate structures that enable tax avoidance is an issue that is highly debated in various forums (UNCTAD, 2016).

Cases in this book will help students to understand the evolving nature of the complex business environment in which regional businesses operate. The cases included in this book have unique business models, management practices, and innovative value-lidden cultures that require analysis, judgement, and customised strategy actions. Cases provide the student with a critical analytical framework for examining the business and management issues confronted by managers in a company. The case study approach to business strategy analysis is an exercise in learning by doing, as this mode of learning provides students with detailed contextual information about the changes and opportunities for different industries and companies in various countries. Case analysis helps students improve their analytical skills and exposes them to the real situations in which company managers perform their strategic responsibilities.

Unprecedented challenge

The last 12 months have been unprecedented in the scale and speed of changes impacting businesses, from the 2019 to 2020 Australian bushfire season starting in late 2019, through to the COVID-19 pandemic impacting Australia from March 2020. These events have impacted businesses in different ways; some industries have been heavily restricted (for example, the tourism industry resulting from bushfire evacuations and border closures due to COVID-19); yet for others, this has been a period of growth or innovation. During this time, there have been many policy announcements, particularly by the Commonwealth and State governments, aimed at supporting businesses. There have also been a variety of government restrictions implemented to help control the spread of COVID-19 (ABS, 2021).

The COVID-19 crisis has caused a serious impact on business investment and disrupted the global value chain. Global FDI flows decreased by up to 40% in 2020, from their 2019 value of $1.54 trillion. It is projected that FDI flow will decrease by a further 5%–10% in 2021 which will represent a 60% decline since 2015, from $2 trillion to less than $900 billion (UNCTAD, 2020). This trend will have a significant impact on businesses in the regional areas due to the cumulative impact of this global shift in investment. It seems that the pandemic is likely to have lasting effects on investment decisions and may reinforce more restrictive measures for foreign investment in some industries (UNCTAD, 2020). This restrictive investment regime will affect regional businesses that are linked with the domestic economic value chain.

As the COVID-19 pandemic wears on, its impact is obviously felt in every region, every industry, and indeed every aspect of life. Nonetheless, some of the pandemic's side effects still have the power to surprise. There has been an explosion in the number of online business transactions, consumers choose to products and services, the acceleration of home-based work practices that reshaped the human resource management practices, changes in buying behaviour, rise of home delivery services, options to purchase online using click and collect e-platform resulting in a huge decline of cash as part of everyday business transaction. According to Australia Post Report (2021), Online shopping growth for the 12 months to 30 June 2021 landed at 31.8% year-on-year (YOY) - almost on par with the previous financial year (33.2%). For the first time in Australian eCommerce history, participation passed the nine million household mark. A total of 9.1 million households purchased online in FY21.

COVID-19 changed how businesses work today. Businesses have moved rapidly to deploy digital and automation technologies. Work went remote, shopping, entertainment, and even medicine went online, and businesses everywhere scrambled to deploy digital systems to accommodate the shifts. These changes in consumer behaviour and business models will persist in metropolitan and regional areas after the pandemic recedes. The pandemic has reshaped the future of work, consumer behaviour, and business management practices. When lockdowns forced consumers to remain at home, e-commerce experienced huge growth in the volume of online demands. Businesses in some sectors were quick to adopt innovative practices to cater for the demands. Regional businesses are required to find alternatives to be connected with this disruptive supply chain network.

It is obvious that the next normal is going to be different. It will not mean going back to the conditions that prevailed in 2019. Indeed, just as the terms 'prewar' and 'postwar' are commonly used to describe the 20th century, generations to come will likely discuss the pre-COVID-19 and post-COVID-19 eras (Lund, Madgavkar, Mischke & Remes, 2021).

Conclusion

This book will assist students and researchers in understanding the processes of industrial localisation. Myriad theories with origins in numerous disciplines have sought to explain how firms in the regional areas can foster regional economic growth through supporting SMEs and increasing the internationalisation of export sector businesses. The case book includes business cases to highlight the background, innovation, local resource leverage, social and entrepreneurial skills, and knowledge of local and international markets used by these businesses. The analysis of the success stories will assist readers in theorising how locational advantages can be used by businesses to withstand competitive pressure and achieve growth in an innovative and sustained manner. The COVIDisation of the world economy has forced organisations around the world to reevaluate many aspects of management and work practices, workforce composition, and workplace layout to avoid risks and avail opportunities.

References

Almeida, P. (1996). Knowledge sourcing by foreign multinationals: Patent citation analysis in the US semiconductor industry, Strategic *Management Journal, 17*(S2), 155–165.

Arvanitis, S. & Hollenstein, H. (2011). How do different drivers of R&D investment in foreign locations affect domestic firm performance? An analysis based on Swiss panel micro data. *Industrial and Corporate Change, 20*(2), 605–640.

Athreye, S. & Cantwell, J. (2007). Creating competition? Globalisation and the emergence of new technology producers. *Research Policy, 36*(2), 209–226.

Athreye, S. & Kapur, S. (2009). Introduction: The internationalization of Chinese and Indian firms — Trends, motivations and strategy. *Industrial and Corporate Change, 18*(2), 209–221.

Australian Bureau of Statistics (ABS) (2021). Household impacts of Covid19 survey. Available at: www.abs.gov.au/statistics/people/people-and-communities/household-impacts-covid-19-survey/latest-release

Baier, S. L. & Bergstrand, J. H. (2004). Economic determinants of free trade agreements. *Journal of International Economics, 64*(1), 29–63.

Baldwin, R. (2011). 21st century regionalism: Filling the gap between 21st century trade and 20th century trade rules. World Trade Organization (WTO), Economic Research and Statistics Division, Geneva.

Baldwin, R. & Jaimovich, D. (2012). Are free trade agreements contagious? *Journal of International Economics, 88*(1), 1–16.

Bhens, S., Lau, L. & Markovitch, S. (2015). Finding the speed to innovate. *McKinsey Quarterly*, McKinsey & Company, 3 (April 1).

Cantwell, J. (1995). The globalisation of technology: What remains of the product cycle model? *Cambridge Journal of Economics, 19*(1), 155–174.

Cantwell, J. & Janne, O. (1999). Technological globalisation and innovative centres: The role of corporate technological leadership and locational hierarchy. *Research Policy, 28*(2), 119–144.

Cantwell, J. & Piscitello, L. (2000). Accumulating technological competence: Its changing impact on corporate diversification and internationalization. *Industrial and Corporate Change, 9*(1), 21–51.

Cantwell, J. & Santangelo, G. D. (2001). Capitalism, profits and innovation in the new techno-economic paradigm. *Journal of Evolutionary Economics, 10*(131–157).

Contractor, F. J., Kumar, V., Kundu, S. K. & Pedersen, T. (2010). Reconceptualizing the firm in a world of outsourcing and offshoring: The organizational and geographical relocation of high-value company functions, *Journal of Management Studies, 47*(8), 1417–1433.

d'Agostino, L. M., Laursen, K., & Santangelo, G. D. (2013). The impact of R&D offshoring on the home knowledge production of OECD investing regions. *Journal of Economic Geography, 13*(1), 145–175.

Dobbs, R., Ramaswamy, S., Stephenson, E., & Viguerie, S. P. (2014). Management intuition for the next 50 years. *McKinsey Quarterly, 1*, 1–13.

Dobbs, R., Manyika, J., & Woetzel, J. (2015). The four global forces breaking all the trends. *McKinsey Global Institute, 11*(4), 1–5.

Dunning, J. H., & Narula, R. (1995). The R&D activities of foreign firms in the United States. *International Studies of Management & Organization, 25*(1–2), 39–74.

Fifarek, B. J., & Veloso, F. M. (2010). Offshoring and the global geography of innovation. *Journal of Economic Geography, 10*(4), 559–578.

Florida, R. (1997). The globalization of R&D: Results of a survey of foreign-affiliated R&D laboratories in the USA. *Research Policy, 26*(1), 85–103.

Kawai, M. & Wignaraja, G. (2011). Asian FTAs: Trends, prospects and challenges. *Journal of Asian Economics, 22*(1), 1–22.

Krueger, A. O. (1999). Are preferential trading arrangements trade-liberalizing or protectionist? *The Journal of Economic Perspectives, 13*(4), 105–124.

Lewin, A. Y., Massini, S., & Peeters, C. (2009). Why are companies offshoring innovation? The emerging global race for talent. *Journal of International Business Studies, 40*(6), 901–925.

Lund, S., Madgavkar, A., Mischke, J. & Remes, J. (2021). What's next for consumers, workers, and companies in the post-COVID-19 recovery. McKinsey Global Institute. Available at: www.mckinsey.com/~/media/mckinsey/featured%20insights/future%20of%20organizations/whats%20next%20for%20consumers%20workers%20and%20companies%20in%20the%20post%20covid%2019%20recovery/whats-next-for-consumers-workers-companies-post-covid-recovery.pdf?shouldIndex=false

Moncada-Paternò-Castello, P., Vivarelli, M., & Voigt, P. (2011). Drivers and impacts in the globalization of corporate R&D: An introduction based on the European experience. *Industrial and Corporate Change, 20*(2), 585–603.

Patel, P. & Pavitt, K. (1991). Large firms in the production of the world's technology: An important case of non-globalisation. *Journal of International Business Studies, 22*(1), 1–21.

Patel, P. & Vega, M. (1999). Patterns of internationalisation of corporate technology: Location vs. home country advantages. *Research Policy, 28*(2), 145–155.

Pearce, R. & Papanastassiou, M. (1999). Overseas R&D and the strategic evolution of MNEs: Evidence from laboratories in the UK. *Research Policy, 28*(1), 23–41.

Rahman, A., Abdullah, M. N., Haroon, A., & Tooheen, R. B. (2013). ICT impact on socio-economic conditions of rural Bangladesh. *Journal of World Economic Research, 2*(1), 1–8.

UNCTAD (2005). World Investment Report, 2005: Transnational Corporations and the Internationalization of R&D, UNCTAD, New York and Geneva.

UNCTAD (2016). World Investment Report 2015: Reforming International Investment Governance, Division on Investment and Enterprise, UNCTAD, New York and Geneva.

UNCTAD (2020). World Investment Report: International Production Beyond the Pandemic, 2020.

Von Zedtwitz, M. & Gassmann, O. (2002). Market versus technology drive in R&D internationalization: Four different patterns of managing research and development. *Research Policy*, *31*(4), 569–588.

2
AGRICULTURAL INNOVATION IN A REMOTE SETTING

Natural Evolution company in Far North Queensland

Elena Konovalov

Introduction

Regional and remote communities and businesses, including agricultural enterprises, are facing a multitude of challenges such as high unemployment rates, limited economic diversity, out-migration to urban metro centres, and fading of traditional industries (Haines, 2016). Entrepreneurship and innovation are seen as key conditions for overcoming these obstacles and ensuring continuing vitality and development of Australian regions. In this view, this chapter will discuss a case of exceptional innovation of a product and production technology pioneered in Far North Queensland.

In 2010, a farming couple from a small rural town in Far North Queensland with a population of 630 started a journey towards developing and marketing a new product, previously not represented in the market that has the potential to become a new food staple worldwide. They developed a green banana flour product from Lady Finger banana variety and associated 'NutroLock' technology for producing it. Previously, even though banana flour was known to the world, it was never produced commercially in large quantities. This type of flour is gluten-free and the richest source of resistance starch (at 40%), which is linked to improving colon health, assisting in the treatment of diabetes as well as lowering cholesterol and triglyceride levels, increasing absorption of minerals and production of serotonin, and improving immune system overall (Department of Science, Information Technology and Innovation, DSITI, 2015). Furthermore, the production of the flour utilises 'waste' bananas that do not meet criteria set by supermarkets, which amounts to astonishing 500,000 tonnes a year in Australia alone (DSITI, 2015). Australia accounts for only 1% of the global banana supply and bananas are the fourth largest agricultural croup in the world (TEDx JCUCairns, 2017). Thus, the developed product combined properties of superfood and sustainable wasteless practices of a circular economy.

DOI: 10.4324/9781003256717-2

This chapter will present the company's history, its products and services, present strategies, and challenges they encountered. The journey of this entrepreneurial family provides many lessons that will be useful for fostering other innovation initiatives in regional Australia.

Company/Business history

Coming from a farming family, the founder of the business Robert (Rob) Watkins has a strong farming philosophy and believes that healthy soil and plants are vital to ultimate nutrition (Natural Evolution Foods, 2019). Rob's family has been growing bananas for many years, specialising in premium Lady Finger variety. Growing this variety is more demanding as compared with ordinary Cavendish bananas; it requires 25%–30% more labour and due to its height 50% fewer plants can be planted per acre.

As they say, necessity is the mother of invention. And true to the outback North Queensland spirit, Rob was always thinking about innovative and effective solutions to his farming problems. In 2008, he designed 'Banana Blankey', a fully recyclable polypropylene carton insert. Banana Blankies reduced costs, handling, and plastic packaging that were required for transporting bananas. The blankies cushioned bananas on their sometimes up to 15,000 km long transporting journey and then were collected and recycled. This invention was featured on Australian Broadcasting Corporation (ABC)'s new inventors show in 2009 and Rob took out the episode winner title. Rob continued innovating and designed machinery specifically for banana harvesting and maintenance. In 2010, for his inventions, he was crowned Young Farmer of the year (O'Sullivan, 2010).

Another challenge that Rob faced in his day-to-day operations on the family farm was that he was discarding tonnes of valuable and perfectly fine bananas as they did not fit strict supermarkets standards. It is estimated that in Australia every week approximately 500 tonnes of bananas get wasted as they do not conform to the supermarket guidelines (Natural Evolution Foods, 2019).

One day a small mishap led to a breakthrough. Rob accidentally drove his truck over a bunch of green Lady Finger bananas that were left in the sun for a few days. He then noticed that it resulted in some white powder and immediately started wondering if this could be some flour. His inquisitive nature led to experimenting with different methods of turning green Lady Finger bananas into flour and before long a small production line was established in the family garage resulting in about 6 kg of banana flour a week. The gluten-free banana flour was sold through the family café, and within the first three weeks demand surpassed the 6 kg a week production. Producing the flour was quite labour intensive as green bananas are very hard to peel. This was another problem that required an out of the box innovative solution.

The ever-increasing demand for the product inspired Rob to refine the production process. Hand peeling green bananas was labour intensive, uneconomical, and prone to accidents. Rob put all his efforts into designing the first-ever banana peeling machine in the world. This was the only way to make the product economically viable and secure an opportunity in the market. The designed machine increased the output to approximately 300 kg of flour per week; however, this was still behind the increasing demand for the product.

Potential of growth

Further development required a significant financial investment. In 2014, Rob was successful in obtaining a $996,270 grant from Commercialisation Australia for establishing the first-ever factory for producing pharmaceutical-grade banana flour (Department of Industry and Science, 2014). The new $3.8 million facilities were established in Walkamin and are producing approximately 2–5 tonnes of pharmaceutical-grade banana flour a week. This patented technology can turn green bananas into powder in under 25 minutes, compared to a much longer conventional drying process.

In 2015, Natural Evolution company was born for selling innovative products developed by the entrepreneurial couple. Natural Evolution Foods is devoted to developing and promoting natural, nutritional, gluten-free superfoods and distributing these products worldwide. Now the company has received requests for purchasing NutroLock technology licence from Africa, Asia and Pacific regions, and is focusing on exploring these new opportunities. The developed mechanical process facilitates the production of up to 1 tonne of powder every eight hours.

Following the success of banana flour, the couple further invested in research and development and developed Banana Ointment, which they regard as 'possibly the largest natural medicine breakthrough we will see in the world' (Natural Evolution Foods, 2019). The ointment possesses anti-bacterial, anti-fungal, and anti-inflammatory qualities and was developed out of a need to treat farming dogs that frequently developed bacterial infections in hot and humid North Queensland climate. The first batch of ointment was developed in a Terminix and had incredible results of stopping the spread of the infections after one application and speeding up healing ten times. After such success, the ointment was used to heal burns, cuts, rashes, and other skin conditions on the farm. Through word of mouth, the information about the ointment spread out and before long the couple was receiving inquiries from North America. Once again, the demand for the product was growing fast and this led to the introduction of the banana ointment to the market. The ointment can be applied to arthritic pains, spurs, wart/sunspot removal and intensive healing, nappy rash, burns, blisters, minor cuts and abrasions, fungal and bacterial skin infections (Natural Evolution Foods, 2019).

The couple's innovative products and practices are well recognised, and they won numerous awards. Among many awards and prizes received by their business is The Innovation in Sustainable Technologies Award, Banksia Food for Sustainable

Thought Award, The Tropical North Queensland Innovation Award, and the prestigious Peter Kenny Medal (Growcom, 2019; Queensland Agriculture, 2018).

In 2017, NutroLock technology that was developed by Rob for producing green banana flour won the prestigious international Edison Award (Gold in Food and Beverage category). These awards that were established in 1987 by the American Marketing Association honour best of the best among world's companies, inventors and academics for their innovation and business success (Edison Awards, 2017). NutroLock is the world first food preservation technology that utilises and processes nutritious food that otherwise would be thrown away due to its appearance or oversupply on the market. Compared to conventional food processing techniques, the NutroLock process has improved nutritional preservation by 20%–50%. The received recognition demonstrates the significance of this technological breakthrough and its future potential to significantly reduce food waste.

In 2018, Krista won the AgriFutures Australian Rural Woman of the Year award (National winner) due to the international recognition of the innovative banana flour products that reduced food waste (AgriFutures Australia, 2018). Krista used her $10,000 bursary to engage with Tablelands sweet potatoes farmers and research alternative use of unsellable produce (AgriFutures Australia, 2018). The award has provided Krista with opportunities to further develop professionally, grow her professional networks, and have the confidence to take on new opportunities and new markets for her business.

Banana flour produced by the farming couple is sold nationwide as well as distributed overseas (Business Enterpreneurs' Program, 2017). The production utilises otherwise discarded green bananas that were grown with dedication and valuable resources and provides banana farmers with a new market for their produce. However, the current supply is still way behind the market demand and there are further opportunities for development and innovation nationally and internationally.

Currently, the Watkins' pharmaceutical grade processing plant in Far North Queensland employs eight staff and turning 50 tonnes of waste bananas into 5 tonnes of banana flour per day as well as processes 20 tonnes of sweet potatoes a month (Farm Online, 2019). Early next year in partnership with other producers the new factory will be complete that will see an increase of processing capacity by 500% and will employ 40+ workers (Farm Online, 2019).

The present focus of the dynamic duo is on the entire food industry and produce/food waste reduction in farming practices. The couple set up a cooperative model that connects groups of farmers with Natural Evolutions' technology and expertise. Through these partnerships, more sustainable and wasteless farming practices are explored and established – produce that is traditionally wasted has now been utilised and processed in innovative ways. The consultations include discussion of market opportunities, processing design, product innovation. The couple urges all the farmers experiencing a large amount of waste of their products due to seasonal oversupply or other circumstances to get in touch and discuss opportunities for utilising Natural Evolution's expertise and technology for developing innovative products from that wasted produce.

Products/Services

The business not only provides food products but also expands to nutraceutical and health supplements and beauty products. Currently, Natural Foods Evolution company produces products in the following categories:

- Health Supplements
- Beauty
- Backing
- Equine
- Healing

While green banana flour is the star product of their range, there are further innovative products that the entrepreneurial couple introduced to the market, including beauty products, sweet potato flour, and broccoli powder. Working with their Japanese partners, the company developed a line of skincare products with extracts from green Lady Finger banana skins including a soap, mister, and a moisturiser.

Sweet potato flour developed by the business is used in mashed potato products and baby food. It can also be used as an ingredient in bread, cakes, biscuits, and as a thickening in soups, stews, and smoothie drinks. Broccoli powder is now used in protein drinks or added as a baking ingredient and is high in iron, calcium, folate, and Vitamin C. It is produced from surplus broccoli from southern Victoria (Gippsland). The range of Natural Evolution flour and powders is now sold in Woolworth supermarkets as well as disturbed through a range of health stores and the business' online outlet (Farm Online, 2019).

Among the new directions for the business is the launch of Green Banana Rum and Sweet Potato Vodka through their partnership with a local distillery, Plantation Brew Co (AgriFutures Australia, 2019). The business is also partnering with other unique Australian food producers to set up personalised Australian food hampers that will be sold online through a gifting website. Additionally, powder trials were completed on the pumpkin, green beans, mushroom, carrot, and beetroot produce and showed positive results. The company now explores market demand and sales platforms for these possible new products.

Furthermore, the patented NutroLock technology developed by Rob and the opportunities it provides for other farmers led to establishing another arm of the business named Evolution Industries. The goal of this venture is to support produce growers with custom business solutions, including design, fabrication, product development, and marketing/sales. Based on the couple's previous experience, they developed a 'business success formula' that can be modified accordingly and applied to other farms. The business provides 'full vertical integration' services that consist of three stages (Evolution Industries, 2019):

1. Investigation of the current waste stream and raw produce assets.
2. Design of customised processing line to utilise waste products and with help of NutroLock technology transform it into valuable long-shelf-life products (expanding shelf-life from weeks to years).
3. Building and installing NutroLock processing line on-site, with complementary test run and training on maintaining and servicing the equipment.

This process enables the farmers not only to develop and introduce new products to the market but also successfully market those products and create the niche demand for them in the market. The plan is to open up multiple processing plants across the country and make a significant positive impact on food waste.

Business strategies

Natural Evolution is a very successful company that just keeps on growing. An innovative idea was developed and build on by the owners to create a unique and successful business with a distinctive competitive advantage. Rob and Krista are natural entrepreneurs and constantly scanning the internal and external business environment for further opportunities. Looking at their journey so far, it can be concluded that the couple employed multiple business strategies to help them succeed. The couple credits the successes of their innovation to obtaining expert advice, a substantial investment of time and funds into research and development, and capitalising on available government support (DSITI, 2015). Specific strategies employed by the owners are described below.

Focus on Australian local produce and partners

While the business has interest from overseas (including Canada, Europe, Japan, South Korea, Singapore, China, America, and New Zealand), they are particularly interested in working with local suppliers and establishing other Australian sites. The business is proud to contribute to Australia's green and clean reputation and provide a high-quality local product with a distinctive competitive advantage over unsafe and unregulated imports (Growcom, 2019).

This strategy is complementary to the recently announced by government 'Go Local, Grow Local' campaign that encourages Queenslanders to support local small businesses and help businesses to promote their locally grown and manufactured products (Business Queensland, 2019). As part of this campaign, governments provide a range of support, tools, and advice for starting, running, and growing small businesses. Provided services include access to information about grants and available financial support, events that provide a networking opportunity, mentoring program, and support services for women in business and Indigenous business initiatives (Business Queensland, 2019).

The company's focus on local suppliers also complements the recent trend in wider economic development towards sustainability, environmental responsibility, and circular economy. The circular economy concept stems from ecological and environmental economics and industrial ecology. The concept is linked to sustainable development and opposes unsustainable perpetual growth strategies. A circular economy implies environmentally responsible production at the company level, greater environmental awareness and responsibility of producers and consumers, renewable technologies, and materials (if possible) and environmentally responsible policies (Ghisellini, Cialani, & Ulgiati, 2016). Put simply, it means that all the inputs to the business are utilised to the fullest in an environmentally responsible way and all the outputs or waste resulting from the business activities are reused and put back into the production system as much as possible.

Similarly, to the Natural Evolution practice of turning waste bananas and produce into flour and powder, a circular economy is focused on turning waste into wealth. Lacy and Rutqvist (2015) specifically clarify that waste implies more than just physical waste or rubbish. They identify four distinct forms of waste that in the view of circular economy can and should be turned into valuable products or assets:

1. Wasted resources such as energy and materials that currently are not regenerated and instead used once in the absence of recycling or reuse facilities/provisions/practices.
2. Products with wasted lifecycles when despite of possible further demand for the products they are disposed of prematurely.
3. Products with wasted capabilities when the existing facilities or products are underutilised and are not used to their full capacity.
4. Wasted embedded values of disposable products when components, materials, and energy used for their production are not recovered or reused.

Virtually any type of modern business or organisation has waste (as it is described above). This underutilisation of resources is resulting in missed business opportunities. Employing innovative solutions to capitalise on these 'waste' opportunities not only provides the businesses with financial rewards but also enables their success and prosperity without ever-increasing consumption of already significantly constrained natural resources.

Diversification

Natural Evolution has a quite diverse portfolio of products. The company actively explored existing market opportunities and invested in developing new product lines. Starting with adding extra products to their backing range, the company expanded in lucrative health supplements, healing, and beauty products. Currently, they are working on introducing new alcoholic beverages to the market. Additionally, the company patented their innovative 'NutroLock' technology and now provides business consultancy services to other produce growers.

The relationship between diversification and performance was the subject of research for many decades, with initial research on the topic first published in the 1940s (Santarelli & Tran, 2016). Most recent research on the topic tends to agree that the diversification–performance relationship is nonlinear, that is while generally, diversification tends to enhance firms' performance, there eventually comes a point where an increase in diversification results in declining performance.

Diversification strategy offers several benefits to the firms that all contribute to achieving better synergies between different aspects of a company. There are three advantages of diversification that were identified by Montgomery (1994):

1. Access to multi-markets and various support networks.
2. Maximising utilisation of existing resources.
3. Being able to allocate funds from currently well-performing products/ businesses to the ones that need more financial investment or outlay.

However, diversification is a strategy that needs to be carefully considered. On one hand, synergies of interrelated business can deliver benefits stemming from sharing inputs, including tangible (distribution systems, technologies, manufacturing facilities, etc.) and intangible (brand name, managerial practices and capabilities, industry expertise, etc.) resources (Santarelli & Tran, 2016). On the other hand, it can lead to slower responsiveness to change, difficult and redundant decision-making process, inconsistent strategy, and lack of control (Wit and Meyer, 2005). Challenges those businesses employing the diversification strategy must face include managing the conflict between existing and newly acquired ventures/ products/services and resolving inevitable tensions among staff and managing personnel (Dess et al., 2003).

However, the case of Natural Evolution and its success demonstrates that this is a worthwhile strategy to consider, especially when expanding to new areas well complements the existing business and area of expertise.

Collaboration and partnership

Rob and Krista formed many business partnerships and relationships. They partnered with relevant government bodies to obtain grants and funds for further development of their processing facilities, they partnered with local and intra-state farmers to form cooperatives and expand their supply chains, and they partnered with local and international complementary businesses to develop new products and diversify their product range.

Cooperation between firms and industries provides means of accumulating additional knowledge and expertise, which delivers valuable benefits to the business in terms of innovation, productivity, and competitiveness (Peris-Ortiz & Ferreira, 2017). Recent research has demonstrated that cooperative and networking behaviour among small firms is one of the key determinants of business success and can result in competitive advantage (Peris-Ortiz & Ferreira, 2017). In the field of organisational research, networking covers a variety of relationships between firms, including strategic alliances, subcontracting, clusters, cooperation networks, outsourcing relationships, industrial districts, consortia, and franchises. Thornton, Henneberg, and Naudé (2013) conclude that networking behaviour between firms can be classified into the following four types:

- Information acquisition behaviours, including acquiring valuable business information via business partners, business contacts outside of existing trading relationships, and business/trade events.
- Opportunity enabling behaviours, including activities/routines/practices utilised by the firms to scan for the opportunities in the external environment and circulate their reputation through purposeful interactions with relevant stakeholders and agents in their business network.
- Strong-tie resource mobilisation behaviours when firms mobilise resources via their direct/established relationships.
- Weak-tie resource mobilisation behaviours, when firms mobilise resources via their indirect, less-established or new relationships.

The cooperation networks tend to facilitate better preparedness for and adaptation to uncertainties in the business environment and increase firms' flexibility and adjustment to inevitable changes (Peris-Ortiz & Ferreira, 2017). Other benefits of networking relationships include sharing knowledge, accelerating innovation, reducing transaction costs, gaining a better reputation, and creating new market opportunities (Lin and Lin, 2016). Hamlin, Knight, and Cuthbert (2015) in their study of farming practices in New Zealand and Canada have found that the development of networks, including horizontal and vertical, as well as forming partnerships and alliances, was among the most common and the most important strategies employed by successful enterprises.

As demonstrated by Rob and Krista, this business strategy can be developed through attending industry events, registering, and becoming a member of relevant business networks, building a vertical and horizontal relationship with relevant organisations and businesses, and nominating your products for suitable industry and government awards.

Innovation and research

Rob and Krista are experienced innovators. They constantly search for better solutions to their everyday farming challenges. When stumbled on an opportunity of turning their wasted produce into flour they pursued it with all their energy. Not only they explored every opportunity with their own farming crop of Lady Finger bananas, but they also tested their developed powdering technology on every other suitable crop. They also pursued opportunities of transforming their produce into beauty products and beverages. And currently working with other farmers, coaching and mentoring them to replicate their success.

Despite such successful examples of innovative products and practices from Natural Evolution, practice shows that innovative initiatives frequently fail. As Pisano (2015) argues, the main problem with innovative improvement efforts by organisations and businesses is the lack of an innovation strategy. That is companies lack the commitment to a set of coherent and complementing policies and/or behaviours that facilitate the achievement of a specific competitive goal.

Innovation strategy allows the companies to consider their intent and commitment to business model innovation or technological innovation. When evaluating potential innovation, it is useful to consider it against the following four categories of innovation (Pisano, 2015):

1. Routine innovation that expands on existing technological capabilities and expertise and aligns with the company's existing business model and customer base. An example of such routine innovation can be the latest model of the iPhone.
2. Disruptive innovation usually proposes a new business model that can be based on a technological breakthrough. This type of innovation challenges traditional business models within an industry and thus creates a competitive advantage. A good example of such innovation is Airbnb.
3. Radical innovation is a purely technological type of innovation (as opposed to disruptive innovation). Examples of such innovation are any new inventions such as electricity, refrigeration, air-conditioning, internet, or electronic payments when it first appeared.
4. Architectural innovation is a combination of technological and business model disruptions. Due to this double breakthrough, this type of innovation poses the biggest challenge and threat to competitors. An example of this innovation is digital photography and emerging of new brands and companies that were selling digital cameras only. This innovation forced traditional photography brands like Kodak and Polaroid not only to master completely new technology but also find new revenue streams besides disposable photography products such as film, photo paper, chemicals for photo printing and printing services.

Given the latest trend towards sustainable development and sustainable business practices, there is an increasing demand for eco-innovations. Eco-innovation can be defined as 'the development of products (goods and services), processes, marketing methods, organizational structure, and new or improved institutional arrangements, which, intentionally or not, contribute to a reduction of environmental impact in comparison with alternative practices' (OECD, 2009, p. 2). Bossle, Barcellos, Vieira and Sauvée (2016) identify external and internal factors that contribute to the development of eco-innovations and eco-innovative practices. Among the external factors, the authors specifically identify government support or lack of thereof as a key condition or restrain for eco-innovations. Other extremal factors include knowledge bases, technological opportunities, and demand conditions. Internal factors that can trigger eco-innovations include cost savings, an adaptation of environmental certification practices, and managerial environmental concern. The authors conclude that eco-innovation and green innovations are growing phenomenon and as the case with any innovation, a key ingredient for success is an organisational commitment in the form of intended strategy.

Challenges to face

Behind every success story, there is a set of challenges that had to be faced and overcome. Like any farmer, Rob and Krista's business is exposed to climate and weather events. At the beginning of their entrepreneurial journey, they experienced two cyclones within five years – Cyclone Larry in 2006 and Cyclone Yasi in 2011. Then in December 2018, the couple's banana plantation was affected by a fire that started in a nearby bushland. The plants and irrigation systems were destroyed; however, luckily their factory and processing line were not affected due to change in the wind. Despite their critical infrastructure surviving the ordeal, the couple were devasted by losing the plants and equipment that they put so much effort and time into. The couple had to cut down all the damaged bananas and plant new plants by hand. Twenty kilometres of irrigation needed to be replaced.

Natural disaster events are an increasing threat to business operations with the latest estimate that there is one natural disaster a week somewhere in the world (Twomey, 2019). These events are no longer something that can only happen once in a lifetime; they are occurring with more and more increasing regularity. Natural disasters result in abrupt changes to business organisations, such as asset damages, increased costs, and operational interruptions, as well as declining revenue and growth (Winn et al., 2011). Thus, it is of extreme importance for any business to have a response and recovery plan in place that assures as much as possible continuity of the business activities. There is a range of resources put together by government and not-for-profit organisations that are free and available online to help businesses develop their emergency plans.

While utilising innovative technology and farming practices is second nature to Rob and Krista, they found that sometimes it can be challenging to inspire other farmers who are used to traditionally doing things to explore new opportunities. Resistance to change is a known barrier to further business development and growth, and sometimes it can be very hard to overcome factor. The following main reasons for resisting change in organisations and businesses can be identified: fearfulness of change and its consequences, feeling of being unable to make a change or been disempowered, and previous unsuccessful experience (TEDxPerth, 2010). To help people embrace change and innovation, Jason Clarke who has extensive experience in consulting government departments, businesses, and not-for-profit organisations suggests thinking about proposed changes in terms of positive, interesting, and negative consequences (TEDxPerth, 2010). This helps people to audit their feeling and emotions about the change. Another helpful strategy includes keeping people informed about the upcoming changes, making it very clear what exactly is going to change and give people authorship of the change (TEDxPerth, 2010). Once those emotions are addressed, facts about the change are clarified and people feel responsible and empowered to take control of the changes, and moving on and embracing proposed changes become significantly easier.

Conclusion

Earth resources are limited. As Lacy and Rutqvist (2015) conclude, some resources, including precious metals and stones, are very limited and have already been greatly exploited. Other types of resources, including freshwater, air and forest, even though renewable, are under increasing stress. Traditional economic models and practices must be modified to ensure that we develop and sustainably improve our societies.

It is estimated that $4.5 trillion can be achieved if current waste is to be turned into wealth by 2030 (Lacy & Rutqvist, 2015). In the food production industry, a staggering 30%–50% of food intended for human consumption is wasted at different stages of food production (Stuart, 2009). Food waste at the farm gate alone represents around 10% of gross food production with an estimated value of $4 billion (Farm Online National News, 2019).

This chapter described an innovative business that is on a mission to transform currently wasted produce into new long-shelf-life products. The founders of the business, Rob and Krista Watkins came to be known as 'waste crusaders' for their enthusiasm and expertise in transforming and utilising produce that is currently wasted by farmers due to various constraints, transporting costs, and supermarkets regulations. Starting originally with their farming crop of green Lady Finder variety bananas, they tested the developed and patented NutroLock technology on various other products, and already successfully introduced new sweet potato flour and broccoli powder to the market. With the help of similarly minded business partners, they also expanded their product range to beauty and health products, and are still exploring further ventures and opportunities. The entrepreneurial couple is establishing farmer cooperative groups in Queensland, Victoria and elsewhere in Australia to help build a network of processing plants which in 25 minutes or less will be turning 'wasted' fruit and vegetables into nutrition-rich food powders (Farm Online, 2019).

What is the secret to their success? According to Rob, the amazing 'Krista and Rob team' were and are essential to the success of their business endeavours (Growcom, 2019). Their passion, enthusiasm, outside-the-box thinking, and ingenuity paved the way to the success they are today. The achievements of this couple are well celebrated with multiple awards under their belt, including Rural Woman of the Year and Young Farmer of the Year. The strategies that the business employs include working with local suppliers and partners, diversification, collaboration and partnership, and investment in innovation and research. Successful synergy of all these strategies and tactics, as well as great and inspiring leadership lead to the business being as successful as it is today.

However, in the ever-changing economic environment, all businesses must be aware of possible risks to their operations. Climate and weather disasters are posing an increasing risk to many different types of businesses. Rob and Krista had to work on the recovery of their operations after two cyclones and a bushfire. The food industry is susceptible to risk associated with global warming and climate change. Therefore, measures and innovative practices need to be put in place to try and counteract possible negative impacts as much as possible.

Looking at the example of Natural Evolution business, we can conclude that constant innovation, absence of complacency, and playing to external environment trends are core elements of business success. The entrepreneurial couple behind the business put their best effort into developing new innovative products and technology, meanwhile addressing the environmental issue of food waste. Given the current environmental pressures, focusing on waste reduction and elimination and turning waste into wealth under circular economy principles should be at the forefront of every business strategy.

References

AgriFutures Australia. (2018). *2018 Winners*. Retrieved from www.agrifutures.com.au/people-leadership/rural-womens-award/2018-winners/

AgriFutures Australia. (2019). *Green Banana Rum? Waste Crusader Krista Watkins Takes on New Opportunities*. Retrieved from www.agrifutures.com.au/news/green-banana-rum-waste-crusader-krista-watkins-takes-on-new-opportunities/

Bossle, M. B., de Barcellos, M. D., Vieira, L. M., & Sauvée, L. (2016). The drivers for adoption of eco-innovation. *Journal of Cleaner production, 113*, 861–872.

Business Enterpreneurs' Program. (2017). *Natural Evolution – Global Opportunity Not Wasted on Innovative Farming Couple*. Retrieved from www.business.gov.au/assistance/entrepreneurs-programme/business-management-customer-stories/customer-story-natural-evolution

Business Queensland. (2019). *Go Local, Grow Local*. Retrieved from www.business.qld.gov.au/starting-business/advice-support/support/small-business/go-local

Department of Industry and Science. (2014). *Innovation Australia Annual Report 2014–2015*. Retrieved from https://parlinfo.aph.gov.au/parlInfo/search/display/display.w3p;query=Id:%22publications/tabledpapers/8065a93e-13a2-4b6c-a3bd-1112dbdd2501%22;src1=sm1

Department of Science, Information Technology and Innovation (DSITI). (2015). *The Innovation Case Study Library: Natural Evolution's Green Banana Flour*. State of Queensland.

Dess, G. G., Ireland, R. D., Zahara, S. A., Floyd, S. W., Janney, J. I. & Lane, P. J. (2003). Emerging issues in corporate entrepreneurship. *Journal of Management, 29*(3), 351–378. https://doi.org/10.1016/S0149-2063(03)00015-1

Edison Awards. (2017). *2017 Edison Best New Product Award Winners*. Retrieved from www.edisonawards.com/winners2017.php

Evolution Industries. (2019). *Services: Full Vertical Integration*. Retrieved from www.evolutionindustries.com.au/services.html

Farm Online National News. (2019). *Qld Couple Go Bananas with Horticulture Co-op Processing Move*. Retrieved from www.farmonline.com.au/story/5971507/trash-to-treasure-food-waste-processors-new-crop-salvage-goal/?cs=4698

Ghisellini, P., Cialani, C. & Ulgiati, S. (2016). A review on circular economy: The expected transition to a balanced interplay of environmental and economic systems. *Journal of Cleaner Production, 114,* 11–32. https://doi.org/10.1016/j.jclepro.2015.09.007

Growcom. (2019). *Edison Award Shines Light on a Visionary Journey.* Retrieved from www.growcom.com.au/portfolio/rob-and-krista-watkins/

Haines, T. (2016). Developing a startup and innovation ecosystem in regional Australia. *Technology Innovation Management Review, 6*(6), 24–32.

Hamlin, R., Knight, J & Cuthbert, R. (2015). Niche marketing and farm diversification processes: Insights from New Zealand and Canada. *Renewable Agriculture and Food Systems, 31*(1), 86–98. https://doi-org.ezproxy.cqu.edu.au/10.1017/S1742170514000489

Lacy, P. & Rutqvist, J. (2015). *Waste to wealth: The circular economy advantage.* Chennai: MPS Limited.

Lin, F.-J. & Lin, Y.-H. (2016). The effect of network relationship on the performance of SMEs. *Journal of Business Research, 69*(5), 1780–1784. https://doi.org/10.1016/j.jbusres.2015.10.055

Montgomery, C.A. (1994). Corporate diversification. *The Journal of Economic Perspectives, 8*(3), 163–178.

Natural Evolution Foods. (2019). *Our Story.* Retrieved from www.naturalevolutionfoods.com.au/story/

Organisation for Economic Co-operation and Development (OECD). (2009). *Sustainable Manufacturing and Eco-innovation: Towards a Green Economy: Policy Brief June 2009.* Retrieved from www.oecd.org/env/consumption-innovation/42957785.pdf

O'Sullivan, M. (September, 2010). 2010 Farmer of the Year Awards Announced. *ABC Rural.* Retrieved from www.abc.net.au/news/rural/2010-09-21/2010-farmer-of-the-year-awards-announced/6196396

Peris-Ortiz M., & Ferreira J.J. (2017) Cooperation and networks in small business strategy: An overview. In: Peris-Ortiz M., Ferreira J. (eds) *Cooperative and networking strategies in small business. Innovation, technology, and knowledge management.* Cham: Springer.

Pisano, G.P. (2015). You need an innovation strategy. *Harvard Business Review, 93*(6), 44–54

Queensland Agriculture. (November 2018). *Agricultural Leaders Recognised.* Retrieved from http://statements.qld.gov.au/Statement/2018/11/21/agricultural-leaders-recognised

Santarelli, E. & Tran, H.T. (2016). Diversification strategies and firm performance in Vietnam: Evidence from parametric and semi-parametric approaches. *Economics of Transition, 24*(1), 31–68. https://doi.org/10.1111/ecot.12082

Stuart, T. (2009). *Waste: Uncovering the global food scandal.* London: Penguin Books Limited.

TEDx JCUCairns. (2017, October 17). *Going Bananas: Krista Watkins.* Retrieved from https://youtu.be/hV38emFiAYk

TEDxPerth. (2010, December 22). *Jason Clarke: Embracing Change.* Retrieved from https://youtu.be/vPhM8lxibSU

Thornton, S., Henneberg, S., & Naudé, P. (2013). Understanding types of organizational networking behaviors in the UK manufacturing sector. *Industrial Marketing Management, 42*(7), 1154–1166, https://doi.org/10.1016/j.indmarman.2013.06.005

Twomey, D. (July, 2019). *UN warns one climate crisis disaster happening every week.* Retrieved from http://econews.com.au/61554/un-warns-one-climate-crisis-disaster-happening-every-week/

Winn M., Kirchgeorg M., Griffiths A., Linnenluecke M.K. and Günther E. (2011). Impacts from climate change on organizations: A conceptual foundation. *Business Strategy and the Environment, 20*(3), 157–173. https://doi.org/10.1002/bse.679

Wit, B. D. & Meyer, R. (2005). *Strategy synthesis.* London: Non Basic Stock Line.

3
BUNDABERG BREWED DRINKS
Regional to global

Quamrul Alam and Rumana Parveen

Introduction

Bundaberg Brewed Drinks (BBD) is a premium brewed soft drink manufacturer located in regional Queensland and is best known for its famous 'Bundaberg Ginger Beer' that is sold in most national supermarkets in Australia. The family owned business grew from a small regional distributor in the 1960s (Bundaberg, 2021a). The company began exporting its products around the world in 1987. BBD global business has tripled since 2006, making it Australia's largest owned soft drink company and the fourth largest in terms of local sales behind foreign-owned Coca-Cola, Schweppes, and Pepsi (Asialink Business, 2014).

During the 1970s and 1980s, the company's focus was on the local market in Bundaberg and Maryborough, in regional Queensland, Australia (Bundaberg, 2021a). It took the family owned company 19 years to start exporting into the global market with no real success. It initially exported its products to New Zealand and later it expanded its operations by exporting to many countries around the world. New flavours were also introduced at this time. In 1997, BBD decided to stop trading with any other brand of soft drink and to focus on their own 'Bundaberg Brewed' brand to market them exclusively – 'taking control of our own destiny', as mentioned by John McLean, CEO of Bundaberg Drinks (Clun, 2017). From some small sales to New Zealand 34 years ago, Bundaberg now sells its drinks in 60 countries including China, the USA, Germany, the UK, and South Korea. Its total sales were AUD 117 million in 2016 (Cullen, 2017; Wheeler, 2020a). In the US, Bundaberg's sales grew from 0.15 million in 1997 to about 24 million in 2017 and offshore sales currently makeup 35% of Bundaberg's total market and are soon expected to outstrip domestic sales (Cullen, 2017).

In 2018, BBD signed a massive distribution deal with the American company PepsiCo. At the time of the announcement, the Chairperson of BBD, Mr Terry

O'Brien, stated that '…the PepsiCo deal is the start of a new era for the company, opening the door for quantum growth in sales and a major step in the globalisation of the company' (Durie, 2018). The company, which has annual net sales of $160 million and employs 250 people, produces 81 million litres of Ginger Beer a year, of which one-tenth goes to the US market, due in part to its deal with PepsiCo.

Product profile: the brew

The company has 16 varieties of soft drinks, all of which are non-alcoholic brewed drinks –even the iconic 'Ginger Beer' (BBD, 2021 b). All BBD is classified as a soft drink (or soda) and is promoted as a delicious alternative to alcoholic beverages. The traditional brewed drinks of BBD were joined by seven brewed fruit-based sparkling drinks in the product portfolio of BBD (BBD, 2021 b).

The local endowment factors of Queensland are key to the success of the company. Cane sugar, ginger, and water are the most significant ingredients for the flagship product. The correct flavour profile has been researched for BBD. Bundaberg Ginger Beer uses organically produced chemicals-free ginger, which grows best in the wet tropical climate and well-drained friable coastal soils of Queensland. These are the most ideal factor for growing high-quality, healthy, flavoursome ginger which is rightly called 'Queensland Gold', as mentioned by the head of farming operations at BBD, Ross Maxwell, who has been interested in growing crops sustainably and organically since 1970 (Gorey, 2019).

The finest ingredients are brewed for as long as it takes to extract maximum flavour to make BBD Ginger Beer. Ginger root is dried using a special process and ground to a coarse flour so that the natural flavour is preserved. The ground ginger is mixed with Queensland Cane Sugar and water – this mixture is called 'Wort' – it is then heated to release flavours. A special yeast is added to the wort for fermentation, which is then brewed up to maturity before it is filtered and carbonated and lastly bottled with the utmost care (BBD, 2021c). The BBD drinks have always been packaged in glass bottles to ensure authentic flavours and taste retains.

BBD has rigorously been involved in maintaining the highest quality of ingredients and authentic flavour coming from the producers of the Australian tropical region. It has invested a considerable amount in research and the practice of best farming of sugarcane and ginger (Gorey, 2019). It is anticipated that the flavour profile will ensure that the US arm of the company will triple its sales over the next few years, based in large part on the PepsiCo distribution deal (Gorey, 2019; Durie, 2018). Last year, Bundaberg Brewed Drinks was rated by Australian consumers as Australia's best soft drink in 'Canstar Blue's first national review' of the soft drink industry which is highly dominated by multinational giants (Bundaberg Now, 2020). Bundaberg Brewed Drinks received the maximum five-star rating on taste and packaging design, which earned it a maximum rating on overall satisfaction. On this award, BBD's CEO John McLean commented 'It was great to see

Australians putting local soft drink producers first' (Bundaberg Now, 2020). More recently, Bundaberg Brewed Drinks has been recognised on the world stage and awarded a platinum medal at the Spirit International Prestige Awards for its Ginger Beer, being the award is an internationally recognised one where the consumers are judging (SIP, 2021).

Non-alcoholic drink industry

BBD is the fourth largest company in the non-alcoholic drink market in Australia. The leading company is Coca-Cola Amatil Limited followed by Asahi Holdings (Australia) Pty Ltd and True Blu Beverages Pty Limited, each having a market share of 39.8%, 15.4%, and 5%, respectively. BBD's market share in Australia is 4.0%. (Yeoh, 2020). Most of the industry's output is sold to supermarkets and other grocery retailers. Fast food shops and takeaway services are other important buyers of BBD products. A weak retail environment and rising health awareness among consumers against sugar-based soft drinks have caused industry revenue to decline over the last five-year period. Additionally, strong competition and aggressive pricing strategies by major players have further contributed to revenue declines (Yeoh, 2020). These trends have been partially offset by the increasing popularity of higher value soft drinks made with all-natural ingredients and fruit-based sweeteners such as those produced by BBD.

BBD has been recognised for its efforts in international expansion, winning the Queensland Premier's Exporter of the Year award in 2013. The US deal is expected to open BBD products to some 400,000 stores, bars, and restaurants through the PepsiCo network and comes on the heels of a booming US and Californian market where BBD is seen as a craft beverage and importantly is the preferred mixer for the Moscow mule vodka-based cocktail.

Non-alcoholic drinks have an evolving threat from Sugar Tax which has been introduced in several countries including the UK, Mexico, and France in an attempt to decrease obesity numbers. Soft drinks have been the main target of the campaign as they have high sugar content and have been judged as being one of the main contributors to obesity and the consumption of a substance with no clear nutritional value (Briggs, Rayner, & Scarborough, 2016). Sugar was found to be one of the leading causes of obesity in Great Britain's population, which now sits at 25% of adults (Colborne, 2016).

The major market failure associated with the consumption of sugar is due to negative externalities and imperfect information available to the consumer. Soft drink consumption has been blamed for the jump in high obesity rates and welfare losses. In California, the tax on soda beverages can range from 1 cent every 30 ml to 2 cents every 30 ml (Roache & Gostin, 2017). It is estimated that taxes of this type will have a significant adverse impact on BBD sales, given that the retail price of Ginger Beer will increase by approximately 12.5–25 cents per bottle. There was approximately a 50% drop in soda consumption in Berkeley, California after a soda tax was introduced in that state (University of California – Berkeley, 2019). Logic

TABLE 3.1 Popular Ginger Beer of UK

	Brand Name of Ginger Beer	Sugar Per 100 ml	Sugar Level
1	Fentimans	7.8 g	Medium high
2	Fentimans Pink	7.8 g	Medium high
3	Fever-Tree	4 g	Medium
4	Bundaberg	4.9 g	Medium
5	Cawston Press	5.4 g	Medium
6	Belvoir	7.8 g	Medium high
7	Waitrose	7.8 g	Medium high
8	Abbotts KA	4.8 g	Medium
9	Old Jamaica	4.9 g	Medium
10	Supermalt	16 g	High

Source: Based on information of My Best (2020).

suggests that having higher sugar content in soft drinks will cause consumption to drop, leading to a decrease in sales revenue and long-term growth for soft drink manufacturers.

In a comparison among popular Ginger Beer available in the UK market, BBD Diet Ginger Beer has been found to have lower sugar levels than many of the brands (See Table 3.1). It has a medium level of sugar, but to be in the lower level, one drink should have 2.5 grams sugar per 100 ml.

The current industry environment has another serious threat from the COVID-19 pandemic crisis. Event cancellations, social restrictions, and limited patrons in food establishments caused by the COVID-19 pandemic have affected both 'on the go' soft drink consumption and 'out of home' soft drink consumption. Despite relaxed restrictions in many states, the hospitality industry is not expected to get back to pre- COVID-9 sales numbers for the next few years. The industry estimates a 5% decline in revenue in the current and next financial year (Yeoh, 2020).

Sustainability practices of BBD

BBD has largely invested in the sustainable production of ginger. BBD farming research managers spend a considerable amount of time visiting farmers around Bundaberg, sharing research-based knowledge to ensure a sustainable farming industry of ginger survives in Bundaberg (Gorey, 2019). Local businesses have increased productivity, efficiency, and streamlined the economic value chain for the product and have been able to sustain the unique flavour profile for BBD Ginger Beer. The head of Bundaberg Research Farm, Ross Maxwell, has been researching and practising the organic way of ginger production since the 1970s, without applying harmful chemicals and pesticides. Ross is not only working for BBD he is also widely advising the local ginger producers (Bundaberg Brewed Drinks, 2021d). BBD traditionally shared its research-based findings with the local farmers and ginger-growers to continue the legacy of the highest quality of ingredients; according to the findings, sustainable farming isn't just great for BBD, it's great for the region too. BBD has been using glass bottles for its product since the beginning. The bottle is its trademark as well as it is working as a sustainable packaging item because glass is the most recyclable material and not harmful to the environment as are plastic bottles (Helen Wise Research, 2017). Even the recyclable plastic bottles mostly end up at landfills and start to pollute the environment at least for the next 100 years (Clean Up Australia, 2021).

BBD has been working on a carbon offsetting project with help of CO2 Australia and Queensland Department of Employment, Economic Development, and Innovation (DEEDI), by establishing a huge forestation field at Moura, Queensland, 300 kilometres west of Bundaberg (Sustainability Matters, 2012). Recently, BBD has invested a commendable amount to upgrade its packaging design with help from Signet packaging company and thus reduced 30% use of plastic in packaging large product containers, which are specially used for the export market (Signet, 2021). BBD has chosen the location for its recent multi-million-dollar expansion project in Bundaberg though there were offers from other locations; this will create at least 221 local jobs (McManagan, 2021).

Market opportunity in the UK

A key factor that determines the success of a product in the beverage industry is the quality of the product. It should fulfil customer needs and expectations and provide customer intrigue (Bere, Sorli, Te Velde & Kleep, 2007; Meher, Bulbul & Khaled, 2017). BBD is positioned in the soft drink and beverage industry in the UK as a competitor that has a strategy to increase its market share.

The biggest competitors in the British soft drink market are Coca-Cola and Pepsi. According to Fortune Magazine (2016), both Coca-Cola and Pepsi have seen considerable declines in their profits since 2014; however, these two giant corporations still have high market share rates at 42.3% (Coca-Cola) and 27.5% (Pepsi). These two companies are in direct competition with BBD 'Ginger Beer' and worldwide the two company's own more than 500 'still' and 'sparkling' brands of soft drink, including some Ginger Beers such as the Coca-Cola UK, owned Stoney Ginger Beer.

According to research, higher consumption of soft drinks has been observed due to the higher temperatures (Oberlander & Játiva, 2019). In 2020, the UK carbonated drinks market commanded a 38.2% market share of the total soft drinks market (British Soft Drinks Association, 2021). The soft drinks industry plays an important role in the UK's economy, contributing £13 billion to the economy, providing jobs to more than 140,000 people and the platform to successfully export products around the globe (British Soft Drinks Association, 2021).

Competitive analysis

Central Queensland University and Solent Southampton University signed an agreement to pursue research opportunities with its students in the UK and Australia. In 2017, UK students developed a marketing analysis for BBD which was passed on to the CEO of BBD. To assist in this marketing analysis, CQUniversity undertook a review of BBD's main competitors, Old Jamaica, Fentimans, and Fever-Tree Ginger Beers. CQUniversity identified these brands as the most likely competition for BBD 'Ginger Beer' due to their placement in the market and where BBD was most likely to expand. Each different brand of Ginger Beer sold in the UK has a specific target market. BBD currently maintains a small share of the UK market. It is mainly sold in Waitrose and Tesco supermarkets and a handful of small restaurants and cafes. Fentimans operates in the same markets as BBD and offers a similar traditionally branded Ginger Beer that is for sale in supermarkets and small restaurants and cafes (Fentimans, 2021). Recently, Amazon noted on their website that BBD is among the top five best-selling Ginger Beer brands in the UK (Amazon, 2021). Unlike Fentimans, Fever-Tree brews drinks are mainly used as mixers for alcoholic beverages and although they focus mainly on tonic water, they also produce three different kinds of ginger mixers and therefore they are in strong competition with BBD. Like BBD, Fever-Tree produces high-quality products that are highly priced drinks in the UK market. The main rival for BBD in the UK market is Old Jamaica, the most widely spread mainstream 'Ginger Beer' in the UK, being sold in supermarkets, corner shops, bars, and restaurants. Old Jamaica is BBD's main competitor due to the size of the organisation and their brand recognition in the UK.

The main strength of BBD Ginger Beer comes from the use of natural quality ingredients, locally grown ginger, and sugar cane, which combine and help the Bundaberg brand to differentiate its products from other competitors. The second relevant aspect that adds strength to the BBD brand is its unique glass bottle design. The glass material gives a more expensive look and at the same time helps to preserve the ginger flavour with elements of the ginger root present in the bottle. The shape of the bottle also helps customers to recognise the brand easily, as no other competitor presents their products in a bottle with a similar shape (all the existing competitors tend to use the classic long and thin bottles or cans).

BBD prides itself on having a strong culture and experience of over 50 years. This is a great asset that shows a strong brand that has managed to satisfy its customers since 1960. Strong branding was an important reason for gaining customer trust in the UK market. Furthermore, distributing its products worldwide was also seen as a key strength in gaining fast recognition in the UK marketplace.

The main problem confronting BBD brand expansion into the UK market was the temperate maritime climate of the UK with lots of rainy days and the abundance of strong competitors that already enjoyed a high percentage of market share. Another issue relates to the fact that Ginger Beer has a specific target market that does not include generation X; young people aged between 18 and 24 years. Ginger

Beer is often thought of as a drink of choice for professionals who would like to enjoy an alcohol-free night out, with a refreshing non-alcoholic drink that will offer a similar experience as to an alcoholic drink. This aspect may affect the soft drinks consumption in the UK compared to other countries where Bundaberg have successfully managed to dominate the markets. In Australia, the climate varies in populated centres from semi-arid to tropical and as a consequence, the demand for soft drinks is always present. In the UK market, Ginger Beer consumption tends to be mostly seasonal (British soft drinks, 2015) and centred around summer festivals. This seasonal consumption pattern will make Bundaberg's journey into the UK market more challenging but does give rise to some opportunities.

The main opportunity for BBD is that Ginger Beer is very well known for being used as a mixer with other drinks to create cocktails. This provides BBD with a great opportunity to form partnerships with other alcoholic and non-alcoholic drinks by promoting BBD products in combination with other products which should strengthen year-round sales. This strategy has the potential to boost BBD brand recognition in the UK and make the product available via direct retail in bars and pubs. Currently, BBD is mainly sold in supermarkets which doesn't offer the reach that BBD is aspiring to achieve. Another opportunity for BBD is to promote its 'Ginger Beer' as the drink of choice at several big festivals that are organised in the UK every summer.

Competition from other products is seen as the most significant threat when entering a new market. Looking at the already existing competitors on the UK market, it can be observed that the soft drink leaders Coca-Cola and Pepsi are dominating, with a high percentage of market share; however, all manufacturers suffer from a similar problem – perceptions around the health of carbonated beverages. This threat is related to the health habits of the population. For the past few years, the UK population has become more concerned regarding the right foods to consume to follow a healthy lifestyle. Soft drinks are seen as a threat to a healthy diet, and most dieticians advise the population to exclude soft drinks from their diets due to their high sugar content (Roache & Gostin, 2017). However, BBD and Old Jamaica Ginger Beer have 4.9 grams of sugar per 100 ml, whereas the Fentimans original brand has 7.8 grams of sugar per 100 ml (McPhail, 2021).

Political factors can have a negative impact on organisations trying to enter a new market. Every country has its own set of regulations regarding the marketplace. Some can be more tolerant, others more demanding. For example, BBD must satisfy the food hygiene and compositional standards and procedures used in the UK and other EU Member States (Food Standard Agency, 2021). BBD needs to respect and adopt the policies and changes that the UK Government impose to create a strong and sustainable living brand for this market. Over recent years, the UK has suffered in a variety of areas. Economic decline influences consumers to reduce their spending habits. The primary cut-back generally happens around reducing the amount of money spent on leisure activities. Consumers are likely to consider purchasing Ginger Beer as a leisure activity whether they classify the drink as a non-alcoholic or alcoholic alternative.

Social factors play an important role in the success of BBD in the UK due to lifestyle changes. Issues related to embracing a healthier lifestyle have been discussed over the past years in the UK. The British population is dealing with one of the highest levels of obesity in all of Europe. At 27.8%, the UK population has the third highest obesity level behind Turkey, at 32.1%, and Malta, with 28.9% and on average 23.3% Europeans are obese (Bell, 2020). BBD Ginger Beer has its present formulation medium to moderately high in cane sugar and this may have a negative influence on the UK market. However, having the option of the diet Ginger Beer might help attract customers who are concerned about their sugar intake levels.

The UK population are keen on social media users. BBD should consider expanding its coverage to actively participate in the UK social media market to reach more customers and build brand awareness. The UK beverage industry has multiple legal obstacles that need to be considered, including the recent 'Sugar Tax'. BBD should be commended for its use of recyclable packaging that helps reduce waste unlike other Ginger Beer packaging on the market that store their products in cans or plastic bottles. Built-in store display cartons also significantly reduce waste.

Potential for expansion in Asia

After continued success in the Australian market, BBD turned its sights in the early 1990s to growing new markets in Asia (Asialink Business, 2014). BBD was initially established in Singapore, which today is its largest Asian market, by focusing on Singapore's significant Australian expatriate community. BBD then launched successfully into Hong Kong, Malaysia, and Brunei. China was next on the list, with a 30% annual growth rate in the Chinese food and beverage industry making the potential for success irresistible. 'China presented a real opportunity for BBD with a rapidly emerging middle-class, large disposable incomes and an increasing appetite for imported food and beverage products', says BBD CEO John McLean. 'However, what we learnt the hard way, is that you really need to take your time' (Asialink Business, 2014). Regarding the expansion policy of BBD in China, the company took some well-thought strategy approaches:

- Don't rush, take your time with Asia. It is easy to rush into Asia to take advantage of the extensive growth opportunities. BBD learnt that you need to explore and understand the market while staying true to your values.
- Find the right partner – do your research and choose carefully. BBD uses a testing and sorting process to determine if a potential partner can develop the brand in the long term, rather than just sell products short term.
- Build a successful partnership. BBD responds to the different business cultures in Asia by setting clear expectations and objectives while developing a strong relationship through guidance and support.

- Don't bite off more than you can chew. It is important to have a clear and achievable entry strategy when considering Asia. BBD segments markets and cities into zones, and only introduces a limited number of products to avoid overwhelming consumers.
- Build your own Asia Recipe. Tailoring your product for a long-term market presence is critical in Asia. BBD is developing an 'Asian Brew' of its Ginger Beer and is researching future unique products for Asian tastes.

BBD entered the Chinese market in the early 2000s, taking on a local partner with limited research or preparation (Asialink Business, 2014). The relationship quickly proved very one-sided, with BBD unhappy with its partner's lack of transparency on sales, distribution, and customer details. Different values, business ethics, and a lack of control also raised concerns. BBD had no input into product promotion and sales, or the ability to manage quality or contribute to strategic direction and eventually terminated the partnership. At the same time, BBD became increasingly aware of similar worries with its other partnerships in Asia. Its initial ad hoc approach to partnerships involved simply selling cartons of Ginger Beer to distributors throughout Asia to get the product into the region. No additional support was provided to partners such as help with branding or relationship-building. It was a basic purchase-order relationship with no product exclusivity. Challenges soon arose, with concerns about its partners' transparency as well as the impact of not having targeted market-entry strategies to take advantage of future growth opportunities. BBD decided it needed to slow down and be more strategic.

BBD past experiences demonstrate that entering Asia and building a strong presence comes with many challenges. The key to expanding into the Asian region is to understand the potential difficulties and adapt to the different modes of doing business. Having learnt from its mistakes in its initial attempt to enter China, BBD is now focused on finding the right Chinese partner who meets its stringent selection criteria. Indeed, its increased knowledge of the complexities of the Chinese market has led BBD to recognise that they might have several partners who will operate in the various regions across China, rather than simply one partnership (Asialink Business, 2014).

The emphasis on growth extends beyond China. BBD has recently secured partnerships in Indonesia and is in the process of finding partners in South Korea. BBD is also increasing its product offerings in its existing markets of Singapore, Hong Kong, Brunei, and Malaysia. Its Asian engagement will be an ongoing learning process, but with its commitment to going slow, understanding the various markets, building strong partnerships, and tailoring its product to the region, BBD aims to build on its success (Asialink Business, 2014).

Future strategic focus

According to reports, the global demand for Ginger Beer was valued at approximately $7.5 billion in 2018 and is anticipated to increase further to $10.85 billion by the end of 2025 with a staggering compound annual growth rate (CAGR) of around 5.4% in a market that is dominated by US consumption (Nutakor, Essiedu, Adadi, & Kanwugu, 2020). BBD has been exporting to the USA since 1998. The business is strong, healthy, and growing fast (International Business Today, 2015). Andrew Shepherd, the General Manager of Marketing at BBD, explained that their strategy to capture market share in the USA is centred on a social media presence through young urban influencers, sampling opportunities, and setting up a strong relationship with distributors, retailers, and logistic companies (International Business Today, 2015, p. 35). Entering its biggest deal for distribution with PepsiCo in the USA in 2018 has been an effective strategy for BBD, helping it to capture a larger share of the global Ginger Beer market. According to Amazon and leading lifestyle-based websites and online platforms, BBD is among the top ten Ginger Beer brands in the US market because of its authentic classic taste, natural ingredients, and lower sugar levels.

BBD's strategy has been transformed, as CEO McLean explains that initially, Bundaberg was shipping from its warehouse to international distributors and simply hoping for the best (Cullen, 2017). 'We changed our focus from being an export business to being an international business and, over the last seven years, we have really focused on that', he says. 'It's not just simply moving the product across the road or across the sea, but how do we help our partner in that country and help them sell that product and sell more'. This strategy meant BBD was able to take control of international marketing, trading in the local currency to have a better handle on the foreign exchange risks and focus on distribution points.

Currently, BBD is hoping to create 221 jobs for the Bundaberg region with the construction of its new $100 million factory. The 44-hector factory is being built in phases to meet the demands of the iconic Queensland drinks international success and is expected to bring $12 million in wages into the local Bundaberg and surrounding economy (McManagan, 2021).

BBD recently invested a handsome amount to establish the first canning line of their own including a Craft-mate filler from Krones to better support its worldwide export market (Krones Service, 2020). Following several years of toll packing, Bundaberg Brewed Drinks deliberately opted for a canning line of their own. To have the canning technology in-house was an important decision for BBD that allowed the company to offer a versatile pack format to satisfy the consumers' demand. This decision was very timely as it wanted to offer options to the consumers for easy-to-carry cans that are also suitable for cooling quicker. This shows the intuitive managerial competencies regarding product differentiation.

The COVID-19 and new challenges

The economic impact of COVID-19 will continue to impact consumer spending habits in 2021–2022. It is anticipated that the pandemic will lead to the rise of a more price-sensitive consumer where mass grocery retail (MGR) players will focus and expand their discount/wholesale operations and for there to be greater strong demand for private label food and drink products (Yeoh, 2020). The spread of COVID-19 has led to greater awareness around food and drink products that support and boost immunity. As a result, more food and non-alcoholic drinks products that are fortified with vitamins and claim to support immune systems will be launched during 2021, and consumer acceptance of these fortified and functional food and drink products will increase (Yeoh, 2020).

In several countries across the globe, the COVID-19 pandemic and its resultant lockdown measures have exposed points of risk within the food supply chains. While the food and drink sector is familiar with supply-side shocks, the pandemic has caused disruptions to production (i.e., labour shortages following travel restrictions and employees testing positive for COVID-19), and manufacturing processes (i.e., production plant shutdowns) and logistics (i.e., transport disruptions), as well as creating unprecedented demand over a very short period due to panic buying and stockpiling by consumers. Due to social restrictions and more people working from their primary place of residence, home food consumption has grown. However, soft drink consumption is often considered as discretionary which means fewer people are consuming soft drinks, despite an increase in in-home food consumption. This trend is confirmed by the Australian Bureau of Statistics (ABS) Household survey (ABS, 2021). The same survey also found a 19% drop in the consumption of soft drinks, cordials, and energy drinks during the pandemic. These trends are expected to negatively affect industry operators although they project an increase in demand that will occur during the festive season.

Changes in real household disposable income influence demand for soft drinks. Higher disposable incomes enable greater spending on items such as soft drinks and other beverages, positively affecting industry revenue and providing an opportunity for the industry to expand. Real household disposable income is expected to decline in 2021 due to the economic downturn driven by the COVID-19 pandemic (Yeoh, 2020). Since March 2020, and the advent of the COVID-19 pandemic, the company has faced many challenges. BBD has taken some operational measures to take advantage of future market potentials (Wheeler, 2020d).

Local sourcing is an advantage

BBD has become one of Australia's most iconic brands of the past 50 years. Not only has the company not forgotten its roots, but it is also entrenched in its DNA just as much as it is in the town that shares its name. The company gets most of its ingredients from local sources, the main exception being sarsaparilla, which must be imported to satisfy one of its root beer offerings. The local farmers are the major strength of BBD because they supply the best natural produce for the brew. The 250 employees who work for the company are mostly local people, many of whom have been connected to the company for generations (Wheeler, 2020a). Although some sophisticated technology came from Europe, most of the heavy machinery for BBD brewery is fabricated in Australia by ME Engineering.

New opportunities in a new normal

BBD thinks that the challenges posed by COVID-19 also offer some opportunities. As Bundaberg's CEO, John McLean said: 'The pandemic has advanced the business from a technological perspective. We used to use Zoom occasionally but now we run entire weeks on the platform' (Wheeler, 2020a).

According to John Maclean, the communication and relationship among stakeholders grow stronger in such a scenario. As he said,

> It has brought customers and suppliers a lot closer because we've all got a common environment to start a discussion from. ... It's been really good in terms of connecting with people. Our business very much believes in relationships. ...I haven't been on a plane since February, but I'm speaking to my customers and other partners more than I ever have by Zoom or telephone, catching up on the way to work, or on the way home from work. I'm also talking to my employees more than I ever have.
>
> *Wheeler, 2020a*

While having local fabricators is good, it is the supply chain where most companies in the processing and manufacturing of products have found problems during the pandemic. While, initially, the company did have issues, forward planning has been essential and helped BBD to thrive. 'At the beginning of COVID it was a bit more challenging because the ports were making boats wait for 14 days before docking', said McLean. 'That really did hamstring our international business and especially our Kiwi business. We've all gotten over that and we have worked out the situation, so the supply chain is now very robust' (Wheeler, 2020a).

Performance in the home country

BBD is rated by consumers as 'Australia's best soft drink' in Canstar Blue's first national review of an industry typically dominated by multinational giants (Wheeler, 2020b) Australian's placed Kirks second, Schweppes fifth, Pepsi sixth, and Coco-Cola seventh. BBD family owned business was the only brand to receive a five-star rating in the following categories: overall satisfaction, taste, and packaging design and they could not be more grateful for the support of the Australian public. 'For the past 50 years we've been the underdog in a competitive industry and are proud to be formally recognised by fellow Australians as their "favourite soft drink"', said BBD CEO, John McLean. 'COVID-19 has been a challenging period for everyone, and we're appreciative of the support Australians have shown us' (Wheeler, 2020b).

Collaboration with other local businesses

In a period where consumers are being encouraged to purchase Australian-made brands, the iconic BBD business is taking things one step further and encouraging

Australian businesses to support fellow homegrown businesses. John McLean, CEO of Australian has led by example and initiated a launch of a network of Australian fast-moving consumer goods (FMCG). The network included iconic Australian brands Vegemite, Four'n Twenty, and Rosella and they aimed to provide guidance and support to Australian FMCG and the broader business community (Wheeler, 2020c). 'Whether you're Australian-owned, manufactured or employing Aussies, our national business community needs to be there for each other', says John McLean. 'If the changes brought on by COVID-19 become the new normal, we need to work together to ensure Aussie brands live long into the future'.

International collaboration

BBD has come together with the New Zealand chocolate manufacturer, Whittaker's to create the new Whittaker's Brewed Ginger Caramel 250 gram Block. Bundaberg's CEO, John McLean commented about the collaboration stating:

> Both family businesses have a long-standing commitment to excellence and are entrenched in the trans-Tasman way of life. It makes sense for Australia's best soft-drink and New Zealand's most trusted brand to join forces, particularly during a time when consumers are looking for affordable ways to treat themselves.
>
> *Wheeler, 2020d*

The silver lining behind the cloud

The deterioration in China-Australia relations both before and during the pandemic has culminated in the imposition of tariffs on wine products and many other commodities. On November 27, 2020, Chinese authorities announced that they would impose import tariffs ranging from 107% to 212% on all Australian wine imports (Sullivan, Birtles & Terzon, 2020). While this represented a major blow to the Australian wine industry it presented an opportunity to the manufacturers of non-alcoholic drinks like BBD to extend their scope of demand into the Chinese market. Every cloud has a silver lining.

The Australian Federal Government has announced very supportive COVID-19 assistance measures for eligible SMEs. Starting from 28 September 2020, the wage subsidy scheme was changed to a two-tier system based on employees' hours worked and lasted for six months. Employees that work for 20 hours or more per week received $1,200 per fortnight, while employees that work fewer than 20 hours per week received $750 per fortnight. From 3 January 2021, fortnightly payments were reduced to $1,000 for employees that work 20 hours or more per week and $650 for employees that work fewer than 20 hours per week. The COVID-19 assistance policies are expected to benefit small soda manufacturers.

Conclusion

Customers are more drawn to companies that show good signs of corporate social responsibility (Hejase, Hashem, Al Dirani, Haddad, & Atwi, 2017). With rising obesity rates, BBD must address the issue of sugar in its beverages. A bottle of BBD Ginger Beer has 4.8 grams of sugar per 100 ml. This is 0.8 grams more than Fever-Tree Ginger Beer, though 0.4 grams less than Coca-Cola (MyBest, 2020). The social responsibility of BBD has been demonstrated in the community of Bundaberg, its hometown. This social responsibility must now be demonstrated on a global scale.

Acknowledgement: We acknowledge the support of Ms Kasey Bion for her insight and inputs that immensely helped us writing this case.

References

Amazon (2021, 11 August). Amazon Best Sellers. Available at: (www.amazon.co.uk/Best-Sellers-Grocery-Ginger-Ale-eer/zgbs/grocery/435560031).

Asialink Business (2014). Bundaberg Brewed Drinks – Case Study. Available at: https://asialinkbusiness.com.au/research-resources/case-study-bundaberg

Australian Bureau of Statistics (2021). ABS Household Impacts of COVID-19 Survey, 24–29 June 2020 Available at: www.abs.gov.au/statistics/people/people-and-communities/household-impacts-covid-19-survey/jun-2021

Bell, V. (2020). The 10 Most Overweight Countries in Europe. How Does the UK Compare? Available at: https://au.news.yahoo.com/10-most-overweight-countries-in-europe-173658813.html?

Bere, E., Sorli, G. E., Te Velde, S. J., & Kleep, K. I. (2007). Determinants of adolescents soft drink consumption. *Public Health Nutrition Journal*, 11 (1), 49–56.

Briggs, A., Rayner, M. & Scarborough, P. (2016). Soft Drinks, Hard Questions. Project Syndicate. Available at: www.project-syndicate.org/commentary/uk-proposed-tax-on-sugary-drinks-by-adam-briggs-et-al-2016-07

British Soft Drinks Association (2015). Refreshing the Nation Our Contribution to the UK Economy. Available at: www.britishsoftdrinks.com/write/MediaUploads/Publications/2015_BSDA_Economic_Report.pdf

British Soft Drinks Association (2021). 2021 Annual Report. Available at: www.britishsoftdrinks.com/write/MediaUploads/BSDA_Annual_Report_2021_FINAL.pdf

Bundaberg Brewed Drinks (2021a) Our History. Available at: www.bundaberg.com/our-history/

Bundaberg Brewed Drinks (2021b). Our Brews. Available at: www.bundaberg.com/our-brews/

Bundaberg Brewed Drinks (2021c). How We Brew. Available at: www.bundaberg.com/how-we-brew/

Bundaberg Brewed Drinks (2021d). Sustaining the Real Difference. Available at: www.bundaberg.com/sustaining-the-real-difference/

Bundaberg Now (2020). Bundaberg Brewed Drinks Rated Best Aussie Soft Drink. Available at: www.bundabergnow.com/2020/10/14/bundaberg-brewed-best-australian-soft-drink/

Clean Up Australia (2021). Available at: www.cleanup.org.au/newpage

Clun, R. (2017). How Three Family-Run Australian Brands Became Global Businesses. Available at: www.oberonreview.com.au/story/4889132/how-three-family-run-australian-brands-became-global-businesses/

Colborne, M. (2016). Britain's "Sugar Tax" tackles obesity. *CMAJ: Canadian Medical Association Journal (journal de l'Association medicale canadienne), 188*(8), E134. https://doi.org/10.1503/cmaj.109-5260

Cullen, G. (2017). Bundaberg Ginger Beer Goes Global. *In The Black*. Published on 1 November 2017. Available at: www.intheblack.com/articles/2017/11/01/bundaberg-conquers-world

Durie, J. (2018, January 8). Brewed Drinks Strikes Deal with Pepsi. *Bundaberg News-Mail*. Available at: www.news-mail.com.au/news/brewed-drinks-strikes-deal-with-pepsi/3305752/

Fentimans (2021). Available at: www.fentimans.com/drinks

Food Standard Agency (2021). Importing Drinks. Available at: www.food.gov.uk/business-guidance/importing-drinks

Fortune Magazine (2016). Another Country Just Imposed a Sugar Tax on Soft Drinks. Courtesy: By Reuters. Published on: March 17, 2016. Available at: https://fortune.com/2016/03/16/sugar-tax-soft-drinks/

Gorey M. (2019). Organic Farming Grows Queensland Gold Ginger. *Bundaberg Now*. Available at: www.bundabergnow.com/2019/04/06/queensland-gold-ginger/

Hejase, H. J., Hashem, F., Al Dirani, A., Haddad, Z., & Atwi, K. (2017). Corporate social responsibility impact on consumer decision. *The Journal of Middle East and North Africa Sciences, 3*(2), 3–20]. (P-ISSN 2412- 9763) - (e-ISSN 2412–8937). Available at: www.researchgate.net/publication/313160723_Corporate_Social_Responsibility_Impact_on_Consumer_Decision [accessed Aug 21 2021].

Helen Wise Research. (2017). Bundaberg Brewed Drinks Delivering Packaging Innovation Through Stakeholder Partnerships. Available at: http://helenlewisresearch.com.au/wp-content/uploads/2017/10/Bundaberg.pdf

International Business Today (2015). Q&A with Andrew Shepherd, GM Marketing at Bundaberg Brewed Drinks. Autumn 2015. Available at: www.export.org.au/magazine/Internation%20Business%20Today%20Aut%2015%20eBook.pdf

Krones Service (2020). First-ever canning line for Bundaberg Brewed Drinks. Published on 28 September 2020. Available at: https://www.krones.com/en/company/press/first-ever-canning-line-for-bundaberg-brewed-drinks.php?cookie=2

McManagan, J. (2021). Bundy's Iconic Soft Drink Raises a Glass to the Town. Queensland Country Life. Available at: www.queenslandcountrylife.com.au/story/7079017/bundy-brewed-drinks-pours-success-back-into-the-community/?cs=4790#

McPhail, M. (2021). Top 10 Best Ginger Beers in the UK 2021 My Best Food and Drink Recommendation Service. Available at: https://mybest-gb.uk/10153

Meher, N., Bulbul, A. & Khaled, M. (2017). Measuring consumer attitude towards soft drinks: An empirical study of selected brands in Bangladesh. *International Journal of Managerial Studies and Research, 5,* 1–8.

MyBest (2020). Food and Drinks Recommendation Service. Available at: https://mybest-gb.uk/10153

Nutakor, C., Essiedu, J. A., Adadi, P., & Kanwugu, O. N. (2020). Ginger beer: An overview of health benefits and recent developments. *Fermentation, 6*(4), 102.

Oberlander L. and Játiva, X. (2019). How Heat Waves Increase Your Craving for Sodas: Findings from Mexico. *The Conversation*. Available at: https://theconversation.com/how-heat-waves-increase-your-craving-for-sodas-findings-from-mexico-119351

Roache, S. A., & Gostin, L. O. (2017). The untapped power of soda taxes: Incentivizing consumers, generating revenue, and altering corporate behavior. *International Journal of Health Policy and Management*, 6(9), 489

Signet (2021). Bundaberg Brewed Drinks Eliminate Transit Damages and Reduce Plastic Usage by 30%. Available at: www.signet.net.au/blog/bundaberg-brewed-drinks

Spirit International Prestige Awards (2021). Available at: https://sipawards.com/entryform/2021brandresults.php

Sullivan, K., Birtles, B. and Terzon, E. (2020). China Puts Tariffs of up to 200 per cent on Australian Wine. Published by ABC rural on Fri 27 Nov 2020. Available at: www.abc.net.au/news/2020-11-27/china-puts-tariffs-on-australian-wine-trade-tensions/12886700

Sustainability Matters (2012). Carbon Offset Project for Brewed Drink Company. Available at: www.sustainabilitymatters.net.au/content/sustainability/article/carbon-offset-project-for-brewed-drink-company-1138028258

University of California - Berkeley. (2019, February 21). Three Years into Soda Tax, Sugary Drink Consumption Down More Than 50 percent in Berkeley: Texas May Be a Promising New Tool in the Fight Again Obesity, Cardiovascular Disease and Diabetes. *ScienceDaily*. Available at: www.sciencedaily.com/releases/2019/02/190221172056.htm

Wheeler, M. (2020a). Meet the Manufacturer: All in the Family – Bundaberg Brewed Drinks' Rosy Future. Food & Beverage. Available at: www.foodmag.com.au/tag/bundaberg/

Wheeler, M. (2020b). Bundaberg Tops Canstar Blue Soft Drink Ratings. Food & Beverage. Available at: www.foodmag.com.au/tag/bundaberg/

Wheeler, M. (2020c). Food Beverage Staples Say Now's the Time to Lend a Hand. Food & Beverage. Available at: www.foodmag.com.au/tag/bundaberg/

Wheeler, M. (2020d). Australian and NZ Icons Whittaker's and Bundaberg Collaborate on New Venture. Food & Beverage. Available at: www.foodmag.com.au/tag/bundaberg/

Yeoh, Y. H. (2020). Soft Drink Manufacturing in Australia Industry Report C1211A, IBISWorld. Available at: www.ibisworld.com/au/industry/soft-drink-manufacturing/1859/

4
REVIVAL OF DECLINING SMALL BUSINESSES IN AUSTRALIA

Sardana Islam Khan, Ho Yin Wong, Tasmiha Tarafder and Parves Sultan

Introduction

This case study sets out to identify the factors influencing the revival of troubled small businesses in Australia based on the perspectives of the key managers. Qualitative empirical evidence was collected from the key managers of 25 Australian small businesses facing a decline in the period between 2006 and 2018. Finally, implications are drawn for the entrepreneurs and managers of small businesses, followed by a conclusion section.

The Australian Securities and Investment Commission (ASIC) defines small proprietary companies, based on the size of annual revenue (≤$25 million), number of employees (≤50), and consolidated gross assets (≤$12.5 million) at the end of the financial year. Having at least two of the above characteristics at the end of the financial year will identify the business as a small proprietary company in the eyes of ASIC (Australian Securities and Investment Commission, 2019). According to these criteria, we selected 25 small businesses, each employing less than 20 people and having an annual turnover of less than AUD10 million (see Table 4.1). The employment size and revenue were recorded as per the 2018 data (for the fully or partially revived organisations) or at the time of exit (in case of non-revival). Australian small businesses enjoy tax benefits as part of government support.

According to Australian Tax Office (ATO) information, most concession policies have been changed gradually to favour small businesses and start-ups (Australian Tax Office, 2019). The threshold of asset and annual turnover is gradually increasing and is designed to arrest the declining growth of small businesses in Australia. These concessions are a deliberate policy change aimed to simplify the reporting process and provide small businesses with direct financial benefits and a sense of protection (see Table 4.2).

TABLE 4.1 Respondent profiles and revival status of 25 declining Australian small businesses

Code	Position	Age	Business	Revival status
R1	Managing Director	62	Medical equipment supplier and manufacturer	Recovering gradually
R2	Commercial Manager	36	News agency	Revived but then sold for a profit. The owner now works as a consultant to the same industry.
R3	Owner/Director	31	Event organiser	Gradually recovering
R4	Owner/Director	41	Training and education	Reviving and growing (expected to be in the growth stage for next 3 years)
R5	Consultant Engineer	58	Electronics	Business revived but then a partnership conflict led to non-cooperation and exit
R6	consultant	64	Electrical/theatrical	Gradually reviving
R7	Owner/Director	55	Property renovation/repair	Exit
R8	Owner/Director	26	Photography	Moderate recovery
R9	General manager	53	Tennis balls	Failed and exited
R10	Owner/Director	68	Air-conditioning	Slowly reviving
R11	Owner/Director	51	Food truck business	Revived
R12	Sales manager	55	International trading	Voluntary exit
R13	Owner/Director	60	Tyre manufacturer	Revived
R14	Owner/Director	55	Solar power	Failed
R15	Owner/Director	29	Video production	Revived
R16	CEO	40	Mining consultancy	Slow revival by choice due to family issues (new child)
R17	Owner - manager	50	Asian Grocery shop	Failed

TABLE 4.1 Cont.

Code	Position	Age	Business	Revival status
R18	Owner-manager	49	Sri Lankan Grocery shop	Increased revenue and then sold out to the best buyer
R19	Owner, manager and Chef	48	Catering	Slowly reviving to a manageable scale
R20	Working partner and one of the key managers	38	Online dating site	Stuck in the iterative loop for three years after the start-up
R21	Owner-manager	55	Grocery shop	Failed
R22	Manager	41	Grocery shop	Revived by changing business partner
R23	Owner-manager	45	Grocery shop	Revived by changing geographical location
R24	Owner-manager	49	Boutique shop	Slowly reviving by changing location
R25	Owner-manager	58	Café and restaurant	Revived and then voluntarily exited by selling out on personal ground

Source: Primary data collected by authors.

TABLE 4.2 The key concession entitlements of small businesses in Australia

Income tax concessions	Asset or turnover threshold or other eligibilities	Impact of policy change on small business
Simplified depreciation rules – instant asset write-off	Turnovers thresh hold≤$50 mil, Asset threshold	Favourable to all small businesses
Accelerated depreciation for primary producers	Fodder storage asset and fencing & water facilities for all small business entities	Favourable to all small businesses
Lower company tax rate changes	≤$50 million for the 2018–19 income year, ≤80% of assessable income is base rate entity passive income (interest, dividends, rent, royalties and net capital gain).	Favourable to all small businesses
Increased small business income tax offset	turnover ≤$5 million. increases to 13% in 2020–21 and to 16% from the 2021–22 income year	Favourable to smaller sole traders, partnership and trust

(continued)

TABLE 4.2 Cont.

Income tax concessions	Asset or turnover threshold or other eligibilities	Impact of policy change on small business
Deductions for professional expenses for start-ups	Deductible start-up costs include professional, legal and accounting advice and government fees and charges	Favourable to all start-up small businesses
Small business restructure rollover	Avoiding tax liability while changing small business's legal structure	Favourable especially to the declining small businesses at the turnaround stage.
Simplified trading stock rules	Free to avoid formally conducting and reporting a stocktake if there is a difference of ≤$5,000 between the stock value at the start and an estimated stock value at the end of the income year	Favourable to all small businesses, especially the ones in trouble.
Immediate deductions for prepaid expenses	Where the payment covers a period of ≤12 months	Favourable to all small businesses

Source: Australian Tax Office (www.ato.gov.au/business/small-business-entity-concessions/eligibility/work-out-if-you-re-a-small-business-for-the-income-year/).

Turnaround decision and responses of declining businesses

The process of business decline and revival

A firm may face significant decline or stagnation in business, with no scope for future growth, but still survive for an indefinite period at a manageable scale of operation. This state is often defined as failure, but many of our respondents viewed it as a successful revival through retrenchment and down scoping. The process of business decline has been outlined by Weitzel and Jonsson (1989) in a five-stage model, with unique managerial implications at each stage. These stages are blinded management, inaction, faulty action, crisis, and dissolution. Others have categorised decline based on its pace (e.g., sudden vs gradual) (D'aveni, 1989). Amankwah-Amoah (2016) outlined the various stages of decline in terms of early warning signals such as declining resources, expertise, and business performance, followed by responses like downsizing, restructuring, and attempted turnaround. These two stages are highlighted by the author as the early stages of decline leading to failure. The later stages of failure are maladaptation (failed response) and dissolution (decision to dissolve or winding up).

Factors influencing the turnaround decision and responses of declining businesses

According to business decline and turnaround-related theories, managerial cognition and the top management team's (TMT) responses or actions are at the forefront of discussion to successfully formulate and implement turnaround strategies (see Lohrke et al., 2004; Trahms et al., 2013). The success of turnaround responses seems to be largely influenced by the managerial cognition of decline severity and the extent to which TMT responses have addressed the external and internal factors causing the decline (D'aveni, 1989, Van Witteloostuijn, 1998; Lohrke et al., 2004). Sheppard and Chowdhury (2005) contend that the ultimate failure or successful revival are not determined solely by the merit of the turnaround strategy; rather the fit between revival attempts and 'environmental jolts' determines turnaround outcomes. Declining a business's resource orchestration capacity is also crucial to attaining a desirable fit (Trahms et al., 2013) and, in the case of small businesses, this capability is largely dependent on the perceptions, capabilities, and motivation of key managers. The demographics of key managers or the top management team (TMT) play a major role in developing managerial cognition and crisis responses in declining Australian small businesses. These factors and processes have informed our case study design and analysis.

The question remains, however: What factors influence a small business's turnaround capacity and how does the managerial perception of such capacity underpin the turnaround decision and responses to successfully revive a declining firm? Extant literature on managerial cognition (awareness, perception, and attribution of decline), strategic leadership (TMTs and Boards of Directors: compensation composition/capability/fit/vigilance), and stakeholder management (ownership, creditors, suppliers, customers, employees, and government) have been identified as influential factors in the selection and success of organisational revival attempts (Lohrke, et al., 2004; Trahms et al., 2013). Trahms et al. (2013) also acknowledged the possibility of an iterative turnaround loop, as opposed to the fixed two-step linear process model of business revival introduced by Pearce and Robbins (1993). In a small firm, one or a few entrepreneurs usually constitute the top management team (TMT). Therefore, the perceptions of key manager's in terms of a declining firm's capacity to revive should logically reflect on turnaround decisions, responses, and outcomes. After reviewing the contemporary literature on managerial cognition, business decline, and the turnaround framework, three major factors (i.e., managerial, organisational, and external factors) plus several sub-factors were identified as having potential implications for the turnaround decision, responses, and the success of a declining small business. The themes presented in Tables 4.3a and 4.3b informed our research design and analytical framework.

TABLE 4.3A Factors influencing the turnaround decision of the key manager(s) and responses of a declining small business in Australia

Key factors	Sub-factors	Frequency (N=25)	Impact on the turnaround decision, responses and successful revival
Managerial factors	- *Managerial cognition*	25	**Structuring & Search/Selection of resources for turnaround**: Depends on the level of managerial cognition, motivation (passion and learning), network (professional community, friends and family) and access to resources (qualification, connections and track record) to build up firm's resource portfolio. **Bundling & Configuration/ Deployment of resources for turnaround**: Depends on managerial skills/capabilities, leadership, innovation, cognition, passion for the business and revival, motivation for exerting efforts to bundle and deploy the acquired resources. **Leveraging & Configuration/ Deployment of resources for turnaround**: Depends on managerial vision, entrepreneurial innovation, enhanced cognition and capability to use resources portfolio to exploit emerging market opportunity and leadership, passion for the business and revival, motivation for exerting efforts to bundle and deploy the acquired resources.
	- Motivation and self-efficacy	25	
	- Managerial capabilities	16	
	- *Network*	12	
	- Leadership and entrepreneurial drive	10	
	- Managerial access to resources	10	
Organisational factors	- *Top-management team (TMT)*	5	These factors have influences on the turnaround response choices and turnaround capabilities of the declining small businesses and
	- *Stakeholder management*	4	
	- *Firm's breadth, depth, and lifecycle*	4	
External factors	- Availability and quality of the support services	4	These factors may moderate the effects of turnaround responses on the successful revival of a small business in Australia.
	- Government support	5	

Source: Based on primary data collected by authors.

TABLE 4.3B Summary of findings from the key managers/entrepreneurs of Australian small business

Stages (decline/ turnaround)	Sub-factors	Response summary
Causes of decline	*Internal*	(i) Flawed human resource management inefficient staffing, poor succession planning, poor performance management systems; (ii) lack of experience; (iii) lack of appropriate skills in marketing, accounting, or IT; (iv) inadequate research; (v) partnership conflict; (vi) lack of professionalism; (vii) lack of innovation; (viii) lack of diversification; (ix) misrepresentation of the product; (x) delayed service delivery; (xi) physical burnout) or severe health issues of key managers; (xii) lack of knowledge transfer and capacity building; (xiii) lack of due diligence of key partners; (xiv) expectation of unrealistic financial return; (xv) lack of understanding and passion for the craft/business; and (xvi) lack of customer orientation.
	External	(i) Decline in demand for various uncontrollable reasons; (ii) intense and unpredictable competition; (iii) global issues; (iv) inefficiency of external financial or advisory services; (v) government policy or legal changes; (vi) unpredictable increase or imposition of external costs; (vii) non-cooperation or corrupt practices of suppliers; and (viii) unpredictable technological advancements.
Early indications of decline	Financial	High-cost low return reflected in the financial reports and books of accounts
	Market feedback	Lost/declining orders, poor customer review, increased complaints and lower loyalty from the regular buyers
	Operational	Visible operational inefficiencies in projected by high absenteeism and employee attrition, slow processing of orders, higher level of conflict, low innovation and slow/ineffective communication.
	Other external sources	Complaints and notices from the suppliers, tax authority, law enforcing agencies or other stakeholders
Turnaround responses	*Structuring & Search/ Selection*	1. to identify/acquire, accumulate, invest or divest the required resources based on their cognition of the nature and severity of decline. 2. to reinvent the business model (may be using ICT or other accessible assets) and restructure the organisation or governance. 3. to use network and to gain access to resources to build up firm's resource portfolio.

(continued)

TABLE 4.3B Cont.

Stages (decline/ turnaround)	Sub-factors	Response summary
	Bundling & Configuration/ deployment	to provide leadership to nurture innovation and coordinate the co-specialised assets in the organisation to stabilise the business, enrich the resources (more training and development activities) and pioneer ideas.
	Leveraging & Configuration/ deployment	to leverage the accumulated and enriched resource portfolio at this stage to create a unique competitive strength and exploit the emerging opportunities in the market.
Firm Actions	*Operational*	- Developing resources - Cost retrenchment
	Strategic	- Acquiring new resources. - Acquiring new market - Repositioning the product. - Down-scoping
Response Outcomes	*Recovery*	- Complete recovery (going back to the normal state with an intension to grow) - Gradual/Slow recovery (aiming stability as opposed to growth) - Recovery and voluntary exit
	Failure	- Stranded in iterative turnaround loop for a prolonged period with no visible efforts to exit or effectively recover - Failure & exit

Source: Based on Authors' discussion.

Findings

The findings of the study have been organised and analysed in the following sections under three themes (a) managerial factors, (b) organisational factors, and (c) external factors (Table 4.3a).

Managerial factors

Managerial cognition of decline severity

According to the respondents, early indications of a business's decline were visible in the accounts, market data, the number of complaints, the visibility of competitors' marketing efforts, or simply by a decline or stagnation in the operations of the business (see Table 4.3b). One of the respondents stated:

> Basically, large costs and lower returns on investments indicated trouble. Certain opportunities were lost to competitors which led me to reassess our position.
>
> R1

In line with the concept of managerial cognition identified by Trahms et al. (2013) as the first aspect of the firm's response to declining, respondents indicated that the key manager's awareness and perception of the severity of the business decline influence their turnaround decisions and capacity during the turnaround process. According to respondent R4, the lack of education of business owners to understand the impact of poor customer service was devastating and to R3 the lack of identifying the importance of financial growth was crucial. Almost all respondents indicated that the key manager's awareness of decline severity has influenced the decision of turnaround responses (attempt vs no response) as well as the effective search and selection, structuring, bundling, leveraging, and configuration or deployment of key resources during the turnaround process. Age, experience, education, and business expertise were identified as the key predictors of the cognitive capabilities of key managers in our study.

Motivation and self-efficacy

The data indicated that the need (source of motivation), availability of alternative employment opportunities, and self-efficacy of key managers influenced their turnaround decision and capacity. For example, R4 stated that "probably one of the most important aspects is knowing myself … if we have fears or doubts regarding the turnaround success, we will subconsciously sabotage that future success".

Some respondents indicated that they made no attempt to revive the business as they believed any such attempt would be a form of financial suicide, or that they just ran out of energy. As for R12 "the partners made a conscious decision not to revive the business as they ran out of energy" and for others; they chose to revive the business because they did not see a better personal alternative in the job market. One owner-manager explained that reviving the business was the only way to stay or permanently migrate to Australia and therefore he used all his available resources and contacts to turn his business around.

In contrast, some respondents suggested that they attempted revival only because closing down was not possible due to legal constraints or because the financial loss of exit would exceed the loss of continuing the business on a small scale. Thus, some owners have been able to orchestrate enough resources to slowly revive the business to a manageable or targeted level.

Managerial capabilities

Marketing, research, Information Technology (IT), networking capabilities, plus the accounting and finance skills of key managers as well as acquiring relevant expertise are deemed important for an effective turnaround response. R12 identified their

TMT expertise in the above areas was not only a key success factor but it was also one of the major reasons for the business decline when some of these managers were forced to retire due to health and age-related issues. The issue of succession planning emerged as a vital cause of non-revival. Succession planning is often more complex for small businesses where performance is influenced not only by the skills of key managers but also by the unique relationship and understanding between the key managers. Such businesses find it very difficult to key managers with the same level of capabilities and fit and therefore lose their advantage for a successful revival. R12's following statement will reflect this fact:

> I would come up with the ideas in what we needed in the software and Mr X was the one who put it together for us. Without him and his expertise, we simply lost our capability to configure, leverage and deploy our other resources to take advantage of market opportunities. Then a core member of staff was diagnosed with a brain tumour. I wouldn't say it was impossible to replace him, but it would have meant enormous time searching, and we didn't have the time for it.

Leadership and entrepreneurial drive

The respondents identified leadership vision, charisma, and passion plus entrepreneurial innovation as some of the factors positively influencing the turnaround decision and capacity during the declining stage.

> Reviving the business was more rewarding than challenging. I thrive with problems and finding solutions and fixing things to the way they should be. In the last 10 years, there had been 4 businesses I revived. I worked for them as the key manager, and my mission was to have that business to where it should be operating, I guess my enthusiasm and positive attitude towards challenges transmitted to others in those troubled organisations.
>
> R13

Organisational factors

Respondents' recollection of their businesses' decline and turnaround process highlighted three major organisational factors that may influence a small firm's capacity and strategic decisions. The TMT composition, dynamics, stakeholder management and firm breadth, depth and lifecycle were the three firm-level components identified in our study.

Top management team

The composition, cohesion, level of engagement, plus the skill and diversity of the TMT were identified as some of the key factors influencing the Revival and

Turnaround (RTA) capabilities of a declining small firm. The extent of the personal and professional networks of key managers was identified by the respondents as an important enabler in the search for crucial resources during the turnaround process. The reach of such networks also seems to have an impact on the business's access to financial and human resource capabilities. While the number of active partners with a diverse range of expertise has been identified as an important RTA strength, the cohesion, team spirit, communication, shared vision, and interest across the TMT were viewed as vital indicators of the capacity of small businesses in the turnaround stage. Strong cohesion between TMT, despite being a strength for a regular organisation, can also be identified as a deterrent to succession planning and subsequent non-revival of some declining firms.

Respondent R16 explains the TMT succession issue:

> My business partner was a working partner with an engineering background and understanding of technical aspects of the mining equipment while I was the marketing expert. We were doing great for a while till my partner started missing meetings and the business started to go downslope. (When resigned), he took some of my clients away, took 25 thousand bucks from the business claiming his contribution to goodwill and left me and the business with the difficult task of recruiting a mining equipment expert We are still in business and wish to continue at a slow pace till I can find a suitable partner again.

Stakeholder management and firm's breadth, depth, and life cycle

Sirmon, Hitt, Ireland, and Gilbert, (2011) argue that a firm's breadth (scope), depth (levels of hierarchy), and life cycle (maturity) affect the resource management decisions of managers in gaining a competitive advantage. Using the same logic, we argue that these three aspects may influence the capacity of a declining small firm in the turnaround process. Our findings reflect the influence of these three aspects on a firm's capacity during revival attempts. As R9 stated:

> I probably should have diversified when my wife wanted me to go into other products. But I didn't want to carry on because I didn't think I had the knowledge. That was probably a mistake because we're not getting enough income to take care of all these costs and that gradually reduced our capability to acquire a new business or expand in the international market even when the opportunity came.

R2 identified the life cycle stage issue as a constraint to capacity during his turnaround attempts:

> News agencies were regulated industries at that time but then the government deregulated it and then gave the business to the supermarkets. It was

good in the 90s but then Officeworks and supermarkets took over....... I was going to dissolve the business as News Agencies were at the declining stage in the life cycle. But then I got everything paid off and when everything was a little more in order, I was able to sell it.

RO actions and focus can vary across the top, middle, and operational levels of management in an organisation (Sirmon et al., 2011). In small businesses, there are usually fewer levels in the organisational structure and even when such levels exist, the small number of employees and the volume of business transactions make it easier to minimise the loss of information in communications across the hierarchy making the synchronisation of resources relatively easier compared to larger organisations. Moreover, during the small business decline and turnaround stage, the first turnaround strategy often involves stabilisation (Lohrke, et al., 2004) and down scoping leading to either hiring new experts in the key management positions or letting go those employees who add little or no value to the business. Therefore, at this stage, in a small business context, the RO decisions and actions are concentrated among the key managers of small firms, posing fewer challenges in resource synchronisation. Our findings indicate that a firm's depth is more relevant when the number of employees is comparatively higher or when the owner-manager is absent or disengaged due to unavoidable circumstances. For example, R2 said:

> When I was sick, I had to employ somebody, and it was costing me a little over a thousand dollars a week. Also, a place just doesn't run as well when the boss is not there. They were going out and buying things they shouldn't have been buying, that cost me a fair bit.

R6 (a key manager but not the owner) stated,

> I joined as the group's general manager of 'Electrical division. (Among two divisions: theatre and electrical) the 'Theatre' division's general manager proved to be dishonest and incompetent ......Once I explained the structural problem and that I also believe there was fraud involved, he (the owner) immediately wanted to sell the business. I said you have a business here that is fundamentally good but is poorly managed, we will rebuild and restore this business.

External factors

The availability and quality of the external support services (such as a lawyer, auditors, accountant consultants, and bankers) and government support have been identified as two of the most important external factors influencing the capacity of a declining small firm in Australia.

As R5 stated:

> ……in the old days, you'd have bank managers who would understand your proposal. I think now it's far more methodical - by the book way and they're not good at analysing the potential of the company or the risk.

R8 who was struggling to revive her photography business stated:

> My feeling is that it was the last budget. They took millions of dollars of grants from the art industries and people just couldn't spend, and I know that some people from similar industries had the same feeling as well.

Turnaround responses

The qualitative findings from this study identified two different reactions at the various stages of decline: (i) revival attempts; and (ii) no revival attempts. Any turnaround attempt could lead to one of five alternatives: (a) full revival of the business; (b) considerable redirection of the business (reinvention); (c) revival at minimum capacity (divesting); (d) temporary revival (smoothly heading towards inevitable demise); or (e) revival leading to a profitable sell-out (continuing operation under new ownership). These alternative pathways to revival or failure are simplified and mapped in Figure 4.1.

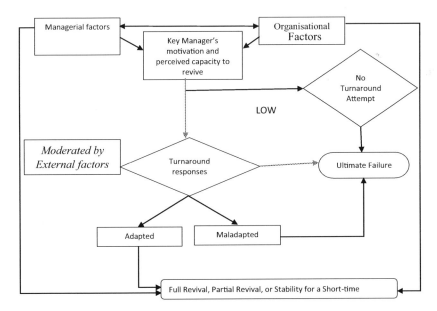

FIGURE 4.1 A flowchart of small business turnaround responses and outcomes

Note: This model has been developed, based on the accumulated findings of this study, to reflect the iterative loop of turnaround responses leading to ultimate failure or successful revival.

One of the respondents stated that he tried to revive the business through intense marketing, greater personal effort and engagement in convincing customers, hiring a more skilled marketing team, using a new website, and self-motivation (R3). In contrast, another respondent stated:

> I put the business on hold and sought employment. Then I was able to earn income and repair my financial status, and all the while I was working in the background on the business about what I need to change or how I need to restructure. I've now incorporated customer service, niched it into a particular industry and hired a marketing expert to improve my concept.
>
> R4

These respondents focused on trying to sell the business and minimise the loss. The business either merged with new owner's or remained in operation under the new management. In case of partnership conflict, one of the partners purchased the share of another and kept the operation going or a new partner replaced one of the old ones and revived the business.

Some entrepreneurs accept liquidation even after attempting to revive the business and some faced bankruptcy during the process. Others still run a limited operation with the help of financial institutions to help pay off existing liabilities. All these revival attempts or non-actions indicate that various response strategies may lead to similar outcomes, whereas similar strategic or operational responses may lead to different outcomes. The complex interaction of managerial, organisational, and external factors and capacity to search, select, bundle, and deploy available resources may help explain these findings (see Table 3a and 3b).

Discussion

The implications and insights from the findings will be discussed in three key sections: (i) factors influencing capacity and turnaround responses in Australian small businesses; (ii) the influence of managerial cognition and perception on the capacity of small business's turnaround responses; and (iii) implications for small business entrepreneurs and policymakers in Australia.

Factors influencing the capacity and turnaround responses of Australian small businesses

Based on the findings we argue that capacity and turnaround decisions and outcomes of declining small businesses in Australia are influenced by managerial, organisational, and external factors (see Table 3a). In Australian small businesses, illness, diminished capacity and motivation caused by ageing (along with no succession plan or knowledge sharing), better opportunities in the job market due to existing or newly gained expertise, and increased family responsibilities have led to the partial recovery, exit/sell decisions by owners. In other words, managerial cognition of asset and resource orchestration capabilities were influenced by key managers' personal motivation, self-efficacy, and alternative employment opportunities. Two respondents said they had to put all their resources and energy into the organisational turnaround process because they had no other option (R10 and R15) which eventually led to the partial recovery of the business.

Influence of perceived capacity and managerial factors on the small business turnaround responses and iterative loop

In line with various models of decline and recovery in the extant literature, our study has identified five different forms of revival. In some instances, the government or financial institutions may step up to help revive the firm or a new owner may successfully revive it while keeping its original identity. In our study, new and inexperienced managers/entrepreneurs were less able to identify decline, assess the situation, and respond effectively at an early stage. However, crisis responses of new and inexperienced managers/entrepreneurs were more flexible than those of experienced or older managers, as proposed in the theory of Lohrke et al. (2004).

The more experienced small businesses entrepreneurs are likely to be resilient or flexible in their response strategies and more likely to sell out to recover or minimise loss. Such responses were in part due to the health of owners or the lack of energy to keep reinventing the business, lack of will to learn and grow, or rigidity in strategic choices. These responses support the theory that career experiences, conflicting goals, and bounded rationality will guide the TMT's strategy (Lohrke, et al., 2004). Key manager's motivation, causal attribution, skills, and abilities influence not only the capacity of the declining small business but also the choice and success of their turnaround responses (Adner & Helfat, 2003). The motivation of key managers to continue their recovery efforts was influenced largely by their capability, resources, efficacy, and self-interest. All these factors were identified as TMT characteristics in Lohrke et al.'s (2004) model.

Theoretically, the three types of TMT resources, i.e., human, social, and managerial cognition (see Adner & Helfat 2003; Lohrke, Bedeian & Palmer 2004), should positively influence and predict turnaround processes and outcomes. However, in the Australian small business context, key managers with superior capabilities (in terms of human and social capital) are more likely to select stabilisation, sellout, retrenchment, or not attempt to recover, despite their higher managerial cognition level. Agency theory or conflict with self-interest (see Lohrke et al., 2004) works differently in small businesses. Highly skilled and capable key managers/entrepreneurs usually increase their involvement in the stabilisation of their declining business. This process further increases their cognitive complexity and this increased social networking and cognitive ability opens up more beneficial new opportunities for them at a personal and professional level and motivates them to recover or minimise the loss from the declining business and exit, rather than continue with the turnaround process.

On the other hand, entrepreneurs with lower social capital and cognitive complexity find it difficult to exit due to a lack of job opportunities in the market and/or lack the resources to pay off existing debt. They keep on applying various recovery strategies to revive the declining business for their own survival. Initially, these entrepreneurs respond with a stabilisation attempt and then gradually apply operational and strategic turnaround strategies. Most of these entrepreneurs manage to revive the organisation to a certain degree by retrenching staff plus other strategic and operational responses. Some other highly capable and resourceful entrepreneurs, who are passionate about their craft, have also managed to successfully revive their organisations, despite having more beneficial opportunities in the job market. Therefore, a complex interplay of managerial cognition, resource orchestration capabilities, firm-level factors, and external causal factors may influence the success or failure of turnaround attempts, processes, and outcomes.

The stages of decline and turnaround responses of small businesses are presented in Table 4.3.

The pattern of turnaround response and outcomes in the Australian small business context

Many severely troubled small businesses use asset sales and retrenchments as a turnaround strategy. Turnaround literature reported contradictory patterns of turnaround outcomes associated with asset sales and retrenchment strategies in a declining business context (see Barker & Duhaime, 1997; Mone, 1994). Most of the declining small businesses included in the current study have revived through down scoping and retrenchment as key managers believed that this is the only way to keep their operation manageable in the long run.

The current study found no noteworthy variations in the revival decision or outcomes across gender except those female entrepreneurs tended to approach down scoping more as a strategic response. A variation was also observed across age groups in terms of revival decisions. The more aged entrepreneurs reported the lack of motivation and energy to rebuild the team and the more experienced ones preferred to explore other options of employment through their professional network instead of attempting revival. Some entrepreneurs who explored alternative means of employment were caught in a prolonged turnaround loop with no real plan or effort to revive their business.

The implications of our findings for Australian small business entrepreneurs are threefold. First, potential small business entrepreneurs should develop their managerial capabilities in the selected industry through education, training, job experience, or by developing networks in the industry. Second, during the declining stage, factors influencing the business's capacity should be carefully measured to select an appropriate turnaround response to minimise loss. Third, organisational capabilities should be continuously developed beyond the capabilities of key managers or entrepreneurs to sustain the business in the long run.

Implications for the small business entrepreneurs and policymakers in Australia

About 10,000 Australian small businesses enter and leave the economy every year (The Australian Small Business and Family Enterprise Ombudsman, 2016). According to the 2013–2014 Australian Bureau of Statistics (ABS) report, only 15% of small businesses have received any kind of government assistance as opposed to the 57% level of assistance received by larger businesses (Australian Bureau of Statistics, 2017). Thus, it seems that the smaller the business, the lower the prospect of receiving external assistance according to the latest statistics. This is largely since it is easier for a small business in Australia to quickly enter the market to exploit an emerging opportunity and then exit when the early symptoms of decline become obvious. These facts support our findings that small business turnaround decisions and success largely depend on managerial cognition, motivation, and their capability to effectively orchestrate the resources as opposed to being influenced by the external forces or other stakeholders.

The ATO concessions (see Table 4.1) have increased over several years (especially after 2015) intending to address the challenges faced by small businesses in Australia. The benefits of such extended concessions are visible in the improved overall economic contribution of small businesses after 2015. More recent policies that extend the asset and turnover eligibility thresholds for concessions to include medium-sized businesses have also helped. These new policies have helped improve the stability and employment generated by medium-sized businesses. Some respondents suggested that they found it difficult to compete with larger organisations due to resource limitations. Extending government concessions to medium-sized organisations may allow small firms to survive the competition. One recommendation could be to provide subsidised education and training opportunities to key managers and entrepreneurs of small businesses to develop relevant skills and capabilities to revive their business and introduce special tax concessions for the severely troubled small firms.

Conclusion

This study used retrospective accounts of 25 key managers during the organisational decline and/or revival of 25 small businesses to further extend an understanding of the capacity of reviving severely troubled Australian small businesses. Informed by the extant organisational decline and turnaround framework we argue that managerial cognition, motivation, and turnaround responses are critical to the successful revival of a declining small business. Our findings also draw the reader's attention to the fact that in a small business context turnaround decisions are generally made by the key managers and their perception of the firm's capacity is important. The perceived capacity and success or failure of revival attempts primarily depend on managerial and organisational factors in the case of small businesses in Australia. External factors like government policy and other forms of support to troubled businesses may also help small firms orchestrate resources more effectively during the turnaround process. The capacity of a declining small business helps predict how the available resources are acquired, bundled, and deployed by the organisation to successfully recover.

The findings from this study will help small business entrepreneurs and managers to examine their context, make pre-emptive moves in the face of potential decline, and explore strategic revival options. The findings of this study will lay a foundation for future research projects focusing on quantitative modelling of perceived capacity, turnaround responses and outcomes in other similar or unique organisational contexts.

References

Adner, R., & Helfat, C. E. (2003). Corporate effects and dynamic managerial capabilities. *Strategic Management Journal, 24*(10), 1011–1025.

Amankwah-Amoah, J. (2016). An integrative process model of organisational failure. *Journal of Business Research, 69*(9), 3388–3397.

Australian Bureau of Statistics (2017). *Counts of Australian Businesses, including Entries and Exits*, Retrieved 26 June 2018, <www.abs.gov.au/ausstats/abs@.nsf/mf/8165.0>.

Australian Securities and Investment Commission (2019), Retrieved 8 June 2019, <https://asic.gov.au/>.

Australian Taxation Office (2019), Retrieved 8 June 2019, <www.ato.gov.au/business/small-business-entity-concessions/eligibility/work-out-if-you-re-a-small-business-for-the-income-year/>.Barker,V. L., & Duhaime, I. M. (1997). Strategic change in the turnaround process: Theory and empirical evidence. *Strategic Management Journal, 18*(1), 13–38.

D'aveni, R. A. (1989). The aftermath of organizational decline: A longitudinal study of the strategic and managerial characteristics of declining firms. *Academy of Management Journal, 32*(3), 577–605.Lohrke, F. T., Bedeian, A. G., & Palmer, T. B. (2004). The role of top management teams in formulating and implementing turnaround strategies: A review and research agenda. *International Journal of Management Reviews, 5*(2), 63–90.

Mone, M. A. (1994). Relationships between self-concepts, aspirations, emotional responses, and intent to leave a downsizing organization. *Human Resource Management, 33*(2), 281–298.Pearce, J. A., & Robbins, K. (1993). Toward improved theory and research on business turnaround. *Journal of Management, 19*(3), 613–636.

Sheppard, J. P., & Chowdhury, S. D. (2005). Riding the wrong wave: Organizational failure as a failed turnaround. *Long Range Planning, 38*(3), 239–260.

Sirmon, D. G., Hitt, M. A., Ireland, R. D., & Gilbert, B. A. (2011). Resource orchestration to create competitive advantage: Breadth, depth, and life cycle effects. *Journal of Management, 37*(5), 1390–1412.The Australian Small Business and Family Enterprise Ombudsman (2016), Retrieved 8 June 2019, <www.asbfeo.gov.au/>.

Trahms, CA, Nodofor, HA & Sirmon, DG 2013, 'Organizational decline and turnaround: A review and agenda for future research', *Journal of Management, 39*(5), 1277–1307.

Van Witteloostuijn, A. (1998). Bridging behavioral and economic theories of decline: Organizational inertia, strategic competition, and chronic failure. *Management Science, 44*(4), 501-519.

Weitzel, W., & Jonsson, E. (1989). Decline in organizations: A literature integration and extension. *Administrative Science Quarterly*, 34(1) 91–109.

5
SOCIAL INNOVATION IN HEALTH RESPONSE

A rare case of social enterprise meeting rural health needs

Lisa A. Caffery, Olav T. Muurlink and Andrew W. Taylor-Robinson

Introduction

Australia's geographical health divide has roots not just in geography but also in policy. Australia's population of almost 26 million (2021) is concentrated in the capital cities of the nation's states and territories, but over eight million live outside those capitals (Australian Institute of Health and Welfare, 2018). While 'regional and remote' Australians, crudely defined as those living outside these capitals, clearly constitute a 'minority', this minority is a critical one to the nation's economy: 67% of the nation's exports come from regional, rural, and remote areas, from labour-intensive sectors such as primary production, and critical industries such as mining and mineral processing. As regional populations shrink or remain stable in absolute terms, as a proportion of the national population the regions are relatively rapidly shrinking, and unable to sustain basic services such as general medical practices let alone offer specialist services taken for granted in metropolitan Australia. The population in rural Australia is thus increasingly forced to commute to receive primary healthcare (Mitton, Dionne, Masucci, Wong & Law, 2011), not to mention more advanced services. Not surprisingly, distance from capital cities in Australia predicts health outcomes (AIHW, 2018); rural Australians are sicker and older than urban-based Australians, have more risk factors, and have higher levels of disability. An additional factor is that although they constitute just 2.4% of Australia's population nationally, Indigenous Australians make up 6% in outer regional areas, 15% in remote areas, and 49% in very remote areas (Baxter, Gray, & Hayes, 2011). Indigenous Australians have a significantly higher incidence of complex health needs (Durey & Thompson, 2012).

This case examines a community-led response to the rural health service deficit. Like many rural centres, the regional hub of Emerald in Central Queensland (population 13,500) faced the consequences related to the speed of access to

DOI: 10.4324/9781003256717-5

care: availability of GPs for initial primary care advice, access to specialist services without heading to larger regional centres, transport difficulties in gaining access to those regional centres, and socioeconomic hurdles in the background.

This case study provides an innovative lens through which to view community-led responses in rural Australia. Herbert and Best noted that as a global society, 'we need new ways of thinking and of working to accommodate the complexity of the challenges in and urgent need for health system innovation and change' (2011, p.31). We examine how a small group of determined community leaders established a new social enterprise that not just addressed health needs in the community but delivered spillover benefits for the local economy. This chapter aims to provide a deeper theoretical understanding of social innovation in health. It illustrates a grassroots innovation that attempts to bridge a gap in health provision.

Emerald is considered a 'medium' rural under Australian classification standards (Australian Government Department of Health, 2021 but with a population of under 15,000 people, it is also the 'capital' of a local government region known as the Central Highlands Region, covering close to 60,000 square kilometres, and a population of almost double that of the town area, with 28,645 in the most recent census. The Queensland Government Statistician's Office shows the area in recent times is showing an almost stat (slightly negative) population growth rate (in contrast to the state of Queensland that has been growing at a rate of 1.6% over the last five years), but the region has a surprisingly youthful profile for regional Australia (25.3% of the population are aged 0–14 whereas across the state that number is 15.7%) and the median age is younger than that of the state. The region has six relatively small hospitals, but substantial population clusters have no access to hospitals – for example, in the Gemfields region of the shire, there are no hospitals, private clinics, diagnostic centres, or specialist services. All non-acute and emergency health services for those living in this region are between 50 and 80 km away.

Overview of CHH

Central Highlands Healthcare Ltd (CHH) traded as the Emerald Medical Clinic and recently changed its brand name to 'Emyria' (Emyria, 2020). It is both a social enterprise and a limited public company with a social purpose. The limited company organisational structure offers limited liability protection to its members. A volunteer board oversees the governance of the company, while a full-time chief executive officer oversees the day-to-day management of the clinic as a business and the medical staff are led by a prominent Sentinel General Practitioner (GP). The senior management team comprise the CEO, the Sentinel GP, a practice manager, a training and education manager, a nurse manager, and a senior receptionist (Table 5.1).

Turning to ownership structure, the company is fully community-owned, and all retained earnings are reinvested back into the CHH operation. The board receives no compensation for their time and no dividends are paid to members. These

TABLE 5.1 Company overview

Region	Emerald, Central Queensland
Country	**Australia**
Service	**Primary Healthcare**
Stage of Development	**Scaled**
Company Established	2012
First Opened	2015
Company Structure	**Private Limited Company with Charity Status**
Company Type	**Social Enterprise**
Company Size	**Small Enterprise (< 50 employees)**
Annual Net Income (2020)	**$3.8 million**
Total Equity (2020)	**$5.3 million**

Source: Emyria Ltd (2020).

characteristics mean that CHH has, unusually, obtained endorsement as a Deductible Gift Recipient with the Australian Tax Office meaning that all donations over $2 are tax-deductible.

Because the operation was set up as a social enterprise, it enabled CHH easier access to government support. Hence, the physical building in which the clinic is housed was fully funded by the Federal Government's GP Super Clinics Infrastructure Program. Many of the other clinics funded under the same scheme received were, strikingly, privately owned businesses lacking the community, grassroots drive that CHH was able to draw on, and have subsequently failed and closed (Australian Medical Association, 2014). The Emerald Medical Clinic is the only not-for-profit, community-owned clinic funded through the GP Super Clinics program and is also an outlier in terms of its sustained success. It's therefore valuable to analyse how The Emerald Medical Clinic has defied this trend (Table 5.2).

Products and services

Social innovation is designed to deliver social impact by finding new ways to address the unmet social need (Mulgan, Tucker, Ali, & Sanders, 2006). At its core, social innovation within the rural health space is a response to complex structural failures that result in people's health needs being unmet (Caló, Roy, Donaldson, Teasdale, & Baglioni, 2019). CHH was first established in December 2012 with the primary purpose to address health gaps in the town of Emerald in rural Central Queensland. The not-for-profit group opened the Emerald Medical Clinic three years later in 2015. Originally, CHH was set up to provide high-quality general practitioner services to local Emerald residents. However, after its first five years of operation, the clinic has more than 23,000 registered patients – in a region that has around a population of 30,000, a remarkable achievement. The numbers demonstrate how the clinic has attracted clients from a wide geographic base and fill a significant unmet need across the entire Central Highlands region and beyond. In the 2019–2020 financial year, the staff at the Emerald Medical Clinic delivered up

TABLE 5.2 Attributes of CHH social enterprise

Enterprise Orientation	• Frontline health services for the general public • Generating revenue and profit • Sustained operation since December 2015
Attributes	• Explicit social purpose orientation • Autonomous local volunteer governance structures • Community ownership • Profits reinvested in business or otherwise for benefit of the community
Scalability	• Model has the potential for replication to other geographical areas or population groups • Business is sustainable through meeting ongoing community need
Competitive Advantages	• Adopting a mission that achieves social value and answers community need • Being flexible and agile to adapt to changing market characteristics and community needs • Working with government agencies to meet government priorities • Maximising limited resources • Skill-based volunteer board

Source: Author's discussion.

to 68,000 individual appointments (including the nurse, doctor, respiratory clinic and telehealth consultations), a 20% increase in three years. It also equates to an average of 186 people seeking a medical consultation at the clinic every single day of the year.

Until the establishment of the clinic, improving health access in Emerald had proven stubbornly resistant to change. 'Intractable problems', as Nicholls and Murdock (2012, p.7) explain, 'are seen as highlighting the failure of conventional solutions and established paradigms entrenched in intractable institutional settings across all three conventional sectors of society'. As the CHH business has developed it has been able to expand not just the quantity element of access (for example availability of standard GP services) but the quality: the range of services offered on-site. Minor procedures are now delivered in its purpose-built surgery. For example, in 2017/18, 36 vasectomies were completed, and 775 patients had suspicious skin lesions removed. A new on-site specialised skin cancer service also meant 25 skin melanomas were identified and removed in the local clinic in the same year. These simple surgical procedures meant 811 people avoided the inconvenience and cost of having to travel to Rockhampton or Brisbane. Other specialist services that patients can now access locally include Cardiology and Endocrinology, which are made possible largely due to remote telecommunications technology. A total of 1,500 telehealth consultations with specialists were conducted at the clinic in 2019/20. In terms of distance, that is roughly three million kilometres that patients did not have to travel to and from Brisbane in a single year alone – all thanks to telehealth technology.

For all social innovations, there is a central theme of achieving impact (Best & Myers, 2017; Hwang, J & Christensen, 2008; Komatsu, 2015). Traditional responses to wicked problems tend to offer 'one size fits all solutions'. Social innovation responses tend to be agile and adaptive to the changing nature of the ecosystem in which they are embedded. The CHH Board has recognised the need to build relational capital and ensure their decision-making processes are embedded in the local ecosystem. Adding additional services has also supported the goal of achieving financial sustainability. The changing health context in the region identified a major service deficit in allied health across the Central Highlands region. In response to this clear need, CHH attracted a range of new allied health services to co-locate at the Emerald Medical Clinic, including audiology, psychology, occupational therapy, physiotherapy, and speech pathology. A benefit of this service delivery model is that the GPs can now build professional relationships with a suite of allied health practitioners and refer directly to a network of on-site clinicians rather than sending patients out of town, which is a standard practice in most non-metropolitan areas.

Key strategies

Social enterprise as a mode of delivering primary healthcare in rural Australia is rare (Wakerman et al., 2008). The sector is typically driven by privately owned GP clinics focused on profit maximisation by servicing the mass market – albeit a smaller 'mass market' than that to be found in larger population centres. Typically, privately owned clinics face a problem faced by rural health providers globally: sourcing qualified personnel willing to live away from major population centres. One aspect of the 'modular' or hub and spoke operation model taken by the clinic is the astute partnering agreements with other medical service providers. Rather than try to attract and retain medical workers or compete with high demand health service providers, the Board have chosen to co-locate these businesses within the medical village precinct. QML pathology collection service was the first business to trial this model and establish a collection lab in the same building as the GP clinic. Since this successful trial, other services have followed and co-located within the Emerald Medical Village precinct. The overarching strategic goal is to provide multiple medical services, previously not available in town, in one location.

The idea of creating social and economic value for the community by addressing a grassroots health challenge is unique (Best & Myers, 2017). The CHH case study demonstrates that a social enterprise business model has the potential to be a viable and sustainable alternative to delivering primary healthcare solutions in rural and remote Australia. The CHH Board affirm three strategic pillars. First and foremost, ensuring safe and high-quality health services. Second, supporting education and training of the current and future primary healthcare workforce in the region. Third, promoting healthy behaviours across the Central Highlands.

The CHH Board, as noted, have taken a modular approach to the business in both design and operation. At the centre of the organisation is the Emerald Medical Clinic and this acts as the main hub. As the business grows, the Board plans to add or 'bolt on' new facilities and services around the GP clinic. For example, in its third year of operation, CHH funded the construction of a new chemist building next to the GP clinic. This second module also added additional clinical space for visiting specialist services and a coffee kiosk. The extra commercial space also establishes a reliable source of secondary revenue for the social enterprise through rent received from lease agreements. As the business matures, there are further plans to add more modules such as a day surgery wing, education and training wing, a palliative and aged care unit, and an x-ray and radiology unit. All of these expansion plans are dependent on several critical factors such as community need, business sustainability, and funding sources.

Innovation

There are several themes to the innovation in this case that demonstrate how business, government, and community can synthesise new ways to create solutions to intransigent social problems.

Drawing on the grassroots

Small towns are not just miniaturized versions of metropolitan communities. The size of small towns can be worked to their advantage, due to potentially greater social capital, cohesion, and ease of social communication. Self-determination is an important concept when considering primary healthcare provision. A core component of this example is the active engagement of community members and other health systems actors to identify issues in the initial instance, then developing and implementing solutions. This radically changed how primary healthcare was delivered in Emerald. The end result was a sense of ownership, and a personalised, engaged, connected, and people-focused business that eliminated significant bureaucratic hurdles.

Design thinking refers to entering the design process with an end-user orientation and involves listening before action (Razzouk & Shute, 2012). The project was originally created for a metropolitan settings and that might not be exactly replicated to rural and remote locations. The CHH Board quickly recognised the need for a bespoke primary healthcare model that involved real consultation with local communities. Because the solution reflects the community, the solution can also not be simply transplanted to other communities…and this uniqueness increases the bond with the community that gave rise to it.

Partnerships

As hinted earlier, the CHH case study is also a clear example of the value of cross-sectoral partnership in addressing a social need. The three main societal pillars – business, government and civil society (community) – come together to address a social issue. In particular, the local government played one of the most critical roles in the early stages of the development of the CHH. Traditionally, health service provisions are seen as a state government function with funding support from the Federal Government. It is not usually a space for local government actors. The Central Highlands Regional Council's (CHRC) contribution to the project development process was principally in-kind but significant – for example, CHRC used internal town planning resources to identify vacant council-owned land that was suitable for the social enterprise to lease and develop, then completed necessary planning approvals, water, sewage, stormwater, and road works so the greenfield site was accessible and ready for development. The Council and Central Highlands Development Corporation (CHDC) (also a non-profit, focused on economic and tourism development) each provided a high-level representative to sit on the CHH Board and the CHDC additionally provided secretariat support to ensure good governance. The local government also played a pivotal advocacy role to secure federal funding for the infrastructure build as well as providing leadership and mentorship about the project within the community.

Transformative governance

The governance structure of a business arguably acts as a framework for innovation (García, Pradel, & Eizaguirre, 2015, and as noted in the previous section, not just the project and its inception, but its governance was respectful of the multiple actors involved. A helicopter view of the company governance structure captures a flexible, competent, and progressive group of entrepreneurs and innovators. The most commonly stated asset of the company was the high calibre volunteer board. This is a group of people with a diverse set of practical skills who know how to run a successful business – an accountant, a property valuer, a real estate developer, two local Councillors, a GP practise manager, and an economic development specialist. The group had broad experience, but a single focus, and that focus.

Synthesis

The CHH case study is a great example of how community, non-government organisations, and government, each with their own restrictions and limitations, can combine to create a powerful solution to persistent local problems. Social enterprises, particularly in small communities, are frequently small and fragile. By aggregating and focusing resources and interests into a single flexible enterprise, the CHH created a significant enough business (within a rural context) to have a critical mass to be sustainable. Beyond sustainability, the clinic has shown that it can grow, and extend its reach to additional services, within the initial health focus. The organisation did not just 'read' the local situation accurately (by including a sufficiently broad range of stakeholders in the initial design thinking) but also included a range of skills (including business, leadership, and governance skills) in the process as it evolved, but retained community input in its business model, leadership, and governance, to ensure that the enterprise did not drift off into yet another 'super clinic' that failed to reflect the community.

Another strength behind the CHH success has been an active and fluid business plan, a loose road map that simply marks some of the key positions but has the flexibility to adapt as the community changes. Finally, we remarked earlier on the use of technology to bridge metropolitan services to rural and remote communities. Seeing those in rural and remote regions as being less willing or able to take up technology can undersell the reality: technology has been a key feature in the CHH business. The Emerald Medical Clinic is not just a medical centre, but a technology hub. The start-up phase of the CHH enterprise involved creative collaboration to access high-speed internet as the National Broadband Network (NBN) was not available in the region at the time. Initially, a microwave antenna was installed on top of the GP clinic roof that had a direct line of sight to the Queensland Rail tower. This microwave link then accessed a direct fibre connection to Brisbane, which has provided a stable and steady supply of data to the business. Access to technological advances coupled with business model innovation has delivered more affordable and convenient health services to CHH patients. Through this pipeline, the clinic can offer enhanced services, as well as remain ready for future developments in e-health.

Conclusion

Rural health access is not a unitary single issue; beneath the challenge lies local diversity and complexity. It is possible to read this case as being an exemplar of the value of initial research: of taking a deep listening, design thinking approach to understanding the nature of the problem that one is seeking to solve. Typically, government and large business takes a top-down approach to problem analysis, and in doing so misses the opportunity to fully understand the problem, as well as design a solution that those being 'helped' feels a sense of fit, and a sense of ownership towards.

A common theme in rural and remote health access, however, is limited access to services due to the withdrawal of public and private health services that are often seen as economically unviable, and the unwillingness of qualified personnel to staff rural and remote sites. This case does not describe a panacea; the lack of health services in rural and remote areas comes with other shortfalls: in educational and social opportunities that those living in large population centres take for granted. However, rural communities have assets that metropolitan centres do not, as this project drew on those assets to create a solution that has proved to be attractive and efficient for medical practitioners. The approach taken showed a richer understanding of what 'strength-based approaches' really mean. Rural 'disadvantage' is often assessed through a 'deficit model' that ignores for example the natural agility of 'small' communities. By drawing on local people, local leaders, and existing local structures, the CHH has proven itself to be economically resilient, while promoting community cohesion and adding value to the local economy through employment, training, education, and even access to technology.

Acknowledgement: The authors would like to acknowledge the assistance provided by Central Highlands Healthcare Ltd.

References

Australian Government Department of Health (2021). Available at: https://www.health.gov.au/health-topics/health-workforce/health-workforce-classifications/rural-remote-and-metropolitan-area

Australian Institute of Health and Welfare (AIHW). (2018). *Australia's Health 2018*. Retrieved from AIHW: www.aihw.gov.au/reports/australias-health/australias-health-2018

Australian Medical Association (AMA). (2014). GP Super Clinics 'Not So Super' [Press release]. Retrieved from https://ama.com.au/media/gp-super-clinics-not-so-super-ama

Baxter, J., Gray, M., & Hayes, A. (2011). *Families in regional, rural and remote Australia*. Canberra: Australian Government. Retrieved from https://aifs.gov.au/sites/default/files/publication-documents/fs201103.pdf

Best, S., & Myers, J. (2017). Prudence or speed: Health and social care innovation in rural Wales. *Journal of Rural Studies*, 70, 198–206 https://doi.org/10.1016/j.jrurstud.2017.12.004

Caló, F., Roy, M. J., Donaldson, C., Teasdale, S., & Baglioni, S. (2019). Exploring the contribution of social enterprise to health and social care: A realist evaluation. *Social Science & Medicine, 222*, 154–161. https://doi.org/10.1016/j.socscimed.2019.01.007

Durey, A., & Thompson, S. C. (2012). Reducing the health disparities of Indigenous Australians: Time to change focus. *BMC Health Services Research, 12*(1), 1–11.

Emyria (2020). Annual Report. Retrieved from www.asx.com.au/asxpdf/20201009/pdf/44njvmh05vpvsx.pdf

García, M., Eizaguirre, S., & Pradel, M. (2015). Social innovation and creativity in cities: A socially inclusive governance approach in two peripheral spaces of Barcelona. *City, Culture and Society, 6*(4), 93-100.

Herbert C, Best A. (2011) It's a matter of values: Partnership for innovative change. Healthc Pap.;*11*(2):31–37; discussion 64–67. doi:10.12927/hcpap.2011.22436. PMID: 21677515.

Hwang, J., & Christensen, C. M. (2008). Disruptive innovation in health care delivery: A framework for business-model innovation. *Health Affairs, 27*(5), 1329–1335. doi:10.1377/hlthaff.27.5.1329

Komatsu, T. (2015). *Libera Terra – creating social and economic value by re-using confiscated assets*. Milano: Politecnico di Milano

Mitton, C., Dionne, F., Masucci, L., Wong, S., & Law, S. (2011). Innovations in health service organization and delivery in northern rural and remote regions: A review of the literature. *International Journal of Circumpolar Health, 70*(5), 460–472. Retrieved from www.tandfonline.com/action/showCitFormats?doi=10.3402/ijch.v70i5.17859

Mulgan, G., Tucker, S., Ali, R., & Sanders, B. (2006). *Social innovation: What it is, why it matters, how it can be accelerated*. London: Basingstoke Press.

Nicholls, A., & Murdock, A. (2012). *Social innovation: Blurring boundaries to reconfigure markets*. Basingstoke: Palgrave Macmillan.

Razzouk, R., & Shute, V. (2012). What is design thinking and why is it important? *Review of Educational Research, 82*(3), 330–348.

Wakerman, J., Humphreys, J. S., Wells, R., Kuipers, P., Entwistle, P., & Jones, J. (2008). Primary health care delivery models in rural and remote Australia – A systematic review. *BMC Health Services Research, 8*(1), 276.

6

RETURN OF THE BUSHRANGERS?

Technological determinism and the collapse and revival of independent Australian rural newspaper publishers

Olav T. Muurlink

Introduction

> Newsprint will decline at least 5% per year, as major publishers continue the loss of circulation and advertising dollars while reshaping, reformatting and redefining the daily newspaper to be less than daily.

The quote comes from John Maine, Vice President of World Graphic Papers at Resource Information Systems, an analysis firm devoted to the global forest products industry (RISI, 2021). Maine was discussing the US market, but the crisis in newsprint (and by extension) print news is global. Prominent, profitable, influential internationally -known titles, such as the 168-year-old *News of the World* (BBC, 2011), and the Pulitzer-prize winning *Tampa Tribune* and the *Cincinnati Post* (Schulhofer-Wohl & Garrido, 2013), have closed – long before COVID-19 accelerated the bonfire. In Australia, where most capital cities boasted at least two daily mastheads in the 20th century, now only two cities can make that claim, the nation's two largest cities Melbourne and Sydney. In the US, the number of cities with a daily newspaper to their name fell from a peak of almost 700 cities to under a dozen by 2010 (Schulhofer-Wohl & Garrido, 2013).

This loss of pluralism has come with a loss of jobs. The journalist is an increasingly marginal profession in developed world countries like Australia: here, the two largest players in the late 20th and early 21st century, News Corp and Fairfax, cut 3,000 jobs between them in 2012 alone (Norrie, 2012), which, while extreme, were dwarfed in both proportion and absolute numbers by the losses in the US and Britain during the same period. In the US for example, in the ten years to 2017, the decline in newspaper newsroom employees fell by 45% (Grieco, 2020).

The loss in title and jobs can also be traced in the numbers that matter most to publishers: circulation. In almost every market, bar India, circulations globally have continued to shrink – ranging from a 48% fall in Brazil in the five years from 2013 to 2018, to a mere 15% in Japan over the same period. All these factors and all these falls can be crunched down into a single measurement alluded to in the opening quote: newsprint. Demand for the paper on which newspapers used to be printed in colossal quantities has fallen globally (EMGE, 2019), with that fall linked to both a decline in the number of publications, editions, and pages being produced globally. Commodity traders project significant further shrinkage in the next 15 years, with only China and India offering resistance to the tide (RISI, 2021).

Technological innovation in print

The assumption that rural newspapers are 'dying' for the same reason that all newspapers are 'dying' is probably wrong. The argument goes that circulation is down due to competition from digital news sources, against a background of an increasingly digitally savvy audience armed with the technology that enables them to meet their needs for free or at least lower cost. However, there are a few problems with this line of logic.

First, digital access in rural Australia is not a given, even well into the 21st century. There is not just a geographical divide between levels of access, but that gap is compounded by the fact that *rural* Australians are also likely to be *older* Australians, less proficient in handling new technology. Thus, there is still a significant gap between levels of access to digital news in rural Australia (Afshar Ali, Alam, & Taylor, 2020).

Second, it is noteworthy that television (and before that radio) did *not* kill newspapers: circulation continued to rise post-1956 in Australia (Tiffen, 2015). While global evidence that digital news has impacted on circulation is solid (Cho, Smith, & Zentner, 2016), there is another reason why the bite of digital platforms is particularly deep when it comes to papers that start from lower baseline circulations – that is, papers in niche markets such as regional Australia.

Regardless of what caused circulation to begin to fall, once circulation falls, it begins to impact on the bottom line of publishers in a non-linear fashion. This factor relates to the fixed costs of producing a single copy of a publication, regardless of geographical location. 'Content' can be spread amongst several titles, and fixed costs related to print can indeed be distributed across and amortised against several titles. But there is a particular set of fixed costs that cannot fall beneath a certain 'floor' level. The costings on newspapers have, up until recently, had a very large, solid, 'iron floor'.

This is a classic case, in one sense, of 'technological determinism', classically defined as a Marxist approach to understanding how technology can act as a driver of history, a causal agent that advantages either one population over another, or makes one outcome more likely than another (Bimber, 1990).

To understand this 'iron floor' to the cost of producing a local, low circulation newspaper, it is necessary to briefly explain the process of producing a newspaper with a traditional printing press with the hypothetical circulation of just one copy.

Newspapers are produced on machines fitted with one, huge (+/− 1,000 kg) 'toilet paper' style reels, that feed through multiple pieces of heavy equipment to produce, very rapidly and with minimum human interaction, a fully printed and folded multi-page copy.

The process is very different to that of an office copier that produces a booklet, one sheet (possibly printed on both sides) at a time.

Newspaper presses are very large, larger than locomotives – and are often situated amid ancillary equipment within factories as large as a small town. These presses are very expensive, but once established, they are capable of producing a dizzying amount of media 'product' – 50,000 or more papers, fully complete, in an hour, numbers which can quickly dwarf the fixed cost of the giant presses that produce them.

However, to produce a *single copy* on these presses requires at the minimum a new set of plates, as well as a certain amount of labour required to clean the press and fix the plates to the press. During this process, the press stops working for a fixed period regardless of whether the newspaper has a circulation of 1,000 or 100,000. Every single run also requires a process of ensuring the plates are using proper colours that make up a full-colour print, and these need to be placed in the exact synchronicity with each other to avoid blurring. As a consequence, during this process of getting the press in the register, it is common to have hundreds if not thousands of copies of the newspaper to be wasted for every single run before printing a single 'finished' copy of a local paper.

Considering these presses require a team of highly paid printers to get the press clean, plated up, and the 'web' of the paper wound through the press, it is not surprising that there has been an industry drive to reduce the waste and increase the speed of 'make-ready' (getting the press ready for print). The result is presses of incredible scale and sophistication, representing tens of millions of dollars of investment. Yet even these sophisticated presses need plates and need to sit idle waiting for the first copy to be produced. Combined with this, fixed costs are squeezed into the price of lower newspaper circulations, where they disproportionately impact the per-copy price. The first copy inevitably costs many hundreds of dollars. Subsequent copies are remarkably cheap. This means as circulations of newspapers drop below 3,000 or 4,000 copies, they become prohibitively expensive to print on traditional presses. This is one of the technical limitations of current technology that has driven the cover price of local papers up. Small rural papers with say 32 pages end up having the same cover price as a thick urban daily newspaper – with customers understandably questioning the value for money. Publishers are caught in a trap, chasing an unchanging fixed cost.

Micro-newspapers and micro-presses

The collapse of News Corp's stable of papers, some of them century-old titles, created an unusual and unusually sudden vacuum in the market, but without press capacity, the vacuum was difficult to fill with traditional newspapers. Using sheet-fed presses not designed for newspapers was an option tried by several small rural newspapers; however, these presses are labour-intensive and thus the newspapers are increasingly reliant on advertising and cost reduction (usually meaning a cut in the number of journalists) to ensure sustainability.

The author was the founder of the *Southern Free Times* web press operation in Southern Queensland, which was mothballed and then dismantled in 2012 as the market changed. From the standpoint of 2020, and now in the role of Associate Professor of Sustainable Innovation at Central Queensland University, he was interested to see how technological innovation had changed the print news landscape, and his research uncovered a revolution underway in Europe. Digital presses drawing on technology first applied to desktop printers (inkjets) had begun to evolve in speed to the point where droplets could be applied to paper moving at a speed similar to the speed at which paper in newspaper web presses travel. This leap in technology lead to the development of high-speed inkjet presses fitted with rolls of paper, as opposed to sheets. What made these presses novel was that they did not require plates, did not require a 'clean-up' between jobs, and could switch between titles instantaneously – that is, they could print a copy of *The New York Times*, and in theory, at least, the next copy to emerge at full speed from the machine could be the *Sydney Morning Herald*. The 'first copy' problem alluded to above had been eliminated.

The first substantial digital newspaper printing application using the new inkjet technology in Europe was the Belgian religious newspaper *Kerk en Leven* (Church and Life), which made the switch in 2013 (GxPress, 2013). The first 'real' newspaper printed on an inkjet web press was a regional British paper, the *Jersey Evening Post*, based on an island with no easy or cheap access to 'mainland' Britain (Print Business, 2016).

In 2017, there was a breakthrough in France that squarely addressed the issue Australia was facing: the decline of small rural and regional titles. The *L'Observateur* group of papers owned by Sogémedia received a total of 2.5 million Euros from the Strategic Press Development Fund (FSDP) for hardware, software, and training, and built a hub and spoke model around digital inkjet presses that embraced rather than avoided 'small' newspapers.

'We could have just waited for [small titles] to die - or do something', Sogémedia's president Jean-Pierre Vittu de Kerraoul told the printing industry publication GXPress 'People are very interested in local news, yet the tendency has been to reduce the number of editions, driving readers away' (2017). Instead of trying to force regional or national news onto local audiences, the inkjet presses allowed the publisher to go in the opposite direction, geo-targeting editions to local readers' local interests. That is, a single newspaper could be 'versioned' so one village would get copies of a newspaper with a piece of different news and advertising mix to the next village. In France, de Kerraoul's firm had a competitor, *La Voix du Nord*, relying on old technology, continued to cut local editions. 'It's good for us, they are running less local news, and we are doing the exact opposite'. The idea has taken root in France. More recently in Montpelier, the *Midi Libre*, which covers the Languedoc

Roussillon and Aveyron areas of central southern France, turned to inkjet. Again, the project was funded by the French government (GxPress, 2019).

Promising as the European case studies are, inkjet presses remain new and thus very expensive technology, beyond the reach of small regional newspaper publishers in Australia. Ink cost per litre or kilogram also remains much higher for inkjet presses than conventional web presses. The new presses thus have high fixed costs and some higher variable costs (per copy), but the 'first copy' problem has been eliminated. These presses, instead, produce a first copy that is cheap, but a 4,000 relatively expensive copy. The Small Newspaper Company (SNC) project (co-founded by the author) was initiated after an exhaustive search for a small affordable inkjet press capable of printing one or two low circulation newspaper titles. The Japanese press was designed for high-volume sheetfed printing – just sufficient to cope with low-volume newspaper printing.

To leverage the low 'first copy' effect, SNC established a daily paid (not free) newspaper, printing only as many as the newsagents required, and sometimes even initiating a reprint of an issue on the same day as it was released – unheard of with traditional presses. With this model, revenue derived newspaper sales exceeded not just the cost of printing, but also exceeded that derived from advertising. Unlike the traditional Australian country newspaper, it was readers rather than advertisers who were paying most of the bills.

The *Daily Journal* was the first greenfields daily (six-day-a-week) newspaper launched in Australia for over half a century, and survived for six months – but it had taken six months to establish, following the closure of the News Corp title it replaced, the *Warwick Daily News* – which itself was the smallest daily newspaper in Australia for decades before its closure during the 2020 'extinction event' (Dickson, 2020). Circulation figures provided to the SNC before launch by local newsagents proved to overestimate demand: it was clear that in the six months hiatus following the closure of the *Daily News*, a significant proportion of readers had developed the habit of 'going without' a daily newspaper; new digital news footpaths had formed, with local single-theme or community Facebook groups springing up and thriving. Even the local council had begun live streaming its council meetings, meaning that the media was no longer the exclusive medium through which critical government information could be accessed by the voter. Low circulation meant low impact for advertisers; advertisers were advertising to support the notion of a daily newspaper rather than because of a return on revenue from readership.

The new title sustained daily publication for six months but only because of significant injection of equity, and the willingness of the founders to invest significant unpaid time to sustain the effort. At the six-month mark, a project review resulted in the founders choosing to create a hybrid model designed to give advertisers the impact they sought while giving newspaper readers the news focus (rather than ad-heavy focus) that they preferred.

A free home-delivered weekly newspaper that targeted rural readers was developed (with a high ad focus), while the daily dropped to a twice-weekly publication ratio, with the free newspaper inserted as a free supplement, in one of the paid editions. Free newspapers, particularly *home-delivered* free newspapers, can 'guarantee' circulation, and thus to some degree guarantee impact for advertisers. While staffing levels were cut, staffing levels *per edition* increased, and thus news content per sold edition improved, leading to a greater perceived value for money – particularly with the edition that included the free supplement. SNC also took advantage of the digital press ability to create low volume 'versions', splitting the single daily title into two twice-weekly titles, one focused on Warwick, and the other on a smaller town to the south, Stanthorpe, that under News Corp also had formerly had its own twice weekly. So a single title was split strategically into three, the *Daily Journal* (Warwick), a free weekly (*The Country Journal*), and a sister twice weekly for the *Daily Journal*, the *Stanthorpe Record*.

Collectively, the circulation subsequently rose for the two days on which the new group of titles was published. Advertising revenue also rose, because advertisers gained the additional impact from the increased circulation of the paid editions and the addition of the free home-delivered edition. The net impact of the loss of circulation income from the loss of four paid editions a week was more than offset by the reduction in costs. With the heavy losses addressed, the new operation has become sustainable and continues to employ more journalists working in the region than any other news media operation with a presence in the circulation area.

COVID-19 and the Australian context

In Australia, the job losses of the previous half-century were minor, when the single year of 2020 is used as a comparator. With lockdowns in April–May 2020 came shut-downs. The year 2020 saw the sudden closure of long-established titles, amongst them daily papers such as the *Queensland Times* (the state's oldest, at Ipswich), the formerly lucrative *Sunshine Coast Daily*, and the *Morning Bulletin* (Rockhampton). Major regional cities and dozens of smaller rural centres saw the closure of their titles, with digital shells and only a skeleton staff (in some cases) retained. The Australian Newsroom Mapping Project provides an overview of the loss of journalistic resources: 194 newsrooms showing a net contraction in staff (Dickson, 2020). While exact, net job losses are difficult to quantify (with small unregulated newsrooms caught in the maelstrom) job losses in the arts and media industry collectively totalled 22,200 in the first four months of 2020, second only to job losses in the hospitality sector (Davies, Butler, Evershed, Nixon, & Capel-Stanley, 2020).

Perhaps surprisingly, the majority of closures were made by a single owner. In May 2020, News Corp Australia, the Australian arm of News Corp globally, controlled 57% of the Australian newspaper market by circulation (Evershed, 2020) made a sudden announcement that caught most journalists off guard. The announcement, to the stock market, saw the closure of 112 titles, with the majority of them being retained as unique digital sites (although this window was also closed in many cases in 2021, with small titles being incorporated into digital offshoots of the main state-based daily site).

Less publicly trumpeted, but equally crucial was the parallel closures of several newspapers print sites. The 'Big Three' newspapers in Australia, News Limited, Nine (formerly Fairfax), and Australian Community Media (ACM) agreed to close several large centralised print facilities in the cause of rationalisation (Robinson, 2020). In the space of a few weeks, the Australian regional newspaper landscape had been changed, and dozens of new 'news deserts' (Abernathy, 2018) had appeared. If one looks back at the origin of Australian regional newspapers, one can see why a rapid response by entrepreneurs to this unprecedented set of closures was almost impossible.

The Australian newspaper market developed a regional and rural presence rapidly, relative to the urban daily newspaper, but 'rapidly' in the early 19th century could still be measured in years. Only in Western Australia was there a substantial delay between the first publication in the state capital and the first publication in country towns (38 years) (Kirkpatrick, 2013). In a vast nation with no road or rail network to speak of, newspapers had to be printed in the town they were published, and thus expanded at the speed with which the heavy iron printing machines could be delivered, usually by bullock cart to entrepreneurial publishers. The publishers tended, as Kirkpatrick notes (2013), to be 'jacks of all trades', turning their hand from everything from advertising sales to journalism, typesetting, printing, and distribution. They were driven individuals.

As distance became a challenge that could be solved at a price, larger and larger presses could be justified. These presses were printing not just for a single town or a single title: they were printing for publications much further afield, amortising the investment in fast imported presses over more publications, more copies. With the amalgamation of print came the amalgamation of titles, beginning the rise of the modern newspaper conglomerates, a small club of powerful national operators, currently, the 'Big Three'. However, in the 21st century, as the 2020 collapse inched into view, the 'Big Three' were not the only operators closing down presses. Analysis shows that in the period 2000 onward, eight web presses focused on newspaper printing closed[1] in South East Queensland alone, with only the News Corp operation at Yandina remaining. For an independent newspaper publisher with an ambition to start a new title, or maintain an old one, only one realistic choice – News Corp – remained.

Analysis and discussion

The COVID-19 pandemic has had a unique impact on the Australian media landscape in ways that the last major pandemic, which began during the First World War, did not. In the first quarter of the 20th century, there was no such fall in either the circulation or the number of newspapers. While this suggests that the 2020 pandemic appears to have struck the industry at a point of vulnerability, the disproportionate loss of titles belonging to the larger players (my analysis of the Australian Newsroom Mapping Project resources show that disproportionate losses of titles occurred amongst the 'Big Three' than amongst the independents (Dickson, 2020)) suggests that something else was afoot. The executive chairman of News Corp, in announcing the closure of dozens of Australian titles, blamed COVID-19 squarely saying it had 'impacted the sustainability of the community and regional publishing' (BBC, 2020). Time has provided evidence that if sustainability is measured in profit, then he was right. With the closure of papers and the shift to digital, News Corp profits recovered from a loss of US$1.26 billion in 2019–2020 to a profit of US$330 million in 2020–2021 (Butler, 2021). News Corp may have just seen the pandemic as a trigger to give in to a commercial trend that had been clear for years: the shrinkage of print, and the expansion of digital.

The closure of News Corp titles opened up a potential market for small print operators, but the simultaneous closure of printing plants meant that these newcomers were forced to technologically innovate, creating newspapers with presses that were not associated previously with newspaper production.

Technological determinism was first proposed by American economist, Thorstein Veblen in the 19th century, and formed a backbone of Marxist theory later in that century. Veblen argued that technology wrought the revolution that shifted the world from the Middle Ages, and the 'era of handicraft' to the 'era of the machine industry'. Veblen would have found newspaper closures and openings in 2020 a curious anachronism: the industry had been marching into a future that looked to be dominated by grand alliances between titles, where the *Sydney Morning Herald* was increasingly sharing resources (journalists, agencies, photographers, even presses) with the *Melbourne Age* (in the same ownership stable) and even with 'the enemy' (titles in other stables). This era looked to be dominated by fewer and few players controlling a greater share of the market using printing machines that were bigger and faster than ever before…and then suddenly, a reversal to an era where small entrepreneurs armed with small machines began, more or less, to be run profitably focusing on small markets once again.

These small newspapers are, however, *not* the same in character, as the ones that speckled the Australian 'bush' in the 19th and early 20th centuries. The case described briefly here is an attempt to replicate the style of these early papers. There was a strong focus in the *Daily Journal* in both its original and modified form on reporting the hard 'real' news that is nevertheless too small to be caught in the nets of the remaining national media networks.

What the *Daily Journal* was attempting was, however, atypical: most of the new newspapers emerging in 2020 and 2021 instead firmly aimed to provide a 'community voice', building or trying to retain social capital rather than serving to reinforce eroding foundations of the Fourth Estate. 'There could be a profile on the new nurse, the owner of the pub, or the backpacker working at the store', one new publisher in a very remote region remarked. 'I am pretty much working on keeping it focused on positive news and people' (Campbell, 2020).

The 'new' Australian country newspaper publishers are also less entrepreneurial in character. Instead, many of these news projects are not driven by individuals but are established as community projects. They lack an activist nature. Not surprisingly, the government has become a key player in resuscitating regional media using the Regional and Small Publishers Innovation Package, a $60.4 million three-year program to bolster small (and sometimes not-so-small) regional operators. 'The media industry is in a significant and sustained transition period, putting the delivery of quality journalism under pressure. This poses challenges for small publishers and small regional newspapers in particular', the announcement of the aid package stated (ACMA, 2020). Government advertising is, additionally, likely to have both a resuscitative impact on regional newspapers' finances and reduce the militancy and radicalism that was often present in the first wave of independent newspapers established in rural Australia some two centuries earlier (Kirkpatrick, 2013). With the high cost of entry to the brave new world of inkjet newspaper presses, it is possible that history could be repeated once again, with those who control the big, efficient presses having effective control of the media landscape.

Note

1 The Goondiwindi Argus press, the Warwick Daily News Press, APN Print at Warwick, the Beaudesert Times operation, the Southern Free Times operation in Warwick, the Horton Media press in north Brisbane, Rural Press' Ormiston operation, and News Limited's Murarrie plant.

References

Abernathy, P. M. (2018). *The expanding news desert*: Center for Innovation and Sustainability in Local Media, School of Media and Journalism, University of North Carolina at Chapel Hill.
ACMA. (2020). Regional and small publishers innovation fund. Retrieved from www.acma.gov.au/regional-and-small-publishers-innovation-fund
Afshar Ali, M., Alam, K., & Taylor, B. (2020). Do social exclusion and remoteness explain the digital divide in Australia? Evidence from a panel data estimation approach. *Economics of Innovation and New Technology, 29*(6), 643–659.
BBC. (2011, 7 July 2011). News of the world to close amid hacking scandal. Retrieved from www.bbc.com/news/uk-14070733
BBC. (2020). Murdoch shuts 112 Australia print papers in major digital shift. Retrieved from www.bbc.com/news/business-52829347
Bimber, B. (1990). Karl Marx and the three faces of technological determinism. *Social Studies of Science, 20*(2), 333–351.
Butler, B. (2021). News Corp recovers from horror year with $445m profit. *The Guardian,* 6 Aug 2021. Retrieved from www.theguardian.com/media/2021/aug/06/news-corp-recovers-from-horror-year-with-445m-profit
Campbell, S. (2020). New newspaper to launch in the Gulf of Carpentaria. Retrieved from www.northweststar.com.au/story/6659326/new-newspaper-to-launch-in-the-gulf-of-carpentaria/
Cho, D., Smith, M. D., & Zentner, A. (2016). Internet adoption and the survival of print newspapers: A country-level examination. *Information Economics and Policy, 37,* 13–19.
Davies, A., Butler, N., Evershed, N., Nixon, T., & Capel-Stanley, C. (2020). Australian job loss tracker: The industries and places most affected by the coronavirus crisis. Retrieved

from www.theguardian.com/business/datablog/ng-interactive/2020/apr/23/australian-job-loss-tracker-employment-unemployment-numbers-industries-places-most-affected-coronavirus-crisis

Dickson, G. (2020). Australian Newsroom Mapping Project. Retrieved from https://anmp.piji.com.au. from Public Interest Journalism Initiative https://anmp.piji.com.au

EMGE. (2019). *World newsprint market: The perfect storm of 2019*. Paper presented at the World Printers Forum Conference, Berlin.

Evershed, N. (2020). Australia's newspaper ownership is among the most concentrated in the world. Retrieved from www.theguardian.com/news/datablog/2020/nov/13/australia-newspaper-ownership-is-among-the-most-concentrated-in-the-world

Grieco, E. (2020). Fast facts about the newspaper industry's financial struggles as McClatchy files for bankruptcy. *Pew Research Center*, Feb 14.

GxPress. (2013). Church puts faith in digital with 'first substantial' inkjet newspaper project. Retrieved from www.gxpress.net/church-puts-faith-in-digital-with-first-substantial-inkjet-newspaper-project-cms-2644

GxPress. (2017). Sogémedia's success sparks new interest in digital print. Retrieved from www.gxpress.net/sog-medias-success-sparks-new-interest-in-digital-print-cms-11277

GxPress. (2019). How inkjet tech and state cash is helping build newspapers' future. Retrieved from www.gxpress.net/exclusive-how-inkjet-tech-and-state-cash-is-helping-build-newspapers-future-cms-12248

Kirkpatrick, R. (2013). *A short history of the Australian country press*. Mackay: Australian Newspaper History Group.

Norrie, J. (2012). Fairfax to cut 1900 jobs, shut printers in huge downsize. *The Conversation*, Jun 18.

Print Business. (2016). Jersey paves the way for a new model for newspaper print. Retrieved from https://printbusiness.co.uk/news/Jersey-paves-the-way-for-a-new-model-for-newspaper-print/104317/

RISI. (2021). New RISI Global 15-Year Paper Outlooks shows demand in North America and Western Europe to shrink 23% and 20%, while Eastern Europe and Asia grows 49% and 39% respectively. *Fastmarkets RISI*. Retrieved from www.risiinfo.com/press-release/new-risi-global-15-year-paper-outlooks-shows-demand-in-north-america-and-western-europe-to-shrink-23-and-20-while-eastern-europe-and-asia-grows-49-and-39-respectively/

Robinson, W. (2020). Print sites to close as newspapers share. *Print21*, 7 August 2020. Retrieved from www.print21.com.au/news/print-sites-to-close-as-newspapers-share

Schulhofer-Wohl, S., & Garrido, M. (2013). Do newspapers matter? Short-run and long-run evidence from the closure of The Cincinnati Post. *Journal of Media Economics, 26*(2), 60–81.

Tiffen, R. (2015). From punctuated equilibrium to threatened species: The evolution of Australian newspaper circulation and ownership. *Australian Journalism Review, 37*(1), 63.

7
MT BULLER'S SNOW BUSINESS

Michael Segon

Introduction

When most people think of holidaying in Australia images of pristine sandy beaches, beautiful coral cays, and Outback adventures tend to come to mind. For most international tourists, iconic images such as Sydney's Harbour Bridge and Opera House, the NT's Kakadu National Park, Central Australia's Uluru, and Queensland's Great Barrier Reef tend to be the most often destinations associated with an Australian holiday. For Australian domestic tourist holiday destinations such as Queensland's beaches, Noosa and the Sunshine Coast or touring along some of the spectacular coastlines in Victoria and WA or visiting the renowned vineyards of the Yarra Valley and South Australia's Claire, McLaren Vale, and Barossa valleys are the 'go-to destinations'. It would be fair to say that most people considering Australian seasonal holidays don't view winter sports such as downhill, cross-country skiing, and tobogganing as on par with these other activities and destinations. Yet Australia does have substantive Alpine resorts that cater to both winter sport and summer activities in the NSW, Victoria, and to some extent Tasmania high country. The winter sports or Alpine industry is dependent, not only on extremely cold weather but also on reliable and substantial snowfalls that enable the range of winter sports activities described above to occur. However, in recent years, the impact of climate change has had a dramatic effect on winter sports and Alpine resorts worldwide. With Australian ski resorts generally being at lower altitudes compared to the Alps of Europe and North and South America, maintaining a sustainable winter sports industry in Australia has become a major challenge. This case examines one of the largest Alpine resorts in Australia, Mt Buller, and how it goes about its snow business, given some of these challenges.

DOI: 10.4324/9781003256717-7

The Mt Buller Alpine resort: history and background

The Victorian winter Alpine destination of Mt Buller with a peak of 1805 metres is located in the south-eastern section of the Australian Alpine National Park and approximately 230 kilometres from the Victorian capital of Melbourne. It is approximately a three-hour drive from the city on the major 'Melba' Highway, making it the most easily accessible Alpine resort in Victoria, if not Australia.

The origins of winter sport activity at Mt Buller date back to 1924 when the Ski Club of Victoria (SCV) built its first accommodation hut near the area on Mt Buller known as Boggy Creek in 1933. The first actual ski lift was a simple rope installed in 1949 that dragged beginner and intermediate skiers some 200 metres up the main ski run of Mt Buller, which is now known as Bourke Street. Since that time the resort has expanded to now include 20 high-tech ski lifts, servicing over 300 hectares of skiable terrain, 80 kilometres of skiable trails with approximately 20% of runs for beginner skiers, 45% catering for intermediate skiers, and 35% for advanced skiers. There are also two toboggan areas for snow play and a cross-country ski trail which joins Mt Buller to its sister mountain, Mt Sterling, which caters exclusively for cross-country skiing that requires no lift systems. There are numerous businesses in the Mt Buller Village including restaurants, ski shops, supermarkets, and travel operators and 183 leased sites and close to 8,000 beds in a range of ski lodges and hotels for ski season accommodation and a range of food, beverage, and entertainment options (ARCC, 2020).

The peak activity for Mt Buller is during the Southern Hemisphere winter months from the official opening of the ski season beginning with the Queen's Birthday weekend in early June, through to the end of September or early to mid-October, depending on snowfalls. This is a relatively short 3–4-month snow season compared to Northern Hemisphere resorts that often have seasons of 5–6 months and high-altitude glacier skiing all year round. Despite being such a short season, Mt Buller receives approximately 400,000 visitors which accounts for almost half of all visits to all Victorian Alpine resorts, the vast majority coming from the city of Melbourne, mostly on weekends when numbers can exceed 10,000 people on the mountain each day (Mt Buller & Stirling Alpine Resort Management Board Annual Report, 2019).

Although it is primarily a winter resort, Mt Buller has expanded its appeal over the past 10–15 years to also focusing on summer activities including the development of mountain bike trails, four-wheel driving, a day spa facility, hiking, horse-riding, bushwalking, and various festivals including cycling, car racing, and 'opera' in the mountains. During these summer months, some 50,000 visitors go to Mt Buller for these events and to escape the heat of the coastal areas and the city with temperatures on average being 5–7 degrees cooler than in Melbourne (Mt Buller & Stirling Alpine Resort Management Board Annual Report, 2019).

Resort management

The Mt Buller Alpine resort is managed jointly by two entities. The first is the Mt Buller and Mt Sterling Alpine Resort Management Board, a statutory authority established under the Alpine Resorts management Act 199, that also fulfils the functions of a shire council in Victoria. Despite both mountains being geographically surrounded by the Victorian Shire of Mansfield, named after the gateway access town of Mansfield, the *Forests Act* 1958 provides for the separate management and administration of Victorian Alpine resorts. Since 1997, Alpine resorts declared under the *Alpine Resort Act* 1983 have been excised from the surrounding municipal district (see *Alpine Resorts Act* 1983, sec. 24)

The main daily operations of Mt Buller are handled by Mt Buller Ski Lifts (BSL), a private company, which was formed in 1993 and was part of the Grollo group of companies. BSL operate the 20 ski lifts at Mt Buller in addition to the Ski & Snowboard School and childcare facility, several hotels bars, and restaurants including the Mt Buller Chalet Hotel and Suites and ABOM Hotel among a collection of other on-mountain hospitality venues at Mt Buller. It also has several Buller Sports retail and rental stores at Mt Buller and in the gateway town of Mansfield, ski specialist store Altitude, and a property development and maintenance business unit (www.mtbuller.com.au). BSL employs over 800 staff including a large seasonal workforce each winter from across Australia and around the world. They were the first Australian ski company to achieve the ISO 14001 standard for Environmental Management and are committed to the sustainable development of Mt Buller as the premier Alpine resort in Australia.

Mt Buller and competitive advantage

As noted earlier, Mt Buller seeks to attract skiers in winter and nature lovers in summer from state, national, and international markets. The basis of any business is to be a more attractive option than like competitors, in other words, to have a competitive advantage. Within Australia, Alpine winter sports are limited to the higher plains of Victoria, NSW and to a lesser extent Tasmania and Table 7.1 summarises competitor resorts and their various attributes.

A review of Australia's primary winter Alpine resort's characteristics indicates that Mt Buller has several significant advantages over its competition in both Victoria and NSW. Perhaps the most obvious is its proximity to the Victorian state capital of Melbourne being only 2.5–3.0 hours' drive time compared to over 6–7 hours from Sydney to the Alpine resorts in New South Wales. Whilst the Victorian resort of Mt Baw Baw is only 120 kilometres away, the travel time from Melbourne is almost the same as that of Mt Buller due to access issues. It is also a much smaller resort with basic infrastructure and lift capacity catering to beginner and family group skiers.

Mount Buller is second only to the NSWs resort of Thredbo in terms of the number of ski lifts, and lift capacity per hour, almost double that of the other resorts. This means skiers get on and off ski lifts significantly quicker, spending less time waiting for access to ski lifts which translates to more time on the snow at Mt Buller compared virtually all other ski resorts. It has a similar skiable area to the

82 Michael Segon

TABLE 7.1 Comparative information of Alpine resort areas

Resort	Highest point	Skiable area ha	No of Lifts	Lift capacity per hour	Longest ski run (km)	Levels (terrain)	Snowmaking	Distance from Melbourne and Sydney
Mt Buller (Vic)	1,805	300	20	40,000	2.5	Beginner: 20% Intermediate: 45% Advanced: 35%	78 ha	263k 2.5–3 hours from Melb
Mt Hotham (Vic)	1,861	320	12	24,000	2.5	Beginner: 20% Intermediate: 40% Advanced: 40%	22 ha	357k 5–6 hours from Melb
Falls Creek (Vic)	1,872	450	15	20,000	3	Beginner: 17% Intermediate: 60% Advanced: 23%	110 ha	5–6 hours from Melb
Mt Baw Baw (Vic)	1,567	30	7	500	.750	Beginner: 25% Intermediate: 64% Advanced: 11%	N/A	125k–2.5 hrs from Melb
Thredbo NSW	2,037	450	14	17,300	5.9	Beginner: 16% Intermediate: 67% Advanced: 17%	25% of the mountains	6–7 hours from Sydney
Perisher- NSW	2,034	1245	47	53,990	3	Beginner: 22% Intermediate: 60% Advanced: 10%	53 ha	6–7 hours from Sydney
Mt Selwyn NSW	1,614 m	450	10	9.500	.800	Beginner: 40% Intermediate: 48% Advanced: 12%	35 ha	6–7 hours from Sydney

Source: Based on the information collected from https://www.mountainwatch.com/australia/resorts; www.mtbuller.com.au; www.selwynsnow.com.au; www.thredbo.com.au; www.mountbawbaw.com.au; www.mthotham.com.au; www.perisher.com.au; www.fallscreek.com.au

other Victorian resorts of Mt Hotham and Falls Creek, far greater than Mt Baw Baw and similar to the NSW resorts of Thredbo, Perisher, and Mt Selwyn. Whilst the NSW resort of Perisher appears to be far bigger, the current Perisher Ski Resort was formed in March 1995 and combining the four separate ski areas of Perisher Valley, Smiggin Holes, Mount Blue Cow, Guthega, so a reasonable comparison is not quite possible. When comparing the diversity of ski runs, in terms of levels, Mt Buller has an even distribution between beginner, intermediate, and advanced levels, potentially catering for a broader range of skiers. It has a similar length of skiable areas, several skiable trails, and a similar length of runs with only Thredbo in NSW having a significantly longer run due to its higher elevation. The other significant advantage for Mt Buller is snowmaking capacity, second only to that of Falls Creek covering over 78 hectares which is the majority of its primary intermediate trails. This means that it can ensure greater coverage of snow in poorer winter seasons compared to most other Australian resorts. There is a clear positive correlation between snow conditions (measured by snow depth) and the number of people who visit Alpine resorts. Furthermore, with an increase in natural snow depth of 1 cm, there is a corresponding 1.8% increase in visitors, and similar increases associated with artificial snowmaking areas result in an increase of 1.6% in visitors and 181 more visitor days. With increases in maximum snow depth, both natural and artificial, not only do a number of visitors increase, but they also stay for longer (ACE-CRC, 2016). In other words, when people know that snow coverage or ski conditions are good either due to natural or combined with artificial snowmaking, they are more likely to visit Alpine regions during winter months to engage in winter sports activities. This raises the importance of global warming and its impact on snow cover and the ongoing sustainability of the industry.

The economic benefit of the Alpine industry and Mt Buller to Victoria

According to the CEO of the Australian Ski Areas Association Colin Hackworth, the annual impact of the Alpine industry on the Australian economy is approximately $2.4 billion (Wiseman, 2021). This would include all Alpine resorts, hospitality, and retail outlets including importation and sale of ski equipment. In 2016, the Victorian Alpine Resorts Economic Contribution Study by major advisory firm Ernst & Young identified that Alpine resorts generate substantial economic activity for the state of Victoria via the attraction of Victorian, Interstate, and International visitors. The total number of ski visitors to Victorian resorts in 2016 was 762,981. On average, each of these spent $456 per day at each of the main resorts. Since this original study, Ernst & Young have continued to provide estimates on the economic contribution of winter and summer seasons to Victoria's economy. In 2019, it determined that the winter season made a contribution of $1,061 million to the Victorian Gross State Product, which was determined to be

TABLE 7.2 Economic significance of snow season in Victoria during 2016–2020

	2016	2017	2018	2019	2020 (Est.)
Gross value added in AUD million	790	945	1,076	1,061	109
Employment (job number)	7,892	9,137	10,471	9,866	960

Source: Alpine Resorts Co-ordinating Council (ARCC, 2020). Annual Report.

TABLE 7.3 Visitor days to Victorian resorts 2011–2020

Visitor days in '000	Mount Buller resorts	All resorts
2011	442.6	1,247.2
2015	473.0	1,386.7
2018	591.8	1,731.7
2019	558.4	1,687.5
2020	77.9	204.1
Previous 10-year average	503.3	1,455.7
% Change 10-year avg to 2020	-85%	-86%

Source: ARCC (2020).

the equivalent of 9,866 direct and indirect jobs (https://arcc.vic.gov.au/publications/economic-reports). Table 7.2 highlights the economic trends of the Alpine Industry to Victoria.

According to the Mt Buller and Mt Stirling Resort Management Board (RMB) from 2016 to 2019, the combined Mt Buller & Mt Stirling Alpine resorts generated an estimated $2,100 million in regional spending, 3,300 full-time equivalent jobs, and $1,061 million to Victoria's Gross State Product. This represents a growth rate of 25.5% over the three years in value-add and a 20% growth rate in employment. This growth rate correlates with the increased visitation to Victorian Alpine resorts which parallels the general population growth rates of the state Melbourne (Mt Buller & Stirling Alpine Resort Management Board Annual Report, 2019).

Alpine visitation and growth of the ski industry

The number of visitors to Victorian Alpine resorts per year has usually been in the range of 600,000–800,000 visitors and 1,100,000–1,300,000 visitor days. As depicted in Table 7.3, there has been a steady increase in the level of visitation to Victorian Alpine resorts, including Mt Buller which grew from approximately 442,000 visitors in 2011 to 558,460 in 2019. Whilst there are peaks and troughs on a year-by-year basis, excluding the 2020 snow season, that was impacted by the COVID-19 pandemic, this represents a 20% increase over nine years. Anecdotal information suggests that the vast majority of visitors to Mt Buller are from the Greater Melbourne metropolitan region, accounting for some 65–70% of daily visitors (ARCC, 2020).

Climate change and winter sports

The viability of the winters sports is dependent on reliable and substantial snowfalls that enable people to engage in the range of winter sports activities such as downhill and cross-country skiing, snowboarding, tobogganing, Alpine touring, and general sightseeing (Pickering & Buckly, 2010; Pegg, Patterson, & Vila Gariddob, 2012). Winter sports tourism and the resulting economic benefits to Victoria and Australia are therefore dependent on regular snowfalls and favourable cool temperatures (Dawson & Scott, 2013; Scott, Gossling, & Hall, 2012; Pickering, 2011; Wolfsegger, Gossling, & Daniel, 2008; Elsasser, Abegg, & Buerki, 2006; Elsasser & Messerli, 2001).

Alpine regions have been identified as particularly susceptible to climate change with global warming being recognised as having a substantial adverse effect not only on total snow cover in mountain areas but also a detrimental effect on the length of snow seasons (Nicolls, 2005; Becken & Hay, 2007; Scott et al., 2008; Roman et al., 2010; Pons-Pons, Johnson, Rosas-Casals, Sureda, & Jover 2012; Gilaberte-Búrdalo, López-Martín, Pino-Otín, & López-Moreno, 2014; Hopkins, 2014).

The experience in Australian ski resorts is showing that the minimum snow depth required for downhill skiing is generally considered to be 30 cm (Hennessy et al., 2008), and a minimum of 60–70 days of operation is considered necessary for a viable season (Pickering, 2011). A report from 2012 addressing the snow coverage in the Victorian high country found that maximum snow depths have declined, and the snow season shortened by several weeks as temperatures have increased across Australia (Bhend et al., 2012). This trend is attributed to human impact on the climate (Bindoff et al., 2013), in particular the continuing production of greenhouse gases. The trend is also likely to increase, thus advancing climate change (CSIRO and Bureau of Meteorology, 2015).

It is estimated that by 2050, average winter temperatures are likely to increase by just over 2°C For every degree of increase in temperature, the snow coverage will decrease by 15% at 1,850 metres and by 12% at 2,350 metres (Beniston 2003; Hantel et al., 2000). Australian skiing typically occurs between 1,000 and 1,700 metres above sea level, given that Australia's highest peak, Mt Mount Kosciuszko is only 2,228 metres above sea level. By contrast skiing in the European and North American alps can be anywhere between 1,000 and 4,000 metres above sea level.

Hantel et al. (2000) note that even the most conservative scenario regarding global warming, being a rise in mean temperature of just 0.9°C by 2020, is predicted to reduce natural snow cover by approximately four weeks at low elevations of less than 580 metres. According to Harris et al. (2016), recent estimates suggest that Victorian ski resorts like Mt Buller will see an increase in average temperatures of between 4°C and 5°C, with up to 20% less precipitation and up to 80% lower annual snowfall given the current global warming trends and emissions. Given the relatively low altitude of Mt Buller and other Australian ski resorts and the already short winter sports season in Australia at just 3–4 months these predictions have dire consequences for the industry in Australia.

The major approaches to deal with the impact of global warming and the reduction of snow cover have been classified as adaption strategies. These largely entail the use of artificial snow in major resorts (Wolfsegger, Gössling & Scott, 2008; Steiger & Mayer, 2008) For example, Table 7.1 highlights that Australian resorts are developing snowmaking infrastructure to guarantee a minimal level of skiable snow. The snow falls and cover predications projections affirm research by the CSIRO that reductions in natural snowfall and shorter seasons length will increase the reliance on artificial snowmaking (Whetton et al., 1996; Hennessy et al., 2008; Bhend et al., 2012).

The global warming adaption strategies of Mt Buller

A review of investments and infrastructure upgrading over the past 15–20 years suggests that the BSL has had clear adaption strategies designed to increase the amount of skiable snow, guaranteeing or extending the length of the ski season via snowmaking, increasing the capacity of the ski lifts to move more people quickly around the mountain. The company went for replacing the old-style drag lifts such as t-bars and slow-paced 2 seater chairs with high speed 4/6 seater detachable chairs, thus increasing the time on skiing and snowboarding for its customers. It has also sought to introduce more environmentally friendly recycling strategies. There has also been a clear strategy to increase the range of summer activities and amenities to attract visitors all year round. Some of the broader strategies adopted by the RMB and BSL include:

- Investment in summer activities and additional licenced tour operators to deliver a broader range of experiences.
- Summer grooming comprising slope works and rock removal so that slopes are evenly graded, well grassed and allow skiing and snowboarding on minimal snow cover.
- Increased trail maintenance and operations focusing on improved snow holding and improved accessibility in low snow conditions.
- Snow fencing to capture and deposit snow during storm events, for harvesting and redistribution over the ski slopes.
- Snow grooming to evenly distribute snow, harvest snow from fences and other locations.
- Installation of significant numbers of conventional snowmaking pumps, compressors and guns to make snow when the ambient wet-bulb temperature is minus 2°C or less.
- Activation of the recycled water plant to produce additional water for snowmaking and firefight during summer months.
- Advancing strategies to develop additional attractions and services that encourage year-round visitation to the resort.

Mt Buller and Mt Stirling Alpine Resort Management
Board Annual Report, 2019

A snowmaking partnership was established between the Mt Buller and Mt Stirling Resort Management Board and BSL in 2015 to develop a coordinated and focused approach. Both organisations equally share all snowmaking costs with a commitment to continued investment and expansion of the snowmaking system (RMB, 2019). The most recent developments were the creation of a 100ML reservoir in 2019, near the base of the Mt Buller summit, at an estimated cost of $11.3 million. Given the extra water this will provide, BSL were able to accelerate its plans for snowmaking on the popular Standard Run at a cost of $2 million, which was completed and operational for the 2020 and 2021 winter seasons. The other recent additions were the purchase of two 'snow factories', the first in 2017 and the second in 2021, that proved crucial on Bourke Street, the Magic Forest, and the toboggan parks at the start of the winter season. Unlike traditional snowmaking that sprays water as a fine mist that falls to the ground like snow in sub-zero temperatures, the snow machines are in effect a giant ice maker which scrapes the ice into a semi-frost that can be piled up in great mounds and then spread over parts of the skiable areas to provide a solid base upon which natural or article snow can fall. This additional capacity means the bulk of the most popular ski trails, including the summit area the ski runs in and around the village and Mt Buller's longest runs of Little Buller spur and Wombat, are now all able to have effective snow cover for the length of the ski season (ARCC, 2021; RMB, 2019).

Table 7.4 highlights the investment made by Mt Buller to increase the capacity of the mountain to accommodate more visitors and to get them moving quicker and spend more time on snow. As evidenced in Table 7.1, this adaption strategy has provided Mt Buller with a clear advantage over its Victorian and interstate competitors through a significantly better ability to cope with a large number of skiers and visitors. However, the strategy is dependent on stable and growing income from visitors across both the summer and winter seasons.

The impact of COVID-19 pandemic

In January 2020, the world was thrown into turmoil with the confirmation of an infectious virus COVID-19 that quickly became a global pandemic with subsequent mutations. The responses of governments worldwide have included the locking down of communities and economies to stop the spread of the infection. The impact of these constant lockdowns and restrictions of movement of citizens has had a devasting effect on tourism and in particular the winters sports industry.

The Victorian State and National government's COVID-19 restrictions resulted in significantly reduced visitation and eventually resulted in early closures of ski resorts due to declared state of emergency status in 2020. These factors produced significant losses for Alpine dependent businesses and organisations, who were already suffering the adverse effects of the 2019–2020 bushfires (ARCC, 2020).

During the 2020 snow season, Victorian Alpine resorts received only 90,000 visitors across approximately 200,000 visitor days. This represents an 88% decrease in visitors and an 86% decrease in visitor days compared to the ten-year average

TABLE 7.4 Summarises the upgrading of lifts, their estimated cost, and their impact on ski capacity

Lift	Type	Est. Capacity per hour	Year replaced	New lift	Est. Cost at time of installation
Burnt Hut	3-person Chair lift	1,000	2012	'Bonza' 4-person chair lift	$3 million
Blue Bullet 1	4-person chair lift	1,200	2019	Bourke St Express 6-person high speed chair	$6 million
Blue Bullet 2	4-person chair lift	1,200	2019	Bourke St Express as above	N/A
Tirol T Bar	2 people drag lift	1,000	2014	New Mid Load Station	N/A
Shaky Knees T-Bar	2 people drag lift	1,000	2015	'The Fox' 4-person chair	N/A
Boggy Creek T-Bar	2 people drag lift	1,000	800	Lift power changed from diesel to electric power-lift shorted	N/A
Grimus	2-person chair lift	800	Proposed 2022–2023		N/A

Source: ARCC (2020).

from 2010 to 2019. In contrast to the previous 2019 winter season, the 2020 figures represent a 90% drop in visitations. BSL were in operation for only 45 days in total, between 24 June and 6 August 2020, and one day at the end of the season in September which is less than half of the usual operations (ARCC, 2021).

Andy Boydell of snow equipment distributor Sports Trade identified that 2020 was a disastrous season on many fronts. Due to the requirement to import the vast majority of ski and snow equipment, most company orders had been placed and paid for in October of 2019 for expected sales in 2020. He suggests that some ski stores in Victoria operated for only 2–3 days for the entire 2020 season (Wiseman, 2021). Colin Hackworth opined that the $2.4 billion income normally generated by the Australian Alpine industry was virtually wiped out in 2020 (Wiseman, 2021). As heightened by the figures in the last column in Table 7.1, the decline in visitation due to COVID-19 on the 2020 snow saw a corresponding decline in direct expenditure and value add by visitors. The results for 2020 are about one-tenth of the economic indicator values estimated in the previous year (ARCC, 2020). The ongoing pandemic in 2021 has seen only a marginal improvement with the Mt Buller resort being open only to regional Victorians and the primary target market of Melbourne, being limited to only one ski weekend in the 2021 season up to 1st September 2021, which had effect snow cover and the majority of the list in operation. It is likely that these two years will have a negative impact on the sustainability of the ski industry in the long term and may result in the deferral of additional planned infrastructure in snowmaking and increased lift capacity.

Conclusion

The future viability of Australian skiing will largely be dependent on the ability to make snow. However, with climate change and global warming now accepted as a matter of fact, not only will this affect natural snowfalls but by 2020–2030 conditions suitable for snowmaking are projected to decline substantially, and the costs of making more snow under warmer conditions are likely to continue rising. Despite these dire predictions, Steiger (2010) suggests that snowmaking should be able to sustain the ski industry until the middle of this century, by guaranteeing starts and extending seasons and helping to maintain the viability of lower altitude resorts such as Mt Buller in the short term to medium term. The COVID-19 pandemic has had a dramatic impact on the visitors to the Alpine regions in both summer and winter. The 2021 ski season has essentially been a repeat of 2020 with lockdowns and social distancing resulting in a decline of almost 90% in visitors and resulting revenues. Whilst Mt Buller had plans for more snowmaking and continued upgrading of its lift system to maintain its competitive advantage, it remains to be seen whether these plans can proceed or will need to be delayed until visitors can return.

References

Alpine Resorts Co-ordinating Council (ARCC, 2021). Victorian Alpine Resorts end of season report winter 2020, ARCC, East Melbourne.

Alpine Resorts Co-ordinating Council (ARCC, 2020). Annual Report. Available at: https://arcc.vic.gov.au/wp-content/uploads/2020/12/ARCC_Annual_Report_2019-20_FINAL_2_Page_Spread-1.pdf

Antarctic Climate and Ecosystems Cooperative Research Centre (2016) "The potential impacts of climate change on Victorian Alpine Resorts. A report for the Alpine Resorts Co-ordinating Council" ACE, Hobart.

Becken, S. and Hay, J. E. (2007). Tourism and climate change: Risks and opportunities, Blue Ridge Summit, Channel View Publications, Bristol.

Beniston, M. (2003). Climatic change in mountain regions: a review of possible impacts. *Climate variability and change in high elevation regions: Past, present & future*, 5-31.

Bhend, J., Bathols, J., and Hennessy. K. (2012). Climate change impacts on snow in Victoria. CSIRO Report for the Victorian Department of Sustainability and Environment. p. 42, East Melbourne, Victoria.

Bindoff, N. L., Stott, P. A., AchutaRao, K. M., Allen, M. R., Gillett, N., Gutzler, D., ... & Zhang, X. (2013). Detection and attribution of climate change: from global to regional. Available at: http://pure.iiasa.ac.at/id/eprint/10552/1/Detection%20and%20attribution%20of%20climate%20change%20From%20global%20to%20regional.pdf

CSIRO and Bureau of Meteorology, (2015). New climate change projections for Australia. Available at: http://www.bom.gov.au/state-of-the-climate/

Dawson, J. and Scott, D. (2013). Managing for climate change in the alpine ski sector. *Tourism Management* 35:244–254.

Elsasser, H. and Messerli, P. (2001). The vulnerability of the snow industry in the Swiss Alps, *Mountain Research and Development 21*(4), 335–339.

Elsasser, H., Abegg, B., and Buerki, R. (2006) Climate change and winter sports: Environmental and economic threats. *Geography Bulletin*, *38*(4), 26–31.

Gilaberte-Búrdalo, M., López-Martín, F., Pino-Otín, M. R., & López-Moreno, J. I. (2014). Impacts of climate change on ski industry. *Environmental Science & Policy*, *44*, 51-61.

Hantel, M and Hirtle-Wielke, L. (2000) Sensitivity of Alpine snow cover to European temperature, *International Journal of Climatology*, *20*(6), 615–640.

Harris, R.M.B., Remenyi, T. and Bindoff, N.L. (2016) The potential impacts of climate change on Victorian Alpine Resorts. A report to the Alpine Resorts Coordinating Council. Antarctic Climate and Ecosystems, Cooperative Research Centre: Hobart.

Hennessy, K. J., Whetton, P. H., Walsh, K., Smith, I. N., Bathols, J. M., Hutchinson, M. and Sharples, J. (2008). Climate change effects on snow conditions in mainland Australia and adaptation at ski resorts through snowmaking. *Climate Research*, *35*:255–270.

Hopkins, D. (2014). The sustainability of climate change adaptation strategies in New Zealand's ski industry: A range of stakeholder perceptions, *Journal of Sustainable Tourism*, *22*(1), 107–126.

Mt Buller & Stirling Alpine Resort Management Board (2020). Annual Report, 2019. available at: https://dc0b3a3e-6027-4943-8bb4-858433a866f2.filesusr.com/ugd/b19fc4_b97d323cb5ec4775ae2db38f0c280e32.pdf

Nicholls, N. (2005). Climate variability, climate change and the Australian snow season. *Australian Meteorological Magazine*, *54*(3), 177–185.

Pegg, S., Patterson, I., and Vila Gariddo, P. (2012) The impact of seasonality on tourism and hospitality operations in the alpine region of New South Wales, Australia. *International Journal of Hospitality Management*, *31*(3), 659–666.

Pickering, C.M. and Buckley, R.C.. (2010). Climate response by the ski industry: The shortcomings of snowmaking for Australian resorts. *AMBIO*, *39*:430–438.

Pickering, C. (2011). Changes in demand for tourism with climate change: A case study of visitation patterns to six ski resorts in Australia. *Journal of Sustainable Tourism*, *19*: 767–781.

Pons-Pons, M., Johnson, P.A., Rosas-Casals, M., Sureda, B. and Jover, È. (2012) Modelling climate change effects on winter ski tourism in Andorra. *Climate Research*, *54*:197–207.

Roman, C.E., Lynch, A.H., and Dominey-Howes, D. (2010). Uncovering the essence of the climate change adaptation problem—A case study of the tourism sector at Alpine Shire, Victoria, Australia, *Tourism and Hospitality Planning & Development*, 7(3), 237–252.

Scott, D., Dawson, J. and Jones, B. (2008). Climate change vulnerability of the US Northeast winter recreation-tourism sector. *Mitigation and Adaptation Strategies for Global Change*, 13:577–596.

Scott, D., Gössling, S. and Hall, C.M. (2012). International tourism and climate change. *Wiley Interdisciplinary Reviews: Climate Change*, 3:213–232.

Steiger, R. (2010). The impact of climate change on ski season length and snowmaking requirements in Tyrol, Austria. *Climate Research*, 43:251–262.

Steiger, R., & Mayer, M. (2008). Snowmaking and climate change. *Mountain research and development*, *28*(3):292–298.

Tourism Victoria and the Alpine Resorts Co-ordinating Council. (May 2014). Alpine Resorts Strategic Marketing Plan 2014–2018.

Whetton, P.H., Haylock, M.R. and Galloway, R. (1996). Climate change and snow-cover duration in the Australian Alps. *Climatic Change, 32*:447–449.

Wiseman, M. (2021). Industry Reflections on Skiing in 2020. *ChillFactor Ski Magazine, Thredbo, NSW,* 24–25

Wolfsegger, C., Gössling, S. and Scott, D. (2008). Climate change risk appraisal in the Austrian ski industry. *Tourism Review International, 12*(1), 13–23.

8

AUSTRALIA POST

A successful government business enterprise

Quamrul Alam and Robert Grose

Introduction

Australia Post was established at the time of the Australian Federation, in 1901, when it was known as the Postmaster General's Department (PMG). In 1975, the PMG was reorganised into the Australian Postal Commission (trading as Australia Post) and the Australian Telecommunication Commission (trading as Telecom Australia, which later became Telstra). In 1989, the Australian Postal Commission became the Australian Postal Corporation under the *Australian Postal Corporation Act* 1989, making it a Government Business Enterprise with the Commonwealth Government as its sole shareholder. Since then, Australia Post has been required to pay the full range of government taxes and charges and to return dividends to its shareholder – the Commonwealth Government (Australia Post, 2005b; Australia Post, 2009). During the past five years, Australia Post has paid a total of $881 million in dividends to the government (The Australian, 2013).

Following the restructuring, Australia Post has long been successfully re-inventing itself into a company that is not only self-funding but also a profit-centre, with a $53.6 million profit before tax in the 2019–2020 financial year (FY) which was an increase of 30% from the previous FY (Australia Post, 2021). Significantly, the increase in profits came amid a technology revolution that has the potential to directly threaten the long-term viability of its core businesses. Deregulation of postal services around the world has presented more opportunities, including diversification, global expansion, partnerships, acquisitions, and mergers, all of which have influenced the competitive dynamics in the postal sector.

Australia Post competes in the postal industry, which is comprised of enterprises involved in the collection, transport, and delivery of addressed mail, packages, and parcels in both domestic and international markets (Johnson, 2021). Operating in a highly regulated monopoly market, Australia Post has radically transformed itself from a government-run organisation to a Government Business Enterprise (GBE). Having diversified its products and services to 12.3 million national delivery points, it has become one of Australia's most successful and reputed public sector entities (Australia Post, 2021). Australia Post maintains its Australian heritage by providing services to over 750 businesses and government organisations through its current 4,330 retail outlets, of which 58% are in rural and remote areas (Australia Post, 2021). In 2013, AMR Rep Track reported it as the second most reputable brand in Australia for delivering trusted services, with an average customer satisfaction score of 9.06 out of 10 (Annual Report 2013). Currently, Australia Post holds 86% of the market share in the postal service sector, followed by Fujifilm Holdings Australasia Pty Limited with 5.1% and the remaining 8.9% by other rivals (IBIS 2013).

Australia Post has three core businesses: (1) letters, (2) parcels and logistics, and (3) retailing and agency services. Australia Post maintains a natural monopoly in its letters business. Contracting reserved letter volumes and rising maintenance costs of collection points' infrastructure have seen revenues and profit margins decline over the past five years.

Major players in the industry

There are several macro-environment factors that can impact Australia Post. These include competition, globalisation, the economy, politics and regulation, demographics, societal values, technology and the internet, and the environment and sustainability. Major competitors for Australia Post are DHL, TNT, FedEx, and UPS (Hubbard *et al.*, 2004). DHL, which is owned by Deutsche Post, has been operating in Australia since 1972. They are the global market leader in international express, overland transport, and air freight (DHL 2008). In 2012, Fujifilm Holdings Australasia acquired the Business Process Outsourcing division from Salmat Holdings to compete for the international mail-outs of bank and credit card statements and other bulk mail services (Johnson, 2021). Salmat focuses on international outsourcing business and Media Force marketing services with 42 operations throughout Australia, New Zealand, Asia, the UK, and the US. The remaining rivals are smaller companies in the bulk mail product and other printing-related services segments (Johnson, 2021). Therefore, Australia Post's three core businesses all have distinct sets of competitors (see Table 8.1).

Globalisation

The pace of globalisation, and its impact on global business competitiveness, public policy formulation, trade negotiations, business transactions, the flow of information and knowledge, and the mobility of people and ideas, has had a significant influence on how public and private sector organisations perform their day-to-day tasks. Due to fundamental shifts in the world economy and its management, we are moving away from a world in which national public entities are relatively self-contained units, isolated from each other, towards a world in which barriers to

TABLE 8.1 Major players in the industry

Business sector	Competitors
Letter delivery	No major players domestically. Australia Post has monopoly control over the whole market for the delivery of mail items weighing less than 250 grams and issuance of postal stamps. However, the market is threatened by substitute services such as email and facsimile.
Retail and financial services	The major players include Officeworks, news agencies (stationery, cards and bill express), governments (local, state and federal), banks (banking), banks (exchanging currency and travellers' cheques), mobile phone dealers, gift shops, and music shops (e.g., iTunes).
Parcels and logistics	Within Australia, the major competitors are Toll Holdings, TNT, and TDG Distribution (Walters, 2000; Way, 2004). Internationally, the main competitors are FedEx, DHL Worldwide Express, United Parcel Service, Fujifilm Holdings, and Salmat Limited, competing heavily in courier services. These multinational players have forced the accelerated adoption of sophisticated technology in Australian bulk mail services.

Source: Authors' discussion based on Johnson (2021) and Skotnicki (2004).

cross-border trade and investments are declining. Distance is no longer perceived as an issue due to advances in transportation and telecommunications technology, and national economies are merging into an interdependent, integrated global economic system (Hill *et al.*, 2008). This global interdependency is characterised by networks of international linkages that bind countries, institutions, and people. The invisible hand of global competition is being propelled by a process that Thomas Friedman referred to as a 'level playing field' among countries or the flattening of the world.

Several macro-environmental factors will have an impact on the current and continuing success of any business operating in the postal service sector. To a large extent, these are factors that the company has only a limited direct influence or control over, but nevertheless, the organisation must be strategically prepared to withstand pressure from these factors. An analysis of Australia Post's macro-environment shows that many factors have influenced the postal industry.

Economic conditions

Australia Post has chosen to focus more on the commercial than on the residential letter market, believing that a stronger economy leads to more business correspondence going through the mail system. As Australia Post expands globally in the parcels and logistics industry, the fluctuating value of the Australian dollar makes its services either more or less attractive to its customers.

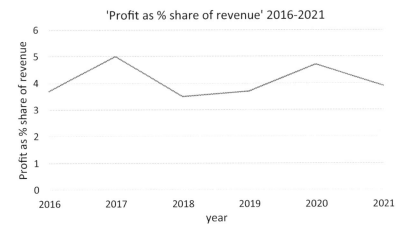

FIGURE 8.1 Postal service industry profit as share of revenue 2016–2021

Source: Based on the information from Johnson (2021).

The postal service industry has seen fluctuations in profit margins in the past five years due to structural changes driven by accelerating technological substitutions in major markets (Johnson, 2021). Rapid growth in online shopping has led to highly profitable parcel services becoming the largest service segment in the industry, which is 50.9% of total services. Some smaller operators have exited the industry to focus on other areas of communication, particularly digital channels (Johnson, 2021) (Figure 8.1).

Despite considerable process automation in the industry over the past decade, it has remained labour-intensive. The operation of postal stores and agencies, and the physical delivery of letters require a large workforce. According to the IBISWorld report in 2021 (Figure 8.2), the industry's wage cost remains above 35% of revenue from 2016 to 2021.

Australia Post normally makes losses on its regular mail services because the volume of sent mail is decreasing but the cost of sending out delivery workers has risen. Additionally, Australia's population growth over the past five years has boosted the number of addresses requiring service. The company is obligated to provide these services by law. Australia Post responded to declining letter volumes over the past five years by investing heavily in infrastructure to make inroads into the growing parcel delivery market and to contain letter-handling costs. However, the profit of Australia Post, as well as the industry, is expected to improve in the coming years in the parcel delivery segment as demand for online shopping has risen strongly since the onset of the COVID-19 pandemic as consumers have become increasingly comfortable with online purchases (Johnson, 2021). Despite stronger performance in the parcel segment, the continued decline in letter volumes is forecast to weigh on Australia Post's performance over the next five-year period. The continued decline of newspaper and magazine publishers and printing firms will

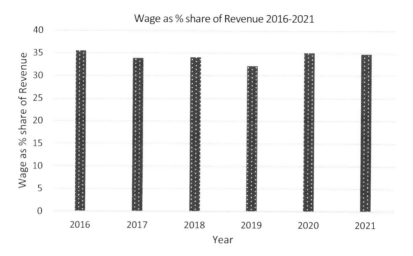

FIGURE 8.2 The wage trend in the postal service in Australia

Source: Based on the information from Johnson (2021).

further reduce the demand for bulk mail and non-regulated mail services over the next five years (Johnson, 2021).

The political environment

In 1994, the Federal Government reduced Australia Post's monopoly level (regarding the delivery of letters posted within Australia) and opened certain postal services up to the competition. These included reducing the weight protection for domestic standard letters from 500 to 250 grams (Hubbard et al., 2004). From July 2000, the Government decided that Australia Post should keep a monopoly on domestic letters weighing up to 50 grams with a charge of 45 cents. The basic postage rate was then increased to 60 cents after the company lobbied for a stamp price increase with the Australian Competition and Consumer Commission (ACCC) in 2010–2011 (IBIS 2013). For international mail, Australia Post is responsible for all deliveries Australia-wide (Hubbard et al., 2004). The Government also decided to allow open competition in business letter services, but Australia Post was free to discount (Hubbard et al., 2004). Australia Post was also forced to comply with the Community Service Obligations (CSO) performance standard to provide universal letter services. This meant that its domestic letter services be made available to all Australians at a standardised price from anywhere to anywhere within the country. Additionally, Australia Post had to deliver mail once a day from Monday to Friday to all locations in the country. While this would result in higher delivery costs in uneconomical rural and regional areas, these costs would be offset by letter delivery revenues in metropolitan areas (Hubbard et al., 2004).

Legislation and regulations

Until 1994, Australia Post had a monopoly on all letters delivered within Australia and those bound for international destinations. In July 2000, the government reduced Australia Post's monopoly on its cash-cow core business of letter delivery. This excluded all business letter services, which accounts for 80% of all letters posted in Australia (*Australian Financial Review*, 2007). As a result, Australia Post had to compete in the open market for approximately 90% of its products and services and faced fierce competition from international courier companies such as FedEx and UPS (*Australian Financial Review*, 2007). As a GBE, Australia Post is committed to providing a service, not just within the heavily populated cities, but in sparsely populated rural areas as well. No matter where a letter is being delivered or the cost of that delivery, the price of a stamp is currently set at $1, and this cannot be raised without government approval. Additional appeal for stamp pricing reform was declined by the Finance Department, despite a 20 cents inflation gap from the basic postage rate (*The Australian*, 2013). There have been calls for the deregulation of the postal industry in Australia, but no official plans have yet been proposed (Kerrin, 2005; Murrill, 2001).

Societal values

Historically and globally, the postal service is seen as a core public service. Societal values, however, are changing and it is becoming more common for governments around the world to de-regulate and privatise their postal services. The European Union planned to liberalise its postal monopolies from 2009, and the UK and New Zealand have already done so (Gray, 2006a).

Rising living standards and the mobility of people across regions and countries have created the need for greater communication services. In 2013, Australia had an estimated 282,400 net migrants from more than 144 nationalities who lived and maintained some form of business and social links with their source countries (IBIS, 2013). This has generated significant growth in transactions, including personal, business-to-business, and business-to-consumers parcel deliveries.

In addition, people have so many communication options available today that traditional mail is competing with many different and ever-changing social multi-media technologies, e.g., Twitter, Google+, Pinterest, YouTube, text messaging, email, chat rooms, and Facebook. Although the volume of personal letters fell at an annualised rate of 3.7% in 2013–2014, this only accounts for a very small proportion (5%) of the total mail delivered (IBIS, 2013; *Australian Financial Review*, 2007). People are also becoming more accustomed to purchasing online, which is adding to Australia Post's parcels and logistics business. There is a growing trend towards mail order and online purchases of items such as electronic goods, books, DVDs, CDs, clothes, wine, and many niches and customised consumer items. In response to the forecast strong growth during the period 2014–2019, Australia Post announced in 2010 a partnership with eBay to roll out its parcel handling services and to integrate into eBay's payment processing system (IBIS, 2013). In

November 2013, Australia Post launched the world's first 'video stamp' with a 15-second personalised video during the pre-Christmas period, to be distributed free with Express Post and Express Courier International products. This is an example of an innovative approach to using social networks to connect its customers during the festive season (www.auspost.com.au).

Technology and internet

During the last decade, postal services in Australia had seen a significant disruptive effect of technological changes. The area that brings the greatest competition to Australia Post is the development of broadband in Australia. Customers' vast use of electronic communication methods such as email, social media messaging services, and mobile phone communication has reduced the demand for letter delivery services and thus limited growth in industry revenue (Johnson, 2021). In 1960, 49% of all communication was conducted by letter mail; in 2004, this had dropped to only 14% (AFR, 2007). The rise of electronic technology has made the postal industry less attractive by eroding the volume of social letters, but at the same time, it has provided opportunities. Rather than being threatened by this challenge, Australia Post has diversified into parcels and logistics, and now delivers more than 60% of the items ordered via the internet (Kirby, 2001). Technology has allowed the Australia Post to improve its distribution and supply chain management systems. It has also made it possible to take on more agency services. Rather than being a threat to its core businesses, Australia Post has committed to looking at how technological innovation can improve its operations and open new business opportunities (Coughlin & Moran, 2007). Technology has also allowed Australia Post to upgrade its address file, consisting of more than ten million Australian addresses, by assigning each address a unique eight-digit number called a 'delivery point identifier' or DPID. Attaching a DPID to each address on a business customer's mailing list through a barcode has reduced costs for both Australia Post and its customers (Hubbard, 2000). Additionally, automated address readers for sorting large letters and flat mail optical character readers were introduced in 2003 (Hubbard et al., 2004).

Realising the need to position itself ahead of the competition in this technology-intensive business, Australia Post launched a four-year Future Ready Program costing $2 billion for new tracking technology to integrate with its existing tracking system. Rolled out in 2013, it invested $71 million on 26,000 handheld scanners supplied by Telstra to provide real-time tracking and improve its Digital Mailbox delivery services (Coyne, 2013). During 2010–2015, Australia Post had invested $2 billion to develop and upgrade capabilities, mostly in terms of technology, to support the transformed business structure of the company (Australia Post, 2015). The company shifted a lot of resources from mail delivery services to parcel delivery services and had to maintain accuracy, security, and customer satisfaction. They achieved this by deploying barcode technology to read and interpret correct delivery addresses automatically. The mail and parcel sorting process is now fully supported with vast automation in Australia Post. The delivery people or posties of Australia Post had previously delivered parcels once in a week during 2013 but with automation (handheld scanners) this had now changed five times a week by 2015 (Australia Post, 2015). With the help of its acquired company, Star Trak, Australia Post provided its customers with several online delivery options. Customers were encouraged to use the MyPost delivery portal where they could track, reschedule, or redirect their parcel deliveries and verify each suppliers' identity (Australia Post, 2015). In 2014, more than 1.5 million customers had downloaded the Australia Post app so that the parcel or e-commerce services of Australia Post could be easily provided to them (Australia Post, 2015). Australia Post has also offered more than 33,000 parcel lockers for customers so that they can collect their parcels across from more than 250 locations in Australia (Australia Post, 2021).

The environment and sustainability

Australia Post participated in the Federal Government's cooperative Greenhouse Challenge program, which focussed on energy saving, waste management, and vehicle fleet fuel efficiency. Examples of Australia Post's commitment to the environment include:

- the use of recycled material in packaging, e.g., most Postpak products are made from recycled materials;
- Australia Post's retail carrier bags, which are made from fully recyclable low-density polyethene;
- Australia Post's standard envelopes are made from 60% recycled paper; and
- a policy emphasis on the use of lightweight packaging products, e.g., Express Post and Parcel Satchels (Hubbard et al. 2004).

During FY2019–2020, Australia Post achieved the emission target to reduce carbon dioxide emission by 25% which is equivalent to 100,000 tonnes of carbon dioxide, which is compatible with taking 41,665 cars off the road (Australia Post, 2021). It also achieved the Reuse and Recycling target to divert 100,000 tonnes of material from landfills between 2016 and 2020. Australia Post successfully introduced plastic sachet with 80% recycled content and mailing boxes that are 100% certified by the forest stewardship council. And it also implemented carbon neutral delivery for all parcel products through retail and MyPost business channels.

Australia Post developed a sustainability 2020–2022 plan which closely follows the United Nations Sustainable Development Goals or SDGs. Within the first 12 months Australia Post had made significant progress in providing customers and communities with more sustainable products and services, which included:

1. introducing carbon neutral delivery for retail customers partnering with Qantas future planet

TABLE 8.2 Diversity profile of Australia Post workforce

Diversity profile	2017	2018	2019	2020
Women	36.7%	36.4%	36.5%	36.9%
Aboriginal And Torres Strait Islander People	1.8%	1.9%	1.9%	3%
People with Disability	4.8%	4.3%	4%	5.7%
LGBTI People	0.9%	1.2%	1.6%	3.1%
Culturally And Linguistically Diverse People	22.4%	22.1%	22.5%	30%

Source: Australia Post (2021).

2. providing market sustainable packaging with plastic sachets made from 80% recycled contents and mailing boxes that are 100% certified by the forest stewardship councils
3. ensuring that packaging is 100% recyclable following the adoption of Australian recycling levels.

Australia Post is using 3,764 electric delivery vehicles and electric-assisted motorbikes for its delivery services and highlights its commitments towards the reduction of fossil fuels in the supply chain. In 2020, the company installed 35,000 LED lights, recycled over 107 tonnes of fixtures and fittings, and in doing so saved $2 million.

Australia Post has a workforce of more than 75,000 people including employees, contractors, community postal agents, and licences. It is committed to the safety, well-being, and health of its workforce. Within the last few years, it implemented state-of-the-art robotics across different facilities to remove 520,000 daily manual handling touchpoints. It also ensured gender pay parity for the last four years in a row. It achieved a commitment to increase the Aboriginal and Torres Strait Islander workforce to 3% of its total workforce by 30 June 2020. The diversity of the Australia Post workforce is shown in Table 8.2.

Australia Post has created 10,802 full-time jobs in regional Australia, contributing $806 million in a year. It has been supporting small local businesses through the MyPost business service. During the COVID-19 pandemic in 2020, 289,000 small businesses registered with the MyPost service to participate in e-commerce and online transactions.

Australia Post and its market position

This section looks at some useful tools that can be used to assist with the strategic analysis of a company. They include Porter's Five Forces model, SWOT analysis, and Value Chain analysis.

Porter's Five Forces model allows a company to look more closely at the immediate industry and the competitive environment in which it operates. It allows a company to assess the actions of other companies within the industry and to think strategically about how to position itself to exploit industry opportunities, shape industry structure, and divide profitability (Porter 2008).

As has been demonstrated above, the attractiveness of Australia Post as a business proposition is low because of high entry barriers and the intense rivalry between competitors. Moreover, the availability of substitutes for the services and products offered is high, which also makes it less attractive to new entrants. Australia Post, DHL, UPS, and TNT can produce their product in large volumes and therefore can lower unit production costs. Mail sorting warehouses, technology, and capital infrastructure investments are high barriers for new entrants. A postal company needs both national and worldwide network access to be competitive (Johnson, 2021). Communication in online platforms is the widely available substitute product; however, there are a few substitutes for parcel delivery services. The bargaining power of both buyers and suppliers is insignificant in comparison to Australia Post's distribution network and huge purchasing power in such a highly concentrated industry.

Postal services, classified as part of the traditional service economy, have invested heavily in technology to improve capital productivity and revenue growth. While this trend should make the industry attractive to outsiders, it could also be argued that advancement in technology could increase the costs of production, since purchasing new technologies can be costly.

Internal analysis is an evaluation of the strengths and weaknesses of a company that considers the company's manufacturing, marketing, technological, financial, and human resources capabilities (Bradmore, 2005). Internal analysis can be assessed using a SWOT analysis, which enables the organisation to better understand its strengths and weaknesses and how it can develop its capabilities into a sustainable competitive advantage. Internal capability analysis is a strategic tool that can be used to identify the features of a business model and help refine strategy in response to external competitive pressures on the firm's internal operations.

TABLE 8.3 Five-year trend – Australia Post

Performance indicators	2016	2017	2018	2019	2020
Revenue – letters ($ million)	2508.6	2554	2433.7	2216.3	1996.4
Revenue – non-letters ($ million)	4053.6	4253.2	4443.3	4773.5	5502.8
Profit before tax ($ million)	41	126	125	41.1	53.6
Profit after tax ($ million)	36.4	95.4	134.2	40.6	42.9
Return on equity (%)	2.3	5.9	7.8	2.4	2.4
Return on average operating assets (%)	1.8	4.0	3.3	1.6	2.9
Ordinary dividend ($ million)	20	63.3	83.1	25.4	27.9

Source: Australia Post Annual Report 2020.

Value networks

Value chain analysis is the collection of activities performed internally by an organisation that together add value to the final product or service. Value chain analysis is a method for decomposing the firm into its strategically important components. A firm's value chain consists of two parts: primary activities and support activities. Primary activities are directly involved in creating and bringing value to customers through a physical product or service, while support activities enable and improve the performance of the primary activities and have an impact on the value delivered to customers (Stabell & Fjeldstad, 1998).

Australia Post's original core business of letters and their associated postal processes have produced a powerful value chain, creating distribution networks and services that enabled the organisation to diversify into unrelated industries through new business alliances. For example, Australia Post's distribution networks and adoption of technology have helped it form alliances with large unrelated organisations such as banks and government organisations to offer a range of bill payment, passport services, banking services, extended identity services (EIS), and taxation services – both online and in-store. The alliance with unrelated organisations has brought synergy gains to Australia Post. Its value chain activities have increased productivity, enhanced service quality, and reduced the costs of deliveries while providing the expertise to deliver a total value-creating solution for many unrelated small- to medium-sized businesses.

Primary activities of Australia Post's value network

The five primary activity categories of the value network are inbound logistics, operations, outbound logistics, marketing & sales, and service (cited in Stabell & Fjeldstad, 1998). These are the critical value activities that provide a basis for understanding and developing a competitive advantage from the perspective of the firm as a whole (Stabell & Fjeldstad, 1998).

Inbound logistics refers to the inputs required to handle, transport, store, and deliver goods to a business from suppliers (Bradmore, 2005). Australia Post deals mainly with the delivery of services to its customers, and to achieve this Australia Post has formed relationships with external manufacturers. In this case, Australia Post uses CorProcure's technology for purchasing everything from vehicles to printer cartridges. Cor procure provides an electronic private marketplace for Australia Post to purchase hundreds of items from pre-approved suppliers, and it generates and sends electronic orders, receipts, and invoices (Australia Post, 2008a). Australia Post's inbound logistics are taken care of by its suppliers.

Operations involve the transformation or manufacturing of inputs into finished products (Bradmore, 2005). This step is also performed by Australia Post's suppliers since Australia Post is the customer who has ordered their products. Scale advantage and cost savings to customers are maintained by an integrated inventory management system and an efficient stock replacement system (Annual Report, 2013).

Outbound logistics includes the storage, handling, transport, and delivery of a firm's product to either distributor or end-users (Bradmore, 2005). In the value chain, this is where suppliers distribute the products to Australia Post Shops.

Marketing and sales. To generate brand awareness and to communicate Australia Post's special features, Australia Post advertise on television, billboards, in newspapers and magazines in addition to online sales channels via its corporate website, which registered 78.6 million visits during 2012–2013 (Australia Post Annual Report, 2013a).

Services are activities designed to enhance or maintain a product's value (Hanson et al., 2005). Australia Post deals mainly with the delivery of services to customers, which include banking, express post, the delivery of letters, the provision of money orders, the delivery of parcels, delivery redirection services, and 24/7 parcel lockers. Access to online orders and delivery tracking through its self-service customer website is also available (Australia Post, 2013a).

Support activities of Australia Post's value network

Support activities enable and improve the performance of the primary activities. These include procurement, technological development, and human resources management.

Procurement. Australia Post uses CorProcure's technology for purchasing everything from vehicles to printer cartridges. It provides an electronic private marketplace for staff to purchase hundreds of items via pre-approved suppliers, and generates and sends electronic orders, receipts, and invoices (Australia Post, 2008a).

Technological development. Australia Post's postal address file consists of more than ten million Australian addresses. Each address has been assigned a unique eight-digit number called a 'delivery point identifier'. Australia Post also employs a 'flat letter program' that uses a flat machine optical character reader (Hubbard et al., 2004). Barcode systems are also used to increase the accuracy of mailing lists and the efficiency of mail processing. Through the launch of its 'digital mailbox' (APDM) and internet-based financial and ERP systems, the efficiency of operations and the protection of sensitive information and bills are achieved (IBIS, 2013).

Human resource management. Australia Post formed a human resource committee to assess major policies, structural and remuneration issues, including recruitment, selection, and succession planning; remuneration; culture and ethics; learning and development; occupational health and safety; terms and conditions of employment; and organisational structure (Australia Post, 2008b). *Australia Post Diversity and Inclusion* was initiated to manage its culturally diverse employees. The focus has been on skills, leadership development, performance, and career management to ensure higher engagement levels, which increased from 69% in 2011 to 77.5% in 2013 (Australia Post Annual Report, 2013a).

Australia Post's business competencies

A business model converts innovation into economic value for an organisation. It describes how an organisation positions itself within the value chain of its industry and how it intends to sustain itself. A core competency analysis is used to identify the features of Australia Post's business model. Core competencies are resources and unique capabilities which enable the firm to deliver customer benefits (Hafeez, Malak & Zhang, 2007). These capabilities should have three attributes such as being rare in the marketplace, inimitable, or difficult to substitute (Hafeez et al., 2007).

Australia Post also uses strategies of cost reduction and economies of scale to cut costs. As a cost reduction strategy, Australia Post maintained a price freeze for several years and only increased the price of stamps from 45 cents to 60 cents in 2011. Despite this 33% increase in price, the volume of letters stabilised at five million in 2011 (Annual Report, 2013). Australia Post has used economies of scale as a management tool; it processes large volumes of mail using the same staff and facilities. This has lifted the productivity of delivery transport, of mail processing facilities, and of the overall delivery network. Labour as a percentage of costs fell from 70% in 1990 to 48% in 2001, and productivity has improved by 67% over the past ten years.

Franchising activities

Australia Post adopted a franchising system to drive costs down, as the government forbids the closing of unprofitable post offices due to Australia Post's community obligation that a certain number of post offices must be kept open. Thus, Australia Post began licencing post offices to private operators, who run them as licenced post offices, usually in conjunction with other businesses such as a news agency, pharmacy, or corner store.

Many differentiated services are provided through these Post Shops including Post Billpay; giroPost; Money transfer services; car procure which enables customers to order products and services online, complete business solutions for companies, and complete end-to-end logistics for business-to-business and business-to-customer transactions; credit management, direct marketing, and database management services for major logistics customers; passport applications and income tax payments for households and small businesses; and Tax File Number (TFN) applications for Australian residents aged 16 years and over.

Strategic alliances

Australia Post has formed alliances with compatible companies to provide new services as well as to increase the efficiency of existing services. Australia Post also offers personalised stamps and other innovative philatelic products at Post Shops. Through alliances with suppliers and handicraft producers, Australia Post sells greeting cards, telephones and accessories, printers, office stationery, gifts, toys, jewellery, children storybooks, and popular learning materials.

Australia Post has built its logistics capabilities with several key acquisitions and joint ventures. The company recognised that its logistic division had the most growth potential and supported this with major investments (McColl, 2002; Hopkins, 2007). Some of the key acquisitions, joint ventures, and partnerships include:

- JR Haulage (acquisition), which was renamed Post Logistics and became the basis for the logistics division;
- State Warehousing & Distribution Services (SWADS) (acquisition) are specialists in moving white goods;
- StarTrack Express was fully acquired from Qantas, a strong national road freight network (Annual Report, 2013a);
- Australian Air Express (a joint venture with Qantas), which has a strong airfreight capacity and international capability (Annual Report, 2007b); and
- DHL (a commercial alliance) for international express services (IBIS, 2013).

To reach international markets, Australia Post has developed alliances with China Post, Hong Kong Post, Japan Post, Korea Post, and the US Postal Service. The objective is to ensure greater control over delivery in these countries. It also has developed unique business links with Jetstar, a low-cost airline (and a subsidiary of Qantas) to sell airline tickets at Post Shops. Customers can manage their mail when they move from one property to another using Australia Post's mail redirection and address notification services. Australia Post also offers a mail-holding service for customers who may be going on holiday or away on business. To make things easier, customers can sign up for free 24/7 parcel lockers which can be found in 400 locations across the country (Australia Post Notification, 30 May 2020). To help the most vulnerable community, Australia Post partnered with Woolworths to deliver the 'Woolworths Basic Box' of groceries across the country. Each box contains meals, snacks, and essential items for those in genuine need. Australia Post also introduced 'Pharmacy Home Delivery Service' to support vulnerable members of the community and those in self-isolation. Under this alliance, pharmacies offer free delivery on prescriptions to their customers.

Australia Post offers services and products for blind people. For example, Australia Post will deliver some items that aid the visually impaired free-of-charge or at concessional rates. Items might include:

> correspondence, documents or literature wholly written in embossed characters as used by the blind, that is, Braille or Moon Aids for the teaching of Braille to the blind; plates for embossing literature for the blind; special paper intended solely for the blind on condition that any communication on the paper is wholly in Braille or Moon; and any form of speech recording for the use of the blind.
>
> *Australia Post, 2008d*

Business alliance and value co-creation

Through the development of its agency services, Australia Post can offer key value chain creating activities of distribution and service (Figure 8.3). This uniquely integrated network is virtually impossible for most businesses or government bodies to match. Furthermore, it can offer to its business alliances a high level of customer service at each of these locations. These services are proving to be very successful, and Australia Post now handles over 12.3 million delivery points across Australia (Australia Post Annual Report, 2020).

As many of Australia Post's capabilities are rare in the marketplace, inimitable and difficult to be substituted for, Australia Post has the core competencies that serve as a sustainable competitive advantage to earn above-average returns compared to its competitors.

Core competencies are activities that a company performs much better than its competitors. They are competencies that give the company an edge or that are central to a company's strategy and competitiveness (Greenwald & Kahn, 2005). They provide benefits to the customer, are hard for competitors to imitate, and can be used across a variety of products and markets (Hamel & Prahalad 1990). The single most important core competency of Australia Post is its logistics management and national network. Australia Post invested $316.1 million as capital investment and made significant adjustments to support communities during the COVID-19 pandemic. It also partnered with supermarkets and pharmacies to deliver essential items during the COVID-19 pandemic. Australia Post also invested $50 million in security including X-ray equipment, explosive trace detection units, and automated conveyer systems (Australia Post Annual Report, 2020).

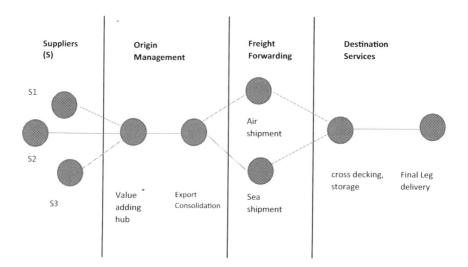

FIGURE 8.3 Australian Post's supply chain – end-to-end capability

Source: Based on Australia Post Annual Report 2006/2007.

Today, Post Logistics can offer end-to-end supply chain capability to customers. Companies can hand over their entire supply chain management with confidence in the ability of Australia Post to not only match their own capabilities but in most cases to exceed their capabilities and add value. This means that a company using Post Logistics no longer needs to spend time, effort, or money on something that is not one of their core competencies and is instead freed to spend more time on its own core competencies.

With the strengthening of its partnerships with international businesses, Australia Post can now offer complete supply chain management for companies working internationally. The standout success in this field is the partnership with China Post that created Sai Cheng Logistics International. Before the recent deterioration in relations, China was the second-largest importer from Australia and has recently become a major export destination for Australian goods.

Australia Post's successes

The success of Australia Post is largely due to its ability to implement its chosen strategies and transit to a technology-based business model. The strategic leadership foresight helped: direct organisational growth, leverage, and continually invest in core competencies through effective organisational culture and control systems (Hanson et al., 2011). In terms of its business-level strategy, Australia Post has effectively determined the values which its customers seek – a highly differentiated service.

Australia Post has also successfully implemented its corporate-level strategies and has enjoyed the benefits of these strategies. A good example of this is the success of Express Courier International, in conjunction with Australia Post's alliance partners. The successful implementation of this strategy has provided its customers with more value, kept its customers loyal to Australia Post, and increased Australia Post's revenues.

Australia Post has worked hard on improving relationships with its staff to effectively implement its strategy. This has included setting up bonuses for staff when deadlines were met, increased investment in training and development, a focus on promotions within the organisation rather than from outside, and a focus on developing team approaches to management (Australia Post Annual Report, 2020. This has led to dramatic reductions in the number of industrial disputes and increased productivity. Most importantly, it has also instilled a greater willingness in staff to accept change.

Maintaining the well-being of stakeholders

By being known as an organisation that looks after, responds to, and adds value to its customers, Australia Post's business keeps growing. An example of how Australia Post has responded to commercial requirements is through its e-Letter service (AFR, 2007; Kirby, 2001). Customers were seeking the convenience of email; yet

TABLE 8.4 Performance against targets 2020

		Targets	Performance
Financial	Profit before tax	$15 million	$53.6 million
	Return on equity	0.5%	1.9%
	dividend declared	$6.1 million	$27.9 million
Service	Deliver on time	94%	97.1%
	postal outlets	4,000	4,230
	rural outlets	2,500	2,520
	street posting boxes	10,000	15,036

Source: Australia Post (2021).

they still wanted the impact that could be derived from paper mail. As a result, Australia Post launched their e-Letter service, which allowed companies to email a letter to Australia Post, who then delivered a paper copy to the end customer.

Australia Post developed a service called Response Post, which could add value to customers' direct mail campaigns through the measurement of each campaign's effectiveness. Also, a barcoding software allowed customers to track in real time exactly their delivery. Recent results indicate that Australia Post has been consistently improving its performance (see Table 8.4). Thus, through technological innovation, by using proven systems, and by focusing on customer service and customer requirements, Australia Post is not only looking after the well-being of its customers but also expanding the quality of its diversified services and setting a new standard for the postal and logistics sector.

COVID-19 impact

Social distancing restrictions announced in response to the outbreak of the coronavirus in early 2020 prompted many Australian retailers to close their in-store operations for some time during 2020–2021. Consequently, demand for online shopping surged throughout the pandemic, increasing demand for parcel delivery services. However, the shift to remote work by many businesses and the increased caution around the physical handling of documents significantly decreased the volume of letters delivered, and this severely affecting demand for related industry services. In April 2020, Australia Post announced that it was reducing the frequency of its metropolitan delivery days to once every two days, allowing the company to divert its resources to parcel deliveries, supporting its revenue growth.

Through the summer of Australia wide bushfires and the uncertainty of COVID-19, the important role of the Australia Post's network was highlighted. As communities faced bushfires on their doorstep it was the local post office that acted as a community hub and as banking systems were cut off for bushfire affected communities it was the local post office that allowed people from these fire-ravaged communities to withdraw cash. During lockdowns, Australia Post moved quickly to work with superstores like Woolworths, Coles, and the Pharmacy Guild of Australia to help deliver the essential items Australians needed (Australia Post, 2021). 'We know so many people are really struggling to get their essential needs during this time, particularly the vulnerable and elderly who may not be able to visit their local supermarket. Making a delivery to people's homes is critical at this time' said Christine Holgate, CEO of Australia Post (Australia Post, 2021).

In dealing with the COVID-19 pandemic crisis, Australia Post made significant adjustments to support communities through 16 pop-up facilities and 17 planes. It made a $50 million investment in security including extra equipment such as contact trace detection units and automated conveyor systems. It launched a workforce verification system that provided a streamlined and efficient verification solution to employers to support them while working from home during the COVID-19 pandemic.

The lockdowns and mandatory restrictions during the COVID-19 pandemic have required businesses and households to adapt. Overall, 56% of goods-related businesses lost revenue during the COVID-19 period from March to August 2020. During this period, online service delivery and e-Commerce initiatives have helped many businesses to remain operating and thus limited revenue losses. In the first seven months of 2020, online spending rose by 72.5% from the same period in the previous year. Australia Post's activities supported this e-Commerce shift and approximately 82% of Australia's e-Commerce by value is delivered by Australia Post's delivery network.

During COVID-19 restrictions and lockdowns in 2020, the bank@Post product of Australia Post has assisted people in regional communities to access emergency everyday financial activities. More than 400 bank branches across Australia closed temporarily during the pandemic, reducing access to core financial services. As automatic teller machines (ATMs) were forced to close off their services to many regional communities, post offices were able to maintain critical services.

According to Deloitte's 2020 report, Australia Post's activities facilitated an additional $4.2 billion in e-Commerce during the height of the COVID-19 and an estimated $1.2 billion of e-Commerce was delivered to regional and remote Australia. They also found that additional e-Commerce supported the growth of new and small businesses.

Conclusion

Australia Post, strategically, is performing exceptionally well. The areas with potential problems are in its high gas emissions from electricity sources and the promotion of paper for direct marketing. By actively marketing the use of paper advertising over electronic or other media, Australia Post runs the risk of having customers question its social responsibility commitment to ecological sustainability.

Australia Post invested $316.1 million across different strategic projects. A major focus of this investment was on network automation and the expansion of the processing and delivery capacity of parcels. This was highlighted by the opening of the new state-of-the-art Brisbane parcel facility complex in Queensland in October 2019. The COVID-19 induced change in retail behaviour has imposed a record increase in parcel volumes in 2020. The company has faced a 7.2% increase in expenditure because of the additional expense involved in delivering the parcels. Around 600 additional employees were employed during 2020 so that the delivery services could be maintained.

As Australia Post is managing significant disruption bought about by COVID-19 induced restrictions, Australia Post is trying to get temporary regulatory relief from the Australian government to help manage the unprecedented parcel volumes. Temporary changes to delivery standards will help Australia Post continue to service the broader needs of the community as quickly as possible. The temporary regulatory relief includes suspending the priority mail letter service, extending the required delivery time for regular Interstate letters to five days after the day of posting, and allowing the delivery of letters in metropolitan areas every second day, freeing up resources to help with the massive demand for parcels.

With the impact of COVID-19 and the aftershocks to remain for some time, the main challenge will be to continue adapting to an ever-changing landscape amid what will continue to be overall tough economic conditions. Australia Post will continue to provide an important community service with post office networks but will need to meet the challenge of increased demand for parcels as Australians continue to become more accustomed to shopping online. Australia Post will continue to trial new products and seek new growth opportunities, particularly in financial and government services and the delivery of international e-commerce, while also looking for opportunities to drive efficiencies.

According to Deloitte's 2020 report, the shift towards online shopping is here to stay, with an estimated 45% of purchases set to be completed online in the future. The purchasing behaviour of regional customers is gradually changing. Deloitte's research found that 38% of regional consumers indicating a willingness to purchase more 'entertainment and hobby' products online in the future, while 24% indicating a willingness to purchase more groceries online. Importantly, as 80% of all customers surveyed stated that they trust Australia Post, future service delivery growth can be expected for the company (Deloitte, 2020).

References

Australian Financial Review (2007). Australian Financial Review case studies: The enduring power of paper as a means of effective communication', Retrieved 25 October 2007, www.afrbiz.com.au/page.asp?3646=431023&E_Page=416389&case=431023&3648=416511.

Australia Post (2005a). Annual report 2004/2005: More than you think. Retrieved 25 October 2007, www.auspost.com.au.

Australia Post (2005b). Heritage strategy. Retrieved https://auspost.com.au/content/dam/auspost_corp/media/documents/heritage-strategy.pdf

Australia Post (2007a). Everywhere, every day. *Annual report 2006/2007*, Retrieved 25 October 2007 www.auspost.com.au.

Australia Post (2007b). Our history, report of operations. Annual report 2006/07, Australia Post, Australia.

Australia Post (2008a). Buying online with CorProcure. *Priority: The Australia Post Business Customer Magazine*, 29.

Australia Post (2008b). Calculate postage rates. Retrieved 7 May 2008, www1.auspost.com.au/pac/int_parcel_select.asp.

Australia Post (2008c). Corporate governance. Retrieved 8 May 2008, www.auspost.com.au/BCP/0,1467,CH3904%257EMO19,00.html.

Australia Post (2008d). For the blind. Retrieved 6 May 2008, www.auspost.com.au.

Australia Post (2008e). Moving services. Retrieved 6 May 2008, www.movingservices.com.au.

Australia Post (2008f). Our products and services. Retrieved 6 May 2008, www.auspost.com.au/IXP/0,1465,CH2118%257EMO19,00.html.

Australia Post (2009). Annual report 2007/08. Retrieved: https://auspost.com.au/content/dam/auspost_corp/media/documents/auspost-annrpt-2008.pdf

Australia Post (2013a). Annual report 2012/13. Retrieved : https://auspost.com.au/content/dam/auspost_corp/media/documents/annual-report-2012-2013.pdf

Australia Post (2013b), 'Future ready', *Annual report 2012–2013*.

Australia Post (2013c). Growth in the digital economy & StarTek acquisition boost Australia Post's income. Retrieved 5 December, 2013, www.auspost.com.au/about-us/annual-report-results-2013.html.

Australia Post (2015). Annual report 2015. Retrieved: https://auspost.com.au/annualreport2015/docs/australia-post-annual-report-2015.pdf

Australia Post (2021). 2020 Annual report. Retrieved: https://auspost.com.au/content/dam/auspost_corp/media/documents/2020-australia-post-annual-report.pdf

Bradmore, D. (2005). *Competitive advantage concepts*, Prentice Hall, Sydney.Coughlin, M. & Moran, B. J. (2007). Special delivery, Outlook. Retrieved 28 October 2007, www.accenture.com/Global/Research_and_Insights/Outlook/By_Issue/Y2007/PostParcelSpecialDelivery.htm.

Coyne, A. (2013). Australia Post spends $71 million on new tracking service', Retrieved 4 December 2013, Itnew.com.au.

Deloitte (2020). Australia's eCommerce revolution: How it saved businesses in COVID-19 and future strategies to thrive. Published in October 2020. Retrieved: https://auspost.com.au/content/dam/auspost_corp/media/documents/ecommerce-report-2020.pdf

DHL Australia (2008). About us. Retrieved 7 May 2008, www.dhl.com.au/publish/au/en/about/dhl_new_zealand.high.html.Gray, J. (2006a). Asian alliances have vital role in delivering more revenue. *The Australian Financial Review*, 7 July.

Greenwald, B. & Kahn, J. (2005). All strategy is local. *Harvard Business Review*, Retrieved September 2005, www.capatcolumbia.com/Articles/FoStrategy/All%20Strategy%20is%20Local.pdf.

Hafeez, K., Malak, N. & Zhang, Y. B. (2007). Outsourcing non-core assets and competences of a firm using analytic hierarchy process. *Computers & Operations Research*, 34, 12, 3592.

Hamel, G. & Prahalad, C. (1990). The core competence of the corporation. *Harvard Business Review*, May–June 1990, 68, 3, 79–91.

Hanson, D., Dowling, P. J., Hitt, M. A., Ireland, R. D. & Hoskisson, R. E. (2005). *Strategic management: Competitiveness and globalisation*, 2nd edn, Thomson, South Melbourne.

Hanson, D. Dowling, P. J. Hitt, M. A. Ireland, R. D. & Hoskisson, R. E. (2011). *Strategic management: Competitiveness and globalisation*, 4th edn, Cengage Learning, South Melbourne.

Hill, C.W., & Hernández-Requejo, W. (2008). *Global business today* (p. 576). New York: McGraw-Hill Irwin.

Hopkins, P. (2007). Australia Post's key division to get more funds. *The Age*. Retrieved 18 October 2007, www.theage.com.au/cgi-/common/popupPrintArticle.pl?path=/articles/2007/.

Hubbard, G. & Koch, A. (2004). 'Australia Post', *Hubbard, Graham Strategic management: Thinking, analysis & action*, 2nd edn, Pearson Prentice Hall, Frenchs Forest NSW.

IBISWorld (2013). 'Postal services in Australia – Industry Report', Retrieved 3 December 2013, http://clients1.ibisworld.com.au/reports/au/industry/ataglance.aspx?entid=5033

Johnson, S. (2021). Postal services in Australia. IBISWorld Australia Industry (ANZSIC) Report I5101. Retrieved: https://my-ibisworld-com.ezproxy.cqu.edu.au/au/en/industry/i5101/about

Kerrin, P. (2005). Time to sell Australia Post. *Business Review Weekly*, July 21–28, 2005, 27, 28, p. 28.

Kirby, J. (2001). Q & A. *Business Review Weekly*, 4 May 2001, 23, 17, p. 77.

McColl, G. (2002). The challenge', *Business Review Weekly*, 7 November 2002, 24, 44, p. 24.

Murrill, M. (2001). The week in review. *Business Review Weekly*, 6 April 2001, 23, 13, p. 18.

Porter, M. (2008). The five competitive forces that shape strategy. *Harvard Business Review*, January, 86(1), p. 79–93.

Skotnicki, T. (2004a). Postal pacts on the way. *Business Review Weekly*, 12 August 2004, 26, 31, p. 28.

Skotnicki, T. (2004b). 'Special delivery. *Business Review Weekly*, 25 March 2004, 26, 11, 22.

Stabell, C. B. & Fjeldstad, O. D. (1998). Configuring value for competitive advantage: On chains, shops, and networks. *Strategic Management Journal*, 19, I5, 413–438.

Walters, K. & Kirby, J. (2000). The fight for e-delivery business hots up', *Business Review Weekly*, 11 August 2000, 22, 31, 76.

Way, N. (2004). Competitors take notice. *Business Review Weekly*, 12 February 2004, 26, 5, 29.

9
GBR HELICOPTERS
Surviving the downdraft of COVID-19

Malcolm Johnson

Introduction

Hindsight. It is tempting to consider COVID-19 as a Black Swan event (Taleb, 2010), one that was unforeseen and unforeseeable. Yet, since 2000, there have been eight other medical-related events that have struck humanity and the stability of global markets. Lest we forget the lessons of Anthrax (2001), SARS (2003), Mumps (2006), *E. coli* and Salmonella (2006), H1N1 swine flu (2009), Whooping cough (2012), and COVID-19 and its variants (2020–2021).

> The plan is nothing; planning is everything
> *(Eisenhower,* New York Times*, 1957)*

Planning relies on perspective. Contingency plans emanating from scenario planning must consider both the likelihood and magnitude of events that might disrupt core operational aspects of a business. How narrow or wide the scope of evaluation is influenced by management and an industry's disposition towards optimism or pessimism. Therein lies the problem. By 'concentrating on the things we already know, we fail to take into consideration the things we don't know' (Taleb, 2010).

Tourism is one sector at the forefront of volatility, and subject to the vagaries of economic cycles, currency exchange rates, geo-political climate, and the challenges of consumer sentiment. Inbound tourism in Cairns and Far North Queensland (FNQ) has developed through several cycles. Dominant in the rapid emergence of the region were tourists arriving from Japan. Initially travelling in groups, this transitioned to free and independent travellers (FITs) who were not tied to the supply chain intermediaries (tour companies) in Japan and Australia. More recently, tourists from southern China started arriving in significant numbers. The commencement of year-round flights by China Southern Airlines between Guangzhou and Cairns

DOI: 10.4324/9781003256717-9

TABLE 9.1 Financial status of experience Co

FY	Revenue	Profit	Return on profit
2016–2017	$90.59M	$9.48M	10.46%
2017–2018	$136.66M	$6.79M	4.97%
2018–2019	$131.11M	(-$48.26M)	(-36.8%)
2019-2020	$92.01M	(-$51.41M)	(-55.87%)

Source: (ASX: EXP).

in December 2017 was received as affirmation that the wave of visitors from mainland China would continue to grow beyond the 218,000 annual visitors reported at the time (Cairns Airport). China Southern Airlines operated five routes to Australia from China, reporting over 100,000 monthly passengers into Brisbane, Sydney, Melbourne, and Perth (Anna Aero, 2016). The direct flights into Cairns followed the demand pattern for visitors to visit the Great Barrier Reef.

> Success is not permanent; failure is not fatal
> *(Winston Churchill, quoted by Wooden, 1973)*

Within the space of two years, China Southern Airlines ceased flying into Cairns. Their departure in December 2019 also severed the link for Chinese tourists to seamlessly visit FNQ from the southern capitals, principally Sydney and Melbourne.

And so it was that Experience Co (ASX: EXP) retreated from its strategy of growth through acquisition, selling its 2017 $20 million purchase of GBR Helicopters to entrepreneur Chris Morris for $17 million in December 2019. At the time, Experience Co (EXP) had seen a fall in its share price from a high of $0.88 in December 2017 to $0.21 at the time of the sale of GBR to Morris. EXP saw its market capitalisation fall from $489 million to $116.7 million during the same period. The outcome of EXP's acquisition strategy, and cessation of visitation by groups of inbound Chinese tourists, revealed revenue and profit levels during this period as follows (Table 9.1).

EXP continues to operate in the leisure sector with sky-diving operations across Australia and New Zealand, island day trips from Cairns and Port Douglas, and rainforest tours around Cape Tribulation in FNQ. These experiential tourism products are attractive to backpackers and adventure tourists. Following the arrival of COVID-19 on Australian shores in March 2020, the company's share price fell to $0.03 valuing the business at $16.67 million. Its current capitalisation has improved to $155.62 million on a share price trading at $0.28 (ASX: EXP, 19 August 2021).]

White Knight or Black Swan?

Merger and acquisition (M&A) activity in Australia is booming during the COVID-19 pandemic. Drivers include low interest rates, distressed businesses, and counter-cyclical investment for cashed-up businesses and entrepreneurs. What follows is a brief recitation of factors at play and thoughtful discussion of strategy.

The sale of GBR's helicopter fleet to Morris Aviation saw it join a portfolio that included the Cairns-based Nautilus Aviation. Operating from five bases across northern Australia, the Morris Aviation fleet now comprises 36 helicopters purposed to tourism and commercial aviation activity. Duplication of assets and service proposition is inevitable; yet, the value of the GBR and Nautilus brands provide an opportunity for service differentiation in the future.

The aviation sector in Australia is replete with a history of entrepreneurial growth and corporate collapse. Notwithstanding aviation regulations, it can be viewed as a fragmented industry, much like that evidenced in the road transport sector. Consolidation strategies (M&A activity) arguably struggle in fragmented industries, with profit margins constrained by intense competition from operators offering an undifferentiated product or service. Helicopter operations per se are not inimitable.

Competitive advantage is consequently more likely to be derived from hidden networks and unique expertise among a range of factors specific to client needs (and risk mitigation). The combination of unique resources and organisational capabilities that meet these needs can provide a dynamic and situational edge but not permanent competitive advantage.

Portfolio investment analysis, with a correlation coefficient approaching '1' is unstable and risky; a market event can positively or negatively impact all businesses. Backward and forward integration in a supply chain represents a doubling-down on such a strategic position. Euphemistically referred to as a 'high commitment' strategy in investment markets, the portfolio of assets held by Morris exhibits this entrepreneurial preference (In addition to Morris Aviation, the Morris Group portfolio includes Orpheus Island Lodge, Mt Mulligan Lodge, Daintree Ecolodge, MY Flying Fish; the Colonial Leisure Group comprising pubs and a brewery). In good times, 'share of wallet' boosts revenue from tourists in parts of the supply chain. In bad times, such as COVID-19 lockdowns and geo-political tensions with China, such a correlation coefficient can lead to increased risk.

Competitive advantage for tourism in environmentally sensitive areas must necessarily evaluate physical assets and processes, and the strategic value and tenure of Government issued operational permits. Companies operating on the Great Barrier Reef have a strong barrier to competitor entry, enforced by government regulation. Over the years, M&A activity has resulted in a handful of companies being able to access the Reef. It is little wonder that some of these companies have sought to maximise their revenue potential through acquiring businesses in the supply chain that offer a diversity of tourism experiences to those same tourists. The challenge from this specialisation is whether there is an ability to repurpose assets that are not being used. Where demand is unlikely to recover quickly, and in the face of financial pressures, divestment of assets, as evidenced by EXP, may become necessary.

Operational diversity, in the form of services provided to different market sectors, is guided by an assessment of business risk. Considering the sectors that Morris Aviation now services through its helicopter operations, the demand conditions are quite different. Tourism demand might rely on inbound and domestic visitations, but commercial success is underwritten by the tenure of permits to operate in specific locations. For other investments in the supply chain, namely hospitality assets, there is no market protection other than booking office influence.

Considering commercial aviation activity, success relies on a different mix of assets, skills, and expertise. Market protection is unlikely unless contracts are in place, or preferred supplier status is achieved, for the provision of services. The prerequisite for this is the depth and quality of networks and personal reputations.

The Founder Factor

Entrepreneurial businesses with significant influence from founders rarely follow corporate approaches to managing portfolios of businesses. Instead, the dominant logic is largely derived from the founder's past successes and current interests. Deep knowledge provides experience curve advantages which is beneficial to a cost leadership strategy. Portfolios that comprise related businesses may tap into that accumulated proprietary knowledge. Stepping out into unrelated diversification may reduce the investment correlation coefficient of the portfolio but it introduces other forms of risk. Specifically, it is more likely to require different operational expertise. The strategic value of a business must include calculation of a business's ability to maintain cash flow from current operations; standard operating procedures and quality assurance underwrite the likelihood of maintaining current profitability. Upside potential from using existing assets to fill product or service gaps in the market is a further consideration. Candid assessment of resources and organisational capabilities will provide insights to help identify commonality across different operational contexts. Also referred to as 'parenting advantage', improving synergies across businesses in the portfolio can boost performance.

Hindsight is only helpful if lessons are learnt from failure as well as unexpected success. Management and strategic behaviour may also be understood through the prism of personal psychology. Specifically, past behaviour is a good predictor of future behaviour. Competitive strategy can be analysed using several proven frameworks: Porter's generic strategies matrix and value chain analysis, Ansoff's corporate strategy, BCG Growth Share Matrix, and the GE-McKinsey Directional Policy Matrix. Beyond the static description these provide, it is the psychology of the strategic actors that largely influences the direction, scope, and implementation of those plans. Growth-oriented managers will flourish in businesses that offer such opportunity through their careers; but they are likely to languish or fail when confronted with contracting markets. COVID-19 has presented both situations across different industry sectors.

Chris Morris has a record of significant entrepreneurial success across more than one industry sector (https://www.morrisgroup.com.au/about/) (Morris Group,

2021). This matters. Unlike publicly listed competitors, whose managers must meet the near-term performance requirements of shareholders, Chris Morris has control of the time frames, how and where resources are deployed, and measures of performance. He can play the long game at his choosing. COVID-19 might be detrimental to short-term cash flow across his portfolio, but it provides opportunities to a variety of potentially inexpensive strategic acquisitions ready for an uplift in market conditions.

References

Anna Aero (2016). China Southern Airlines flew 45% of traffic between China and Australia in 2015; capacity between nations grows 30%; next stop Adelaide. Available at: www.anna.aero/2016/09/02/china-southern-airlines-flies-45-percent-of-traffic-between-china-and-australia/

Morris Group (2021). About the Morris Group. Available at: www.morrisgroup.com.au/about/

New York Times (1957). *President draws planning moral: Recalls army days to show value of preparedness in time of crisis* by William M. Blair, Quote of Dwight D. Eisenhower, published on November 15, Page 4, Column 3, New York.

Taleb, N.N. (2010) *The black swan: The impact of the highly improbable*. New York, NY: Random House.

Wooden, J. (1973). *They call me coach*, Epigraph of Chapter 17 as Quote of Winston Churchill, p. 112, New York, NY: Bantam Books.

10
AUSTRALIAN MACADAMIA INDUSTRY
A community-supported regional industry

Quamrul Alam and Rumana Parveen

Introduction

Macadamia is a genus of four species of trees Indigenous to Australia and is part of the Proteaceae plant family. They are native to northeastern New South Wales, central Queensland, and southeastern Queensland. Many people think the macadamia tree originated from Hawaii, but the Macadamia nut crossed the Pacific, and became a Hawaiian icon and then returned to thrive in its original home of Australia (Allan, 1989). There is something unique about the taste, texture, and goodness of macadamia nuts grown in their natural home. The very essence of Australia, it is a magical product of the perfect soil, climate, and seasons, nurtured by passionate Australian growers. Approximately 50 macadamia cultivars have been undertaken in a number of countries including Australia, California, South Africa, and Hawaii (Hamilton, et al., 1983).

The macadamia nut is the only native Australian crop that has been developed and traded internationally as a commercial food product. Today macadamia nuts are the third largest Australian horticultural export. The macadamia industry in Australia is particularly fortunate in having forged a strong and effective organisation, the Australian Macadamia Society Limited (AMS). The AMS was established in 1974 by a small group of enthusiasts eager to share the benefits of their experience and their innovative ideas. It has responded to needs and opportunities across the whole industry and fosters the dissemination of information through its bimonthly News Bulletin, website, MacGroup meetings, field days, and annual conferences.

The macadamia industry has achieved many targets in a short period due to the dedication of growers. Very little was known about the commercial production of macadamia nuts in the early years of the industry, and many challenges have been solved through Australian ingenuity and the sustained passion of a few people who could see the potential of the magical macadamia (Stephenson, 1990). It is

DOI: 10.4324/9781003256717-10

important to note that it is the growers themselves who continue to invest up to $3 million each year in research and development through the AMS.

As a world leader, the Australian macadamia industry takes its responsibility towards future generations seriously. It is not surprising that Australian macadamias are preferred by millions of people around the world and right here in Australia.

Industry evolution

Around 60 million years ago, in the fertile soil of Australia's northeast coast, the world's first macadamias evolved. It was not until the early 1960s, when the Hawaiian macadamia industry was already well established, that efforts were made to develop the Indigenous macadamia as a commercial crop in Australia. Colonial Sugar Refiners (CSR) imported superior selections and technical expertise from Hawaii. (Stephenson, 2005). Before European settlement, aboriginal people gathered on the eastern slopes of Australia's Great Dividing Range to feed on the seed from two evergreen trees, one of which they called *Kindal,* or as it is more commonly referred to as – the macadamia. Aboriginal people had other names for macadamia including *Boombera, Jindill, & Baupal.* Macadamias were considered a delicacy and were treasured and collected wherever they were found. They were also traded between tribes and used as unique ceremonial gifts at inter-tribal activities. It was not until the 1850s that Australian macadamia trees attracted the attention of European botanists Walter Hill and Ferdinand Von Meuller when they were struck with the majestic beauty of the trees they found growing in the rainforests of Queensland.

While the first plantation was established in the 1880s, it was not until the development of successful grafting techniques and the introduction of mechanical processing that commercial production of the tough nut became feasible. Macadamia enthusiast 'Norm Gerber' pioneered the grafting techniques that enabled the development of the business aspects of the industry, and he is often referred to as the founding father of the Australian macadamia industry.

After decades of hard work and careful development, the Australian macadamia industry is now worth more than $200 million annually, employs thousands of people, and contributes millions of dollars to regional economies. It is an essential sector of the Australian horticultural industry, with about 750 businesses generating an annual gross value of production of $215 million at the farmgate. The industry is valued at $336 million at the factory gate and $650 million at the retail level (National Residue Survey, 2018–2019). More than 700 growers are members of the AMS and the entire supply chain includes processors, investors, marketers, suppliers, consultants, researchers, and administrators.

Industry structure

The macadamia industry has a long-term growth trend that is supported by a rising health consciousness among customers. The high nutrient value of macadamia has

TABLE 10.1 Australian macadamia production and export trend

	2011 actual	2018 actual	2021 forecasted	2025 forecasted
Production in tonnes	28,500	52,900	60,139	70,494
Farm gate value in AUD million	88	297	338	396
Export in tonnes	28,271	42,455	48,111	56,395
Export value in AUD million	71	266	320	400
Total nut export of Australia value in AUD million	232	750	1,031	1,309
% of macadamia export of total export	30.6	35.5	31.0	30.6

Source: Information collected from Australian Nut Industry Council (2019).

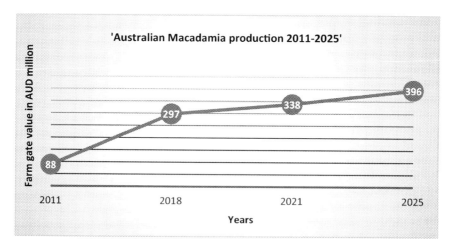

FIGURE 10.1 Australian macadamia production

Source: Based on information collected from Australian Nut Industry Council (2019).

boosted both domestic and global demand for the nut (Chapman, 2020). The production of the nut in Australia has been growing steadily during the last 20 years with both domestic and international demand having the greatest support (see Table 10.1 and Figures 10.1 and 10.2).

According to IBISWorld's latest industry report, the industry is experiencing a steady expansion and it is still in the growth stage of its lifecycle. Export demand has been and will be the most important driver of growth in the industry. Macadamias are Australia's second biggest nut export, after Almond, and are predicted to be worth $400 million by 2025 (Australian Nut Industry Council, 2019).

As the industry requires high levels of investment, long lead times for harvesting and unique climate conditions for production, the entry barriers are high. A competitive rivalry is not strong because Australia and South Africa have many natural competitive advantages and are the two largest producers in the global market

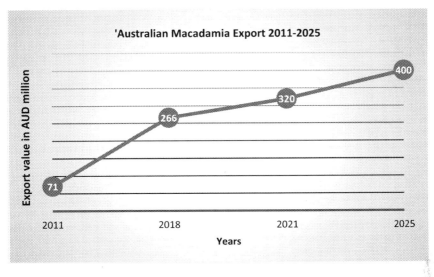

FIGURE 10.2 Australian macadamia export

Source: Based on information collected from Australian Nut Industry Council (2019).

(Chapman, 2020). The Australian macadamia industry enjoys government assistance and a supportive regulatory environment. The industry's major strength lies in the collaborative relationships among producers.

The product and the supply chain

Macadamias are predominantly grown along the eastern seaboard of New South Wales and Queensland, from Nambucca Heads in the south through to Mackay in the north. There are approximately 750 macadamia growers in Australia. Production in 2017 was 46,000 tonnes of Nut In-Shell (NIS) (at 10% moisture) from a production base of around 22,000 hectares. The industry is still growing, with significant new plantings underway. Around one-third of macadamia trees currently under cultivation are yet to reach full production. Australia now produces about 30% of the world's macadamia crop. The Australian macadamia nut breeders have produced a harvest of 43,500 tons in the shell at 3.5% moisture (46,600 tons in the shell at 10% moisture) for the 2019 season. The Australian Macadamia Handlers Association (AMHA) plants macadamia to the end of October and this accounts for over 90% of the entire macadamia nut culture in Australia. Australian macadamia growers are dedicated to expanding output volume while continuing to deliver an outstanding quality product. The industry's farm gate value has almost tripled in the last ten years, and it has only just begun. Australia has a young but innovative macadamia industry, and the cutting-edge orchard management practices will continue to deliver robust and stable supply in the coming years. The 25,000 hectares currently planted are forecast to expand to 30,000 by 2025, with Bundaberg the fastest growing region. With a third of macadamia trees presently under cultivation in Australia yet to reach full production, the stage is set for a long-term, sustained productivity. The Australian macadamia industry is a proactive and open industry that continues to grow each year and is supported by a wide range of businesses that help take Australian macadamias to the world.

It can take 10–15 years before a macadamia tree reaches maturity and achieves maximum yield. Mature trees grow to heights of between 12 and 15 metres and have shiny dark green leaves (Hamilton et al., 1983). Macadamias are mostly grown in northern New South Wales and southeastern Queensland in sub-tropical climates. Recently there have also been significant increases in the plantings of trees in the Bundaberg region. These locations are endowed with perfect conditions for growing this native Australian nut because of all the factors influencing macadamia growth and productivity, with the temperature being the most important factor (optimum growth occurs between 20°C and 25°C). Macadamias are fertile producers with each tree bearing sprays of long, delicate, sweet-smelling white or pink blossoms. Each spray of 40–50 flowers produces between 4 and 15 'nutlets', which will eventually ripen into adult nuts. Flowering occurs in early spring with nuts forming in early summer and, by early autumn, clusters of plump green nuts appear. The nuts grow encased in a hard, woody shell, which is protected by a green-brown fibrous husk. Shell hardening takes place in early December, followed by rapid oil accumulation in late December and January. Between March and September, the mature nuts fall to the ground and are harvested regularly with purpose-built mechanical harvesters. The fibrous outer husk of the macadamia is removed within 24 hours of harvest to reduce heat respiration and facilitate drying. The husk material is usually recycled as organic mulch. Macadamias are available all year round, but because they contain a high level of oil, they must be stored carefully to minimise exposure to oxygen and moisture. From a consumer's point of view, vacuum-packed macadamias are the best choice. Alternatively, look for macadamias that are plump, crunchy, and light-coloured. Refrigerate unopened nuts in an airtight container for up to 6 months or freeze for up to 12 months. Once opened, store macadamias in an airtight jar, refrigerate, and use them within two months.

Macadamias are sold mainly as grain, which is processed for snack food lines and as an ingredient in confectionery, cereals, ice-cream, and bakery products. The macadamia nut is known as the 'world's finest nut' and is renowned for its versatility. The Australian market consumes about 30% of total Australian production, more than 90% of which is sold as seed (Stephenson, 2005). There is continued strong demand in Australia and Asia with trade interest and consumer awareness growing. Market development campaigns are underway in Japan, South Korea, Taiwan, and China. Consumption of macadamias in China continues to grow, and already a vibrant seed market is appearing. Purchases of macadamias in the shell are increasing in China, and this market is expected to grow significantly over the next few years.

Macadamia growers sell directly to processors or in-shell handlers who take the product and dry it. The product is either sold as in-shell or cracked to produce seeds. In-shell handlers and processors manage over 95% of macadamias produced in Australia. There are 12 Australian macadamia processors/handlers. Secondary marketers include those businesses that repackage under proprietary or private label brands; companies and manufacturers that change the product's form, including packaged food products, such as cereal, confectionery, and ice cream; and retailers who sell all types of products, including macadamias. Secondary marketers largely control the development and market positioning of macadamia products and their macadamia content. Macadamia milk has gained a share of the non-dairy milk sector which is currently dominated by soy-based beverages. Most macadamias are sold in seed form. However, there are expanding export opportunities in markets that prefer macadamias nut-in-shell such as China.

Business sustainability: increased market demand and others

Effective marketing programs drive demand, underpin the premium paid for Australian macadamias and the price received by levy-paying growers. The Australian macadamia industry supplies more than 40 export destinations with core markets in Australia, Japan, Europe/Germany, the United States, and China. Taiwan and Korea have been identified as important potential new core markets. The industry has a positive view and has forecasted significant increases in world production, embracing the challenge of increased supply through a program of market development. Australian macadamias are over-represented in the snacking category such as retail packs of whole fresh kernels. The growth of newly manufactured products that use Australian macadamias offers the opportunity for growth in the macadamia market. Products manufactured with macadamias are less sensitive to high prices, potentially making use of different grades of nut and, once launched, are less prone to be discontinued by retailers than products in the snacking category if the price of macadamias changes.

In 2016, growers received a favourable $5.20 to $5.60 per kilogram NIS. Favourable nut prices are due, in part, to the growth in the China market. In 2007, prices fell to between $1.20 and $1.50 per kilogram NIS, which for most growers at the time was below the cost of production. Current Australian macadamia yields have recovered from the lows recorded after the 2007 price drop. Faced with unprofitable production and adverse weather conditions, growers cut inputs, and the average yield fell to 1.9 tonnes per hectare NIS. The restoration of price together with favourable seasonal conditions and a joint extension program have helped yields recover to about 3 tonnes per hectare. As past research results are being implemented, the return might grow to an average of 4 tonnes per hectare NIS. Even more encouragingly, it is hoped that new research will boost returns of 6–7 tonnes per hectare NIS on some commercial blocks. In historical terms, current prices are high, but as world supply increases, some price correction is anticipated.

The Australian macadamia industry has many unique characteristics, that combine, to help it remain a world leader in the industry. These characteristics will remain and even strengthen in future, thus contributing to an even stronger position.

Geographical and historical advantage

The macadamia is the native produce of the lowland rainforests of subtropical Australia (south-east Queensland and northern New South Wales) and the scientists have research-based predictions that all the commercially produced macadamia has shown to have very close genomic relationships among their species (Nock et al., 2019). A joint research project of Dr Catherine Nock (Southern Cross University) and Dr Craig Hardner (University of Queensland) mapped back chloroplast genome of Hawaiian varieties to trees in the wild in Australia and their research suggested that the global macadamia industry may have originated from seed collected from a single tree (Southern Cross University, 2019). The seeds for the first commercial production of macadamia date back to the 1920s in Hawaii; these were taken from Australian origins. The unique geography, weather, and huge available land for cultivation provide a good competitive advantage for Australia. Australia has the only natural germplasm resources for cultivation, and it has spent $10 million during the last ten years on a comprehensive breeding program (Australian Macadamia Society, 2017) to enhance this resource. The new varieties are expected to have a 30% increased yield and will be planted in 2021.

Strong support for research and innovation

The Australian Government has supported macadamia researchers to help growers breed thinner shells for bigger kernels and tougher husks for resisting pests. These combined attributes will further boost Australia's $270 million industry, which earns $190 million in export income annually (Topp, 2021). The $2.2 million National Macadamia Breeding and Evaluation Program (funded by Horticulture Innovation Australia), in collaboration with the University of Queensland, plus AMS-funded research and development actions are helping to improve the cultivation, productivity, and marketing of macadamia.

Highest sustainability standard

Macadamia orchards use 70%–100% of naturally falling rainfall. This represents a huge advantage because water from irrigation requires more water to achieve similar results which, in turn, creates huge pressure on water resources (Neville, 2021). Jolyon Burnett, CEO of the Australian Macadamia Society, when talking with Belinda Neville in 2021, stated that macadamia orchards in Australia absorb more carbon than the whole industry is producing. Thus, it is more than carbon neutral – it is a carbon positive industry. Burnett added that the AMS should take the opportunity to trade the carbon credits they have in store. The industry has been 100% compliant with the chemical usage and disposal laws, which is significant given its proximity to the Great Barrier Reef. Macadamia growers pay a combined research levy of about $3 million a year, some of which is invested into sustainability relevant research.

Australia's macadamia industry is a global leader in sustainability practices (Henderson, 2020). 'From water use efficiency to carbon sequestration, minimization of carbon outputs, recycling of by-products and world's best biological control, the macadamia industry really is kicking goals in this space', says Lynne Ziehlke, General Manager, of Marketing for the Australian macadamia industry (Henderson, 2020). Because of their biological traits, nut trees are intelligent users of water – they do not use more water than is required and they survive well during droughts. Growers ensure every part of the macadamia tree and nut is either reused or recycled, with nothing going to landfill. Macadamia shells are used to generate electricity, made into stock feed, and any organic matter such as branches or foliage is returned to the earth beneath the tree to be reabsorbed by the soil from which they originally grew (Henderson, 2020).

Industry strengths

Industry life cycle – growth stage

Australia's macadamia industry has experienced huge production growth and will enjoy more expansion in demand in the coming years (Charleston, 2020). Macadamia nuts have grown in price in recent decades, the highest price over $6.20 per kilo achieved in 2020. A decade earlier, the macadamia price was $1.30 per kilo. The industry is expected to grow further and enjoy stable profitability as Jolyon Burnett (CEO of the AMS) says, 'It's still a relatively new product and demand outstrips supply'. Australian macadamia orchards have thousands of trees that still have not arrived at their full productive potential.

Weather resilience of the crop

The AMS declared in December 2020 that the yield of macadamia orchards in Bundaberg had significantly contributed to a higher than expected 2020 national crop of 50,300 tonnes in-shell which was higher than the forecasted yield (Ross, 2020). The year 2020 has seen extremely hot weather, less rainfall, bushfires, and floods; however, macadamia crops have shown good resilience against these natural events. The high resilience of macadamias is a great strength. As Lynne Ziehlke, General Manager of Marketing for the Australian macadamia industry recently noted: 'This in-built resilience makes it a certain crop, even in uncertain times' (Henderson, 2020).

Market appeal

The AMS latest market research has shown that 80% of consumers look for the source or origin of nuts and they view Australian products as being both safe and green. The Australian macadamia is an iconic product and its 100-year-old history also has special appeal to Asian customers, especially in the Chinese market (Price,

2020). Macadamias are the number one nut source of the good monounsaturated fats vital for heart health, they are low in carbs, and also contain dietary fibre, protein, magnesium, thiamine, copper, iron, and antioxidants. The high food value makes it a preferred choice for health-conscious customers. There is no doubt that Australians are *macadamia mad*. Australia has the highest per capita consumption of macadamias in the world, followed by the United States (Charleston, 2020). The strong local market is also a strength for the industry.

Industry opportunities and threats

Tariff free market in China

Before the China-Australia Free Trade Agreement (ChAFTA), China applied a 24% tariff on macadamia nuts and a 10% tariff on mixed nuts. Since ChAFTA came into force in December 2015, these tariffs have been progressively reduced and in January 2019, the tariffs on these exported products were eliminated, providing the opportunity for macadamia exports to gain duty-free access into China (Australian Trade and Investment Commission, 2017). China is a big market and its demand for premium Australian products continues to grow and represents a huge and growing market going forward for Australian macadamia growers.

Product innovation

Macadamia is a very popular snack for health-conscious consumers. It is increasingly being used in the bakery industry to bake bread, cookies, and to make healthy drinks. The use of the macadamia nut in confectionery and snacks globally has increased by 20% in the last few years (Charleston, 2020) and the industry continues to find new uses for the versatile nut. Not only is it contained in shampoo, cooking oils, and face creams, but there have also been recent trials with macadamia oil to heal the skin of burn victims (Charleston, 2020). Burnett, CEO of the AMS, noted, 'I understand the trials are in the early stages but it just goes to show how versatile the macadamia nut is. It is so much more than just a tasty snack'. The recent market report by AMS (2020) shows that total new product launches using macadamias increased 3% in the 12 months to March 2021, despite the tumultuous impact of COVID-19.

The growing mid-income level consumers of Asia are interested in Western world healthy foods such as nuts. The huge markets of China and India pose a great opportunity for untapped demand (Ross, 2020). Chinese people like in-shell nuts, because they like to sit in groups, chat while cracking shells of nuts. So they offer the opportunity of in-shell exports which reduce the carnelling costs (Ross, 2020).

Industry growth through collaboration

The AMS is the representative umbrella organisation of the Australian macadamia industry. It has more than 700 members who are the growers, individuals and businesses covering nurseries, consultants, researchers, processing companies, marketers, and commercial suppliers. These members produce more than 85% of Australia's total macadamia yield (australianmacadamias.org, n.d.). The organisation was established in 1974 to help growers improve productivity and profitability. The AMS has worked tirelessly to create a sustainable macadamia industry with strong cooperation in the areas of marketing, management, and research. The AMS works as a source of information that helps growers move forward with farming practices, business goals, and production. The AMS meets growers and suppliers at group meetings to enhance industry relationships. From humble beginnings over 40 years ago, the AMS has grown to become an extensive member network. An AMS membership is an investment in both macadamia-related businesses and industry, and the partners also receive support to achieve the business goals.

The AMS represents a strong lobbying power to negotiate on issues like disaster relief, local environment plans, vegetation guidelines, coal seam gas, tariff reductions, and the backpacker tax. In more recent years, as the industry undergoes substantial expansion, the AMS has played a significant role in promoting the industry to potential new growers and investors and take responsibility for ensuring new entrants have the information and contacts they need to build strong businesses. The AMS has the vision to generate $1 billion in farm gate value within the next ten years (AMS, 2021). It wants to maintain a farmgate gross margin of 50%, plant 1,000 hectares per year to achieve 35,000 hectares of productive orchards by 2030, and adopt innovative and sustainable practices and technologies in cultivation.

Management collaboration

Macadamia Farm Management (MFM) was established in 1987 in response to the increasing demand for specialist and high-quality farm management in the macadamia industry. MFM is now Australia's largest manager of trees for both private individuals and companies. Over 25 years of industry experience is the key to successful long-term investment in Australian farming. The standard of water, granary, housing, fencing, roads, and sheds also needs to be factored into price negotiations as community facilities and support are essential elements in staff retention and resale values within the macadamia industry. The analysis of farm financial performance and land values highlight the opportunities that exist in the industry and ensure partners avoid the pitfalls of purchasing a property with minimal possibility of an acceptable financial return. The experienced team work with partners to develop an annual farm program to manage these risks and thus benefit from the seasonal and price upside.

Marketing collaboration

The Australian macadamia industry's marketing program is coordinated by a Marketing Development Manager (MDM) in consultation with industry marketers and processors to ensure that the program is closely aligned with the commercial sector. Over the last five years, the Australian macadamia industry's marketing processes have evolved considerably from a generic marketing program that was historically based on short-term promotional sales tactics. It now pursues a long-term strategic program, designed to protect and build the value of the industry and maximise long-term returns for all growers and industry stakeholders. The overarching aim of the program is to optimise the value of the Australian macadamia industry across the supply chain and directly influence productivity and farm gate profitability. Farmgate revenue has more than doubled since 2010, while grower profitability has risen threefold (Akinsanmi & Drenth, 2012). Wholesale and retail value has also grown significantly. Of the 70% of production that is exported, the majority attracts a price premium, signalling a high level of global competitiveness. New investments have grown substantially, and the industry is expected to grow by approximately 15,000 hectares by 2022, providing long-term industry growth prospects and making the sector more sustainable by providing customers with greater surety of supply.

The Australian macadamia industry has benefited from a sound export-focused growth program. In 2015, Australia exported 70% of its total production. Although Australia exports macadamias to 40 countries, there is a significant opportunity for further export growth. Major export markets include Europe, Japan, and the United States. Growing markets include Taiwan and Korea, while China is a considerable NIS market. With successful Free Trade Agreements in place, strong growth in China, Japan, and Korea is forecast. The Australian macadamia industry regards the domestic market as just one of its key revenue sources. Most countries currently have low per capita macadamia consumption and macadamias account for less than 1% of the world's nut supply. The AMS aims to identify and exploit other market opportunities in line with an agreed marketing plan and available funds.

Research collaboration

An industry levy is collected from all Australian macadamia growers to raise the necessary funding research, industry development, and marketing in those projects which are essential for ensuring the macadamia industry remains healthy and thriving, both now and into the future. There would not be a grower or other participant in the Australian industry who has not benefited from research, marketing, and trade development made possible by the levy. The levy is mandatory and is paid through processors and the Australian Government to Horticulture Innovation Australia (HIA), an all of-horticulture, grower-owned company that administers the expenditure of levies. Current projects being funded by the levy include a sophisticated breeding program, research into reducing chemicals, and improving sustainability. It is estimated that over 80% of Australia's wild macadamias have been lost since European settlement. The Macadamia Conservation Trust (MCT) has been working for the protection and conservation of wild species of the macadamia and also their native habitat for future generations (Crisol-Martinez et al., 2016).

The Australian average productivity of macadamia nuts is well below that of other industry leaders. The AMS is working to lift the average industry yield from three tonnes per hectare NIS to five tonnes per hectare by 2022. International collaboration to generate better information and a collective understanding of research and development and the marketing challenges and related solutions is an overarching goal of the AMS.

The potential threat of oversupply

It is estimated that Australia's macadamia production will double by 2025 to 400,000 tonnes a year and is still expected to grow further and might reach 600,000 tonnes by 2030 provided the number of plantations increase and yields grow (Brown, 2020). The demand for the macadamias might also increase with the help of targeted promotion and marketing campaigns, and a further increase in health-conscious trends. However, with the threat of COVID-19 hanging over like a dark cloud and the possibility of tariff barriers on exports, there is a danger that the industry could be hit by an oversupply of macadamia nuts.

The potential threat of price decline

The price per kilogram of macadamia dropped by more than $1 after a year of record-high prices. After paying $6.20 in 2020, the country's largest macadamia processor has announced a notional price of $5.10 per kilogram nut-in-shell for 2021 (Honan, 2021). Some producers and wholesalers say the market is still profitable and steady and they expect no further decline, while high demand will allow growers to make good profits (Honan, 2021).

The impact of COVID-19 pandemic

The growing and processing arms of the macadamia industry have quickly adapted to restrictions caused by the COVID-19 pandemic and remain largely unaffected (Charleston, 2020). 'It's been business as usual for the most part. Although there has been some minor disruption to our international shipping, as is the case with most export industries', says Jolyon Burnett, CEO of the AMS. Australia's 2020 macadamia crop remains on track to reach the forecasted 36,500 tonnes in-shell at 3.5% moisture, or 39,000 tonnes at 10% moisture. According to Burnett, harvesting conditions have been largely favourable over the last few months. Best of all, Burnett goes on to say that the nut quality is very good, despite the hottest and driest year in Australia's recorded history in 2020.

The AMS recently received a grant of $58,620 from the Queensland Government which it will use on a project to improve microclimate monitoring and digital data for decision making in the macadamia industry.

The grant to Australia Macadamias Society will support a $118,960 project that will help:

- install weather stations and sensors, including connectivity to collect vital decision-making data;
- create a new online dashboard platform for growers;
- develop and run an industry survey on the adoption rate of digital solutions.

The Federal Government of Australia has announced a huge grant to lift the export performance of the nut industry (Stock Journal, 2021). The Australian Nut Industry Council (ANIC) received the grant to help launch a market expansion program in a bid to develop nut industry exports. It is hoped the program will help bolster market diversification and sustainability, as well as grow Australia's clean and green reputation in the nut industry. It will definitely assist the export market for macadamia nuts.

The AMS recent market report (June 2021) notes that the impact of COVID-19, the unfavourable weather conditions such as the flood in New South Wales, and the associated harvest delays and infrastructure damage were minimal. In fact, Australian kernel sales in the 12 months to February 2020 were up 1% compared to the prior year, driven largely by solid sales in the domestic market, Japan, Korea, and Europe. Australian in-shell sales were 9,609 tonnes, a significant increase from the prior year. This was in part driven by the faster than expected post-COVID-19, economic recovery in China and a strong Chinese New Year result. That said, the macadamia industry has taken some strategic moves through mergers and collaborations to help protect itself against future disruptions.

Australia's largest macadamia processors and marketers were recently relaunched under the new brand Marquis Macadamias. The new entity consolidates the Lismore-based Macadamia Processing Company and its wholly owned subsidiary, Bundaberg's Pacific Gold Macadamias and their marketing company, Brisbane's Macadamia Marketing International, which is jointly owned by South Africa's Global Macadamias (AusFood News, 2020). Marquis will grow, process, and sell 48% of Australia's macadamia production and will be responsible for 22% of global kernel sales, whilst handling over 16% of the world's NIS production. More recently the leading Australian macadamia processor, Macadamias Direct and a global business – Finasucre Group have entered into a merger agreement. The merged business will become one of the largest growers, processors, and marketers of macadamia in Australia (Macadamias, 2020).

Conclusion

The macadamia industry is one of the most significant horticultural economic contributors to the many regions of Australia in which it operates, injecting millions of dollars into these economies every year. In some areas, the macadamia industry contributes as much as 40% to local businesses. The AMS is also committed to giving back to local communities by supporting local food festivals, speaking at local schools, and working with community groups to protect endangered species like the koala. The forecasted production and export of macadamia certainly show growth, which might be a little lower in practicum because of international transport interruption caused by the COVID-19 pandemic. However, the same pandemic has infused more consciousness among customers about healthy eating and thus will push the demand for highly nutritious and healthy food such as macadamia.

References

Akinsanmi, O. A., & Drenth, A. (2012). Economic returns from fungicide application to control husk spot of macadamia in Australia is influenced by spray efficiency, rates and costs of the application. *Crop Protection, 41*, 35–41.

Allan, P. (1989). Macadamia cultivar evaluation in Natal. *South African Journal of Plant and Soil, 6*(3), 149–153.

AusFood News. (2020). World's largest macadamia marketer and producer launches Wednesday. Posted by media release agency on 13 February 2020. Available at: www.ausfoodnews.com.au/2020/02/13/worlds-largest-macadamia-marketer-and-producer-launches-wednesday.html

Australian Macadamia Society. (2017). The Australian macadamia industry: Information for new and potential growers and investors. Available at: https://app-ausmacademia-au-syd.s3.ap-southeast-2.amazonaws.com/factfigure/2aiPVX1RCf9znwNX2ESoBzxZRBvx0L8xafvCcQja.pdf

Australian Macadamia Society. (2020). June 2021 market report. Available at: https://trade.australian-macadamias.org/june-2021-market-report/

Australian Macadamia Society. (2021). A plan for the Australian macadamia industry 2020–2030. (2021). Available at: https://app-ausmacademia-au-syd.s3.ap-southeast-2.amazonaws.com/page/1617236404_Macadamia%202030%20strategic%20Plan%20External%20Feb%202021.pdf

Australian Macadamia Society (AMS, n.d.) available at: https://australianmacadamias.org/industry

Australian Nut Industry Council. (2019). Growing for success. Available at: http://nutindustry.org.au/wp-content/uploads/2021/02/Growing_Success_2019_Email_LoRes.pdf

Australian Trade and Investment Commission. (2017). Australian macadamias crack China's market. Available at: www.austrade.gov.au/news/success-stories/australian-macadamias-crack-chinas-market

Brown, J. (2020). Can demand maintain pace with increased plantings? *The Land*. Available at: www.theland.com.au/story/6912717/nut-marketers-keen-on-china/

Chapman, W. (2020). Tree Nut Growing in Australia. Industry Report Od5544. IBISWorld.com. available at: https://my-ibisworld-com.ezproxy.cqu.edu.au/au/en/industry-specialized/od5544/about

Charleston, L. J. (2020). Our thriving macadamia industry. *Aus Biz Media*. Available at: https://ausbizmedia.com/macadamia-industry/

Crisol-Martinez, E., Moreno-Moyano, L. T., Wormington, K. R., Brown, P. H., & Stanley, D. (2016). Using next-generation sequencing to contrast the diet and explore pest-reduction services of sympatric bird species in macadamia orchards in Australia . *Report, 11*(3): 1–19. doi:10.1371/journal.pone.0150159

Hamilton, R. A., Ito, P. J., & Chia, C. L. (1983). Macadamia: Hawaii's dessert nut, Cooperative Extension Service, College of Tropical Agriculture & Human Resources, University of Hawaii.

Henderson, T. (2020). How Australian grown macadamias are meeting the sustainability demands of the conscious consumer. Snack, food and wholesale bakery. Available at: www.snackandbakery.com/articles/94626-how-australian-grown-macadamias-are-meeting-the-sustainability-demands-of-the-conscious-consumer

Honan, K. (2021). Macadamia nut prices down for 2021 due to pandemic, strong Aussie dollar. *ABC Rural*. Available at: www.abc.net.au/news/2021-03-08/australian-dollar-forces-macadamia-prices-down/13205594

Macadamias. (2020). New merger in macadamia industry. Available at: www.treecrop.com.au/news/new-merger-macadamia-industry/

Neville, B. (2021). Sustainability in the macadamia industry – An interview with Jolyon Burnett. Nuts for Life Podcast episode 8 on June 2021. Available at: www.nutsforlife.com.au/resource/episode-8-sustainability-in-the-macadamia-industry/

Price, J. (2020). Seed to snack with the mac. Food and drink business. Available at: www.foodanddrinkbusiness.com.au/news/seed-to-snack-with-the-mac

Ross, C. (2020). Bundaberg the macadamia capital of Australia. *Bundaberg Now*. Available at: www.bundabergnow.com/2020/12/11/bundaberg-leads-macadamia-national-crop/

Southern Cross University. (2019). A single Australian tree may be the source of the global macadamia industry. Available at: www.scu.edu.au/engage/news/latest-news/2019/a-single-australian-tree-may-be-the-source-of-the-global-macadamia-industry.php

Stephenson, R. A. (1990). The macadamia: From novelty crop to new industry. *Agri. Sci.* 3:38–43.7.

Stephenson, R. A. (2005). Macadamia: Domestication and commercialization. *Chronica Horticulture*, 45(2), 11–15.

Stock Journal. (2021). Australian Nut Industry Council gets $550,000 to lift Aussie nut exports. Available at: www.stockjournal.com.au/story/7362714/federal-funds-flow-to-boost-nuts-market-share/?src=rss

Topp, B. (2021). Cracking a tough nut for macadamia growers. Queensland Alliance for Agriculture and Food Innovation, University of Queensland. Available at www.uq.edu.au/news/article/2021/01/cracking-tough-nut-macadamia-growers

11
HARVEY NORMAN
A competitive business model

Quamrul Alam and Robert Grose

Introduction

Harvey Norman Holdings Limited is a retail icon in Australia, specialising in a wide variety of home and office goods. The company operates as a franchisor and grants franchises to independent businesses that trade as part of the Harvey Norman (HN) complex. Franchisees sell products across a range of categories including Electrical, Computers & Communications, Small Appliances, Furniture, Bedding & Manchester, Home Improvements, Lighting, and Carpet & Flooring (Harvey Norman 2021a). Harvey Norman operates as a publicly listed company and is administered from its head office in Homebush West, New South Wales (NSW).

Harvey Norman grants franchises to independent proprietors in Australia under three leading registered brand names: Harvey Norman, Domayne, and Joyce Mayne. Harvey Norman has a total of 194 franchises in Australia; 168 franchises under the HN banner, 30 under Domayne and 7 under the Joyce Mayne brands (Harvey Norman, 2021a; Dean, 2021).

In addition to its Australian business, HN has 96 company-operated stores in New Zealand, Ireland, Northern Ireland, Singapore, Malaysia, Slovenia, and Croatia, which trade under the HN brand (Harvey Norman, 2021b). Harvey Norman Holdings Limited's retail operations in overseas markets differ from that of the Australian franchised system as the retail complexes are company-operated stores trading under the HN brand name.

In the 2019–2020 financial year ending 30 June 2020, HN reported a $661.29 million profit which was 15.1% higher than the $635.60 million in 2019 (Harvey Norman, 2021c). According to the company, this is the highest profit the company on record. The company declared a 24% dividend per share with a 39.19% earnings per share which grew 15.5% from 33.94% in 2019. The franchising operations in Australia have experienced a 40.3% growth in profit since

DOI: 10.4324/9781003256717-11

2019 whereas stores operating in overseas have experienced a 17.3% growth in profits (Harvey Norman, 2021c). The franchisee aggregated sales revenue of the company grew to $6.16 billion in 2020 from $5.66 billion in 2019. The company-operating sales revenue also grew from $2.23 billion in 2019 to $2.29 billion in 2020 (Harvey Norman, 2020).

Retail industry for Harvey Norman in Australia

Harvey Norman is a key player in the Australian retail industry. Although the company operates in several retail sectors, it mainly competes in three retail segments in Australia – computer and software retailing, furniture retailing, and domestic appliances retailing. In these three markets, HN is one of the market leaders and has the highest or second highest market share (see Table 11.1).

Furniture retailing industry

Retailers in this industry sell furniture across several household categories, including bedroom, dining, lounge, and kitchen. The sale of mattresses, blinds, awnings and antique-reproduction furniture is also included (Dean, 2021).

The furniture industry is expected to operate in the mature phase of its life cycle over the ten years from 2016 to 2026 and sales revenue is expected to decline

TABLE 11.1 Harvey Norman's market positions in the retail industry

Retail industry segment	Market share (%) of Harvey Norman	Market position	Competitor's market share (%)
Furniture retailing	23.1	Market leader	• Greenlit Brands Pty Ltd, market share: 11.6% (brand Names: Freedom, POCO, Snooze, Fantastic Furniture, Plush, Original Mattress Factory) • IKEA Pty Limited, market share: 11.1% • BBQSAM Holdings Pty Ltd, market share: 7.1% (brand names: Amart Furniture, Barbeques Galore
Computer and software retailing	16.4	Market 2nd	• JB Hi-Fi Limited, market share: 23.1%, market leader • Wesfarmers Limited, market share: 12.4% (brand name: Officeworks)
Domestic appliances retailing	18.9	Market 2nd	• JB Hi-Fi Limited, market share: 33.2%, market leader (brand names: JB Hi-Fi, JB Hi-Fi HOME, The Good Guys) • BSR Australia Limited, market share: 3%

Source: Based on the information from Burgio-Ficca (2021a, 2021b) and Dean (2021).

by 1.7% in the same period (Dean, 2021). The industry's mature life cycle status can be attributed to the slow rise in industry value-added, the minimal change in establishments, and the well-defined product market (Dean, 2021). Industry operators have faced a medium level of competition over the past five years. Driven by trends in price, product range, and promotional deals, the trading landscape for furniture operators has become a veritable battleground for the consumer shopping dollar (Dean, 2021). While product quality and Australian-made items have featured prominently as a means for retailers to differentiate themselves from others, the industry has faced intense competition from external players such as department stores and online retailers ((Dean, 2021). According to the IBIS Industry Report, during the COVID-19 pandemic, sales of household goods, including furniture, actually increased. In addition, prevailing declining interest rates have allowed people in Australia to become homeowners, and this has required many of them to spend more on items such as furniture. A projected rise in household numbers will likely support demand for essential furniture.

Computer and software retailing industry

Retail companies in the computer and software retailing industry offer a broad range of computer and software products, including desktops, notebooks, laptops, tablets, scanners, printers, keyboards, and packaged software (except game software). The sale of computer game consoles is also included in the industry (Burgio-Ficca, 2021a).

The industry has a medium level of concentration, with the major players estimated to have over 50% share of the market in 2020–2021 (Burgio-Ficca, 2021a). The trading landscape for computer retailers in Australia has come under increasing pressure over the past five years. The key basis of competition for computer retailers has been price. Consumers in the market for computers and software compare prices by different operators and ultimately choose the one that offers the best value for money. An operator's range and quality of products also influence where consumers shop. The larger the product range, the wider the potential number of consumers. As a result, the increased focus on price has led retailers to cut margins, which has affected their underlying profitability (Burgio-Ficca, 2021a). In addition, a growing number of smaller operators have been affected by the dominance of larger players like HN, which can offer bundle packages and discounted excess stock sales (Burgio-Ficca, 2021a). IBISWorld anticipates that the relevant market share of the major players will increase as they expand their network of stores. This is expected to be the detriment of small independent players, with increased competition leading to their demise, or a merger with or acquisition by larger operators (Burgio-Ficca, 2021a).

In addition to increasing internal competition, industry retailers are facing competition from external players like department stores, domestic appliance stores, and online retailers (Burgio-Ficca, 2021a). Department stores offer a range of computers and software as part of their electronics departments. Domestic appliance stores have also become a notable competitor by stocking an extensive range of computer peripherals, equipment, software, and accessories. Furthermore, online retailers and auction websites have grown considerably, largely due to the confidence of consumers when placing orders online (Burgio-Ficca, 2021a).

According to IBISWorld's recent industry report, ongoing advances in computer hardware and internet capabilities are anticipated to boost demand. Computers have become an integral part of life due to changing work requirements as a result of the lockdown many employees have had to endure in recent times. However, the rapid growth in online shopping and strong price competition have negatively affected the industry and software providers have turned to and adopted cloud services, reducing software retail sales. Further, an anticipated appreciation of the Australian dollar is forecast to support modest profit growth during 2021 (Burgio-Ficca, 2021a).

Domestic appliance industry

Operators in this retail industry offer a broad range of domestic appliances, including TVs, audio, and home theatre goods; kitchen, laundry, and floor-care products; small appliances; and communication products. These products are purchased from manufacturers and wholesalers before being sold to consumers at retail stores (Burgio-Ficca, 2021b). The industry is currently in the mature phase of its life cycle.

Over the ten years from 2016 to 2026, industry value is estimated to contract by an annualised 2.6%, with an expected 2% growth in sales revenue (Burgio-Ficca, 2021b). The decline in value-added for the industry relative to the overall economy can be largely attributed to significant price and margin erosion across the industry due to strong price-based competition.

The industry's large players (Harvey Norman, JB Hi-Fi, and BSR Australia Limited) control a major share of the domestic appliance market and compete against smaller chain-store operators and independent stores for consumer spending across a range of industry products (Burgio-Ficca, 2021b). According to the IBIS Industry Report, intensifying industry competition has dominated the operating landscape and eroded industry revenue. Underperforming industry players have merged, been acquired by the larger players in the market, or exited the industry. Industry revenue is forecast to be threatened by increased competition from online-only retailers, strong price-based competition, and volatile consumer sentiments against high-priced technologies. However, demand for smart TVs and other home appliances has been strong due to the growing popularity of streaming content and stay-home rules imposed during COVID-19 lockdowns. Industry revenue is expected to benefit from residential building construction growth in Australia and growth in home automation is anticipated to help drive demand for new appliances (Burgio-Ficca, 2021b).

The main features of Harvey Norman's business model

A company's business model is management's 'story line'. It depicts how the company's strategy is implemented to make a profit (Thompson *et al.*, 2014).

A business model should be expressed lucidly and not be too complex. It should state the main methods an organisation will use to make a profit. Mullins and Komisar (2009) state that there are five components of a business model: the revenue model, the gross margin model, the operating model, the working capital model, and the investment model.

Harvey Norman's business model is simple but effective, and can be represented by six simple points:

1. a large, diversified range of items – where consumers are enticed to visit a store looking for one item but then buy things from other categories;
2. competitive prices;
3. a franchise ownership system – to ensure an added motivation and expert knowledge in each category;
4. its people, with their product knowledge, sales efficiency, and customer service;
5. advertising and promotions – to increase brand profile; and
6. property investment and development – to ensure the longevity of the company and cost savings on rent.

From the outset, HN chose to create stores that stocked a wide range of popular items and then sold them at lower prices than their competitors. This philosophy ensured a large turnover of stock and substantial profits. Harvey Norman was able to use its purchasing power to the utmost when it came to higher profit items such as furniture and non-electrical items, as suppliers were most disjointed in this area (Koch & Hubbard, 2003). It could be said that HN initially followed a low-cost strategy that attracted price-sensitive consumers, but by 2003 HN's pricing was not as competitive and their focus changed to concentrate on a wider range of items and on customer service (Koch & Hubbard, 2003). By selling computers, furniture, and appliances in the one superstore, HN became a 'one-stop shop' for its customers. This strategy can be classified as a broad differentiation strategy (Thompson *et al.*, 2014) and is discussed in detail in this case.

A crucial part of their business model, and the most significant difference between HN and other retailers, is their franchise setup. The franchising model (see Figure 11.1) adopted by HN has some significant differences when compared with the standard franchising models used in business. A brief comparison of the HN franchise model and a standard franchise model is provided in Table 11.2. Each section of the HN store is allocated to a different franchisee that pays rent and passes on a percentage of their sales revenue to Harvey Norman Holdings. Harvey Norman's format has proven to be extremely effective, with each category within its superstores run by people who know the business. This format means that franchisees have a vested interest in making their segment of the superstore a success.

Most consumers are familiar with the catch phrase 'Go Harvey Norman, Go!'. Koch and Hubbard (2003) noted that HN would spend 3–4% of turnover on advertising, including one or two catalogues per month. Harvey Norman

TABLE 11.2 Differences between Harvey Norman and standard franchise models

Harvey Norman franchising	Standard franchising
Franchisees are personally chosen.	Franchisees choose the franchise they want to purchase.
Franchisees are required to work in a store for at least six months before being awarded a franchise.	Franchisees are not required to work in the business before they purchase the franchise.
Franchisees are allocated premises.	Franchisees choose the business location.
There is no upfront fee to acquire the franchise.	Franchisees pay an upfront fee to acquire the franchise.
The store warehouse entity receives, stores, and delivers goods on behalf of each franchisee.	Franchisees control their own stock.
HN reserves the right to withdraw a franchise.	The franchise can be withdrawn if there is a breach of the conditions of the contract.
Franchisee pays ongoing fees based on a percentage of sales. This is estimated to be 50% of profits.	Franchisee pays ongoing fees in the form of royalties or a franchise service fee, usually based on a percentage of gross or net income.

Source: Stockport (2006).

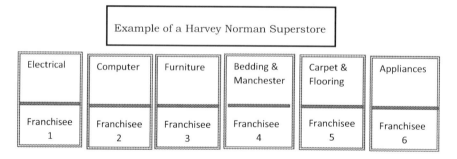

FIGURE 11.1 Franchising model of Harvey Norman

Source: Authors' discussion.

recognised early that they needed to build their brand and invested heavily in advertising, which has resulted in a higher profile for their stores than many of its competitors.

As stated earlier, HN has made some sound investments and made it a policy to own the land where the superstores have been built. Their property portfolio alone is worth a staggering A$3 billion (Harvey Norman, 2021). This investment will help ensure the longevity of the organisation during difficult or testing times.

Core competencies of Harvey Norman

A core competency could be described as a key factor or foundation that defines the collective learning within an organisation (Hamel & Prahalad, 1990; Lahti, 1999; Ljungquist, 2007). A core competency becomes more valuable than a competence as it has a place in the company's strategy and generates tangible contributions to a company's success in the marketplace (Thompson et al., 2014). HN shows this by accumulating its corporate knowledge and sharing this across the entire business. Their information systems are considered superior to those of others in the Australian retail sector.

Numerous examples have been cited in identifying core competencies. Hamel and Prahalad (1990) suggest that there are three tests to identify a core competency. First, opening potential access to a variety of markets; second, the end product accentuates significant customer benefits and the way they are perceived; and lastly, it is difficult for competitors to copy. Halley and Beaulieu (2009) pursue the last point, contending that competency is core when an organisation has developed efficiencies greater than those of its competitors, and when these capabilities are prized and sought after by its customers. Harvey Norman in 2003, according to a competitor, had purchasing efficiencies of 4% greater than its rivals (Koch & Hubbard, 2003). Their superior purchasing discounts set them above their competitors and were very difficult to match. Superior discounts immediately put competitors on the back foot and at a disadvantage in pricing campaigns. In an industry where well-informed consumers (because of the internet) can shop around for the same product, HN's well-placed superstores, price, marketing clout, and service became a sale motivator.

In addition to HN's purchasing power and corporate knowledge, its franchise system is another core competency. It meets the first test in opening access to a variety of new markets by offering entrepreneurs a successful system. Harvey Norman, through its superstores, now offers multiple retail stores under one roof which appeals to the broader market, while internal franchisees drive each category under the stewardship of HN's regional management. Sales efficiencies that include their IT systems fall under the second test, which provides customer benefits through quicker service and supply chain management proficiency. Harvey Norman's strong management team and its leadership by Gerry Harvey are exceptional and difficult for competitors to replicate. In fact, all the items discussed above are fundamental to HN's business operations and are difficult to reproduce. The ability to nurture and shape the core competencies over time gives an organisation the ability to secure a competitive edge. Out-strategising and outperforming the market with resource strengths unique and/or centric to the defined business makes it very difficult for competitors to enter the market, or to match sustainable operational excellence (Thompson et al., 2014).

Harvey Norman's strategies to reposition

Broad differentiation strategy

The essence of a broad differentiation strategy is to offer unique product attributes that a wide range of buyers finds appealing and worth buying (Thompson et al.,

TABLE 11.3 Distinguishing features of Harvey Norman's broad differentiation strategy

Dimensions	Porter's differentiation strategy in the context of Harvey Norman
Strategic target	Target a broad cross-section of the market from the singles, couples, families, and small business.
Basis of competitive advantage	Offers its customers a 'big box' home solution covering a variety of areas as a one-stop shop.
Product lines	Provides a wide product range with various price points within flooring, bedding, Manchester, domestic appliances, computer and software, photography service, and furniture.
Product emphasis	Sources reliable brands and are known to be first to market with emerging products.
Marketing emphasis	This is the only store that offers this wide range; regularly advertises financing options; charges a premium for customer service; and the ability to offer finance.
Keys to sustaining the strategy	Marketing resources, strong brand and image, ability to bring new and innovative products to market first.

Source: Authors' discussion.

2014). A differentiation strategy calls for a customer value proposition that is unique. The strategy achieves its aim when a large number of buyers find the customer value proposition appealing and become strongly attached to a company's differentiated attributes (Thompson et al., 2014). Harvey Norman's competitive strategy can be classified as a broad differentiation strategy. This differentiation strategy can be demonstrated using six dimensions (see Table 11.3).

Harvey Norman is a unique retail chain that offers a wide range of product variety (i.e., computers, furniture, appliances, and many others). They compete in these various categories by positioning themselves in a leading role, through price and quality compared to others within the retail industry. It also has wide geographic coverage. The only retailers that cover most of the HNs product range are JB Hi-Fi, Good Guys, David Jones, and Myer, but they are very different competitors. Harvey Norman's position amongst its competitors in the furniture, domestic appliance, computer/software, and department store retailing segments is shown using strategic group mapping in Figure 11.2.

Omni-channel strategy

The omnichannel strategy is a multi-channel retailing strategy that fully integrates HN's digital, store, and distribution channels. The omnichannel strategy requires HN franchisees to invest in their people and deliver the best consumer experience by focussing on the core mantras of 'quality', 'value', and 'service' in every communication, transaction, and service with the customer (Harvey Norman, 2013). Consumers are delighted with the HN franchisee click, pay, and collect in-store

Harvey Norman: a competitive business model **141**

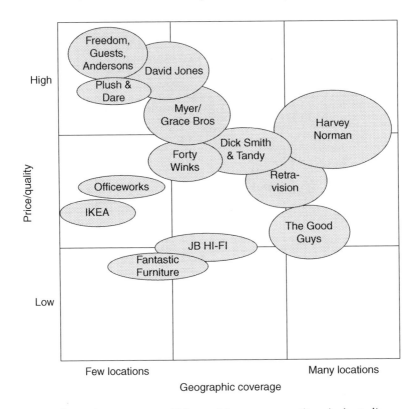

FIGURE 11.2 Strategic group map of Harvey Norman competitors in Australia

capability. This operating model enables HN franchisees to deliver products and services to customers through the established wide network of HN stores in metropolitan, regional, and country areas. The integration of digital communication and transactions with physical franchised stores is a significant competitive advantage for HN franchisees (Harvey Norman, 2013).

The omnichannel strategy (Figure 11.3) is robust and the most viable format to effectively compete in evolving markets. According to HN's Annual Report 2013 (Harvey Norman, 2013), this strategy and initiatives provide several strategic advantages over its competitors including:

1. The operating model is flexible and resilient, which enables HN franchisees to diversify and tailor product offerings in the homemaker and technology categories.
2. A strong balance sheet underpinned by real, tangible property assets – as, at balance date, the company has a total asset base of $4.07 billion, which is inclusive of a property portfolio valued at $2.21 billion. Such a strong balance sheet affords access to capital and the ability to seize opportunities in the marketplace as they arise.

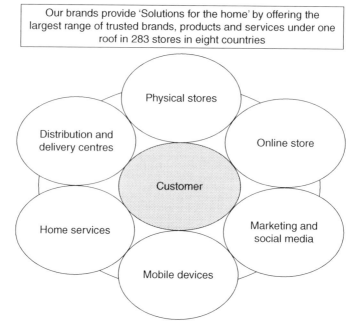

FIGURE 11.3 Omni-channel strategy for Harvey Norman

Source: Harvey Norman, 2021c.

3. The company's strong asset position and prudent management of working capital allow them to conservatively manage its debt levels and maintain a low net debt to equity ratio of 27.69%.
4. The integration of digital, e-commerce, and physical stores enables complete customer choice and satisfaction with a click, pay, and collect in-store capability.

The strategic leadership role of Gerry Harvey at Harvey Norman

Shrivastava and Nachman (1989) challenge the notion that only the CEO provides strategic leadership in organisations, and classify strategic leadership patterns into four conceptually meaningful areas: entrepreneurial, bureaucratic, political, and professional. Gerry Harvey, as executive chairman of HN, embraces the entrepreneurial approach. He assumes the role of guiding the organisation's strategy using classic leadership traits – including confidence, entrepreneurship, energy, aggressiveness, and knowledge – employing personality and charisma to influence people. While the culture at HN is multi-faceted and difficult to define because of the nature of the franchise system, there is an entrepreneurial spirit embedded in franchise operators. However, each franchisee has their own management style and therefore a different culture. This entrepreneurial spirit is created through Harvey's approach to management – he gives you a desk and the resources and says: 'go to it'. When staff need advice or a chat, it is rare for him to decline (Harvey Norman, 2012).

Gerry Harvey always made it clear that he wanted to be 'number one in the retail industry'. He holds a personal commitment to excellence, a desire to drive profits and to produce high shareholder returns (Koch & Hubbard, 2003). Harvey's fundamental management beliefs are simple: know your business and yourself before you start your business; help your people get the most out of themselves; find the best way to do it, and keep on searching (Koch & Hubbard, 2003).

In 1982, Gerry Harvey and Ian Norman (the founding owners) realised that the future of retailing lay in small owner-operated stores, where the owners' dedication and expertise could be backed up by the financial muscle, buying power, and management services of a larger organisation. The strategic decision to move from company-operated stores to franchise-operated stores was based around people. Harvey felt that, when franchisees were given a piece of the business, they suddenly reached new skill levels. They leveraged this to demonstrate that sales could be a first-class career and to provide greater possibilities for advancement (Koch & Hubbard, 2003).

Kaplan and Norton (2008) suggest that effective business processes and satisfied customers will lead to success from a financial perspective; however, none of these will take place without a high performing culture supported by strategic expertise, strong leadership, continuous learning, and sharing of knowledge. Harvey believes that the company's success grew from its corporate culture and emphasis on people. Managers mentor each other, Harvey believes that the company's success grew from its corporate culture and emphasis on people where managers mentor each other. He also believes those with a business gift need to be given freedom (Koch & Hubbard, 2003). With this in mind, little direct training is provided to franchisees, and, while systems are controlled by HN, franchisees manage their own business from both a product and a staffing perspective.

Conversely, for all the success of HN's franchising model, it is interesting to note that Harvey himself says that six out of ten franchisees do not work out and are asked to leave. Van Buren and Safferstone (2009) raise the concept of the 'quick wins' paradox, where new managers and leaders are faced with the pressure to produce quick wins to prove that they are right for the role. They suggest that this creates pressure, and they caution organisations and executives that mastery of management does not occur overnight. In this regard, HN's expectations appear high. But, while little direct training is provided to franchisees, if a franchise was losing money, HN would not take a cut of the sales or charge full rent until they became profitable.

Gerry Harvey is both chairman and a major stakeholder of Harvey Norman Holdings. He runs his own franchise store to help him keep in touch with the issues involved in running a business at the franchisee level. He interviews prospective franchisees, selects new store sites, negotiates leases, selects merchandise, and appears in TV advertising (Koch & Hubbard, 2003). Montgomery (2008) notes that watching over strategy, day in and day out, is not only a leader's greatest opportunity to outwit the competition but also a great opportunity to shape the firm itself.

Future challenges

One of the biggest challenges for HN and similar other big retailers in Australia is overseas retailers who sell similar products online. Overseas retailers are exempt from import duties and the Goods and Services Tax (GST) on purchases under $1,000. The activities of overseas retailers will have an impact on HN's sales and revenue. Although Gerry Harvey did not agree there was such an impact on HN's sales and revenue, he raised his voice in favour of abolishing the GST exemption on imported goods, adding his voice to a chorus of retailers rallying against the tax-free threshold (Wilkins, 2013). Speaking to shareholders at HN's annual meeting, the chairman said that, although the retailer was not directly affected by the $1,000 tax-free exemption, the policy should be changed. Mr Harvey said: 'this is totally unfair. It won't make any difference to us, but it is totally unfair' (Wilkins, 2013). The threat is not only a matter of the GST issue but also a matter of how quickly HN can embrace online technology. It means that the internet has forced retailers to change the way they operate. JB Hi-Fi has responded the fastest and most successful so far, operating a comprehensive online store alongside its popular bricks and mortar stores (Mudie, 2013). David Jones, Myer, and HN are slowly improving their online offerings but they continue to be outperformed online by overseas and online-only Australian companies (Mudie, 2013).

Concerning internationalisation, HN's expansion into some foreign markets (e.g., Slovenia and Croatia) will face tough challenges from the external business environment. In particular, sales revenue from the company-operated stores in Slovenia and Croatia decreased by €1.21 million (a decrease of 1.9%) relative to the prior year. Sales in Slovenia decreased by €4.29 million, whilst sales in Croatia increased by €3.07 million (Harvey Norman, 2013). The adverse effect on sales during the 2012–2013 financial year was due to a fall in consumer confidence as a result of negativity associated with the government, state-owned banking sector governance issues, and European Union (EU) pressures (Harvey Norman, 2013). These issues resulted in extreme discounting and competition from cash-flow struggling competitors, driving down retail margins. Despite this intense competition, HN continued to grow its market share in all key categories and attempted to minimise the impact of such negative issues by renewing its focus on cost control and management (Harvey Norman, 2013).

Lastly, Gerry Harvey's departure from the company could be a threat to the leadership of the group. Gerry's vision and stewardship of the company have exited the domestic market, and shareholders have benefited. While Gerry himself says that he is in no hurry to vacate his role, he has built up a formidable team around him, including his son, to help steer the company now and in the future. Strong management is a testament to the business success seen over the past two decades. As Sarros and Santora (1994, p. 20) state: 'Tomorrow's business leaders are today's hard-working and visionary managers'.

COVID-19 impact on Harvey Norman

Harvey Norman's 2020 Annual Report (Harvey Norman, 2021c) described how the COVID-19 era positively impacted the business, which is the opposite to what has occurred to most other businesses in the last financial year. The COVID-19 pandemic presented different challenges in each of the eight countries HN operates. COVID-19 has been a fast-evolving and significant challenge globally and many governments around the world have supported the economies during this extraordinary time. Australian franchisees were supported by the Government with the job keeper program assisting franchisees to retain their employees. In aggregate this support amounted to $7.6 million.

In overseas countries, many governments mandated the temporary closure of non-essential stores like HN and staggered their reopening. The temporary closures resulted in a significant decline in the turnover for each HN overseas business and based on the eligibility criteria of COVID-19 assistance packages, HN stores applied for and received wages support totalling $22.28 million. All these wage support packages were passed onto the employees, and no employee in any of these stores lost their job. The offshore businesses also received property-related support and assistance including rent discounts from landlords totalling $9.8 million. The assistance received from governments and landlords ensured most of the businesses were able to survive and thrive after the lifting of mandated lockdowns. Importantly, it insured workers continued to get payments necessary to meet their personal obligations even though businesses were in hibernation.

The continued impact of COVID-19 is still unknown. Harvey Norman seems to have escaped much of the pain inflicted by the COVID-19 pandemic crisis and even thrived. There has been elevated importance of family, a study from home, cooking and entertainment from home. Harvey Norman brands are well-placed to take advantage of these trends. The sales growth of the company in the last quarter in Australia was accelerated in July 2020 and has continued in September 2020 notwithstanding metropolitan Melbourne's stage 4 lockdown. Harvey Norman's overseas sales improved quickly as stores reopened to the public. The improved sales trend continued in the September quarter of 2020.

In the early part of FY 2020, the sales trend of HN was not very promising. The company reported a reduction in revenue and profits in the half-year ended 31 December 2019. The fall in franchising operations revenue was directly attributable to changes in accounting standards, a challenging and competitive retail environment, and the adverse effects of unforeseen and unprecedented natural disasters such as bushfires. In January and February, the franchising operations segment continued to follow the same downward trends; and sales fell by approximately 3%, primarily due to the prolonged severe impacts of natural disasters. In response to the COVID-19 pandemic, in March 2020 there was a transition to remote working for many employees and remote learning for students.

Strong sales during March 2020 were primarily driven by essential technology and appliance which helped to reverse the sales reduction in January and February. Following the directive of the Australian government to businesses to keep Australia running, steps were immediately taken to ensure the HN franchisees remained opened. Except for a two-week closure for two franchises in Tasmania 194 HN franchising complexes throughout Australia have remained open throughout the definition year 2019–2020. Appropriate social distancing measures and cleaning practices ensured customer safety and enabled trading to continue. In the quarter beginning, April 2020 sales growth in franchisee operations continued to grow as the Australian public invested in their homes, home appliances, and technologies. Total franchise sales for the 2020 FY in Australia were up by 8.9% on the previous year's figures. During the first half of the 2020 FY, sales revenue growth was a mere 0.11%; however, this skyrocketed to 18.6% in the second half of the 2020 FY. Things were looking up.

References

Burgio-Ficca, C. (2021a). Computer and software retailing in Australia. IbisWorld Australia Industry (ANZSIC) Report G4222. Available at: https://my-ibisworld-com.ezproxy.cqu.edu.au/au/en/industry/g4222/about

Burgio-Ficca, C. (2021b). Domestic appliance retailing in Australia. IbisWorld Australia Industry (ANZSIC) Report G4221a. Available at: https://my-ibisworld-com.ezproxy.cqu.edu.au/au/en/industry/g4222/about

Dean R. (2021). Furniture retailing in Australia. IbisWorld Australia Industry (ANZSIC) Report G4211. Available at: https://my-ibisworld-com.ezproxy.cqu.edu.au/au/en/industry/g4211/about

Halley, A. & Beaulieu, M. (2009). Mastery of operational competencies in the context of supply chain management, *Supply Chain Management: An International Journal*, 14, 1, 49–63.

Hamel, G. & Prahalad, C. (1990). The core competence of the corporation. *Harvard Business Review*, 68, 3, 79–91.

Harvey Norman 2012 Annual Report: Available at: http://clients.weblink.com.au/news/pdf2/01338168.pdf

Harvey Norman 2013 Annual Report: Available at: http://clients.weblink.com.au/news/pdf2/01447892.pdf

Harvey Norman (2020). Annual report 2019. Available at: https://static1.squarespace.com/static/54803162e4b08e1b8a472201/t/5dac405a64fbcd1ae7b3bd58/1571569849947/HVN+2019+Annual+Report.pdf

Harvey Norman (2021a). Annual report 2021. Available at: http://clients.weblink.com.au/news/pdf2/02428459.pdf ALSO Change "staggering A$3 billion" to A$3.7 billion.

Harvey Norman (2021b). Overseas market. Available at: https://www.harveynormanholdings.com.au/overseas-market

Harvey Norman (2021c). Annual report 2020. Available at: https://static1.squarespace.com/static/54803162e4b08e1b8a472201/t/5f7548b27a7dba1ef4c5bfb9/1601521983870/HVN+2020+Annual+Report

Kaplan, R. & Norton, D. (2008). Mastering the management system. *Harvard Business Review*, 86, 1, 62.

Koch, A. & Hubbard, G. (2003). Harvey Norman: Unparalleled success in a tough industry. *Strategic management: Thinking, analysis and action*, 2nd ed, Pearson Prentice Hall, pp. 423–431.

Lahti, R. (1999). Identifying and integrating individual level and organizational level core competencies. *Journal of Business and Psychology, 14*, 1, 59–75.

Ljungquist, U. (2007). Core competency beyond identification: Presentation of a model. *Management Decision, 45*, 3, 393–402.

Montgomery, C. (2008). Putting leadership back into strategy. *Harvard Business Review, 86*, 1, p. 54.

Mudie, A. (2013). The next online threat to Myer, JB Hi-Fi and David Jones. Retrieved from www.fool.com.au/2013/10/11/the-next-online-threat-to-myer-jb-hi-fi-and-david-jones/

Mullins, J. & Komisar, R. (2009). *Getting to Plan B: Breaking through to a better business model*. Boston, MA: Harvard Business Press.

Sarros, J. & Santora, J. (1994). Successful CEOs in tough economic times. *International Journal of Career Management, 6*, 14.

Shrivastava, P. & Nachman, S. (1989). Strategic leadership patterns. *Strategic Management Journal, 10*, 51–66.

Stockport, G. J. (2006). Harvey Norman. *The Management Case Study Journal, 6*, 1, 100–120.

Thompson, A. A., Peteraf, M. A., Gamble, J. E. & Strickland III, A. J. (2014). *Crafting and executing strategy: The quest for competitive advantage,* 19th ed, New York, NY: McGraw-Hill/Irwin.

Van Buren, M. & Safferstone, T. (2009). The quick wins paradox. *Harvard Business Review, 87*, 1, 54–61.

Wilkins, G. (2013). Gerry Harvey Joins the Fight Against Online Imports. *The Sydney Morning Herald*. Retrieved from www.smh.com.au/business/gerry-harvey-joins-fight-against-online-imports-20131126-2y83p.html.

12
HUMAN RESOURCE MANAGEMENT INNOVATION IN REGIONAL AUSTRALIA

Linda Colley and Upamali Amarakoon

Introduction

This case study investigated the challenges of attracting and retaining staff in regional labour markets. It outlines how a regional company thrived, expanding in a competitive market, and confidently deciding to compete not on cost but on a different value proposition for its employees and its clients.

As part of our research agreement, we committed not to reveal the identity of the company and will refer to it as *RegionalOrg* and identify its head office location in North Queensland referred to as 'HeadOfficeNQ'. Our case study is based on several sources including RegionalOrg documents and interviews and focus groups with 16 key personnel who knew of the organisation's human resource (HR) practices. Five interviews were conducted with those engaged in recruitment policy and process, including the Manager Corporate Services, the Resource Coordinator, and three members of the recruitment teams (for both professional and service staff). Three focus groups were conducted with operational staff responsible for recruiting and managing staff and representing different professional areas (e.g. professional and services corporate employees, professional employees, and services employees).

Despite regional skills shortages (Houghton, 2019), RegionalOrg has been successful in attracting and retaining quality staff. This chapter sheds light on RegionalOrg's HR recruitment and retention strategies and challenges. The case study begins with an outline of key information about RegionalOrg and its deliberate business strategy and proceeds with identification of how it weaves that business strategy and value proposition into its attraction and retention of employees, with sections focused on employee attraction, employee relationships, and employee engagement and development.

The case study organisation

RegionalOrg is a medium-sized organisation in the resources sector, founded in the early 1990s and remaining in private ownership. It operates in industries across the resources sector, from mining to infrastructure to agriculture. It specialises in industrial asset management, and the provision of expert staff for trades, maintenance, project management, and other customised services.

Ownership and management structure

The founder continues to be involved in the organisation's management and brings extensive knowledge of the resources sector. The chief executive officer (CEO) also brings extensive knowledge and experience in mining, heavy vehicle, power and energy, and automotive industries. The senior management team includes a Chief Financial Officer, and managers responsible for (1) a services division responsible for specialised trades services, (2) an asset management division responsible for professional services, (3) a corporate services division, and (4) compliance and safety.

Business strategy

RegionalOrg retains its head office in its original regional location, referred to as HeadOfficeNQ.

The cornerstone of RegionalOrg's business strategy was different to many of its competitors, with a deliberate differentiation through a value proposition relating to clients and employees. One element of the value proposition is flexibility and tailoring of solutions for each unique situation or project. Another key element of the value proposition is to treat client relationships as more than just a transaction, with a focus on understanding client needs and being flexible in delivering tailored solutions.

RegionalOrg extends this value proposition to employee relationships, with a high level of engagement with its permanent and temporary workforces. This value proposition, together with its focus on safety as good business and good management, has enhanced its reputation in its field. It is a distinct point of difference especially in the resources sector where many competitors are focused purely on price and transactional relationships with employees.

RegionalOrg is now widely known for this value proposition, and its reputation has supported a growth strategy to expand beyond mining into commercial ports and infrastructure sectors, which is also important to buffer against the cycles synonymous with the resources sector.

This growth required some restructuring, and it now has a team of corporate service staff in HeadOfficeNQ, supporting two distinct divisions of Asset Management and Professional Services, and with employees living and working across Australia and overseas. Since its inception, RegionalOrg has grown to a team of sometimes over 500 employees working in Queensland, Australia and overseas (although numbers are fluid with many of these employees on contracts).

Attraction strategy: employer branding for clients and employees

One of the most prominent themes in our case study was how RegionalOrg deliberately positions itself to be more than just a labour-hire company, for both its clients and its employees.

For clients, the message was clear that RegionalOrg was focused on building relationships beyond a particular transaction, understanding the client's short-term and longer-term needs and being flexible in meeting those needs. RegionalOrg is clear about this value proposition when communicating with clients, explaining that they offered this higher level of service which could also mean higher overheads:

> .. it's all-around positioning. We say we're not labour hire. We don't operate like labour hire. We are not structured with the overheads to compete with labour-hire. The service we offer is different. We see ourselves more as a fully-featured organisation, as a resourcing partner.

The senior management group extended that value proposition to their employees and believed that 'anyone who works for us would say that'.

> ...if you go to a labour-hire company, they don't take care of your accommodation. We take care of the accommodation … none of our employees has to worry about that. That's all of us. It's the small things that we do that hopefully attracts people and we offer vehicles as well, which labour-hire companies don't do.

Many clients appreciated value-added services such as the creation of account managers. Account managers worked closely with the clients to understand longer-term horizons, looking beyond the next contract to the planning of future opportunities. For example, RegionalOrg would ask each of its clients what the next 12 months looked like for the client, to get a sense of the work schedule and potential overlaps between clients demands for skilled individuals or teams. This also had benefits for workforce planning and ultimately for employees, as RegionalOrg could make longer-term commitments about potential work.

Our conversations with managers and employees confirmed that they had been drawn to RegionalOrg due to its reputation for caring for its employees. Some were attracted following the word of mouth recommendations from friends and colleagues. One employee applied on the recommendation of a friend who worked for RegionalOrg and identified them as 'a really good crowd'. Other indicative quotes included:

> ...had the reputation for being people-friendly rather than corporate-ish people... Their focus, to me, was on the people that worked for them and how to protect the people to the client as a resource. That's one of the things that I do like about it and they do look after you. If you're willing to do the right job and help out.
>
> What attracted to me to [company name] was more of that personal touch. So we're not a labour-hire business. We're a professional services business. We're not about just putting bums in seats, we're about attracting the right people who are skilled in the area that they're going to be working
>
> I didn't want to work at maybe at [a competitor], for instance, where it's numbers-driven and it's very focused on bonuses.
>
> This had led to some loyalty amongst some employees, who said just ring me up any time and I am there!

Several employees noted that RegionalOrg's expansion meant they had moved beyond just mining, to include work with ports, aviation, defence services. One employee confirmed that they were drawn to the organisation due to the different opportunities it offered within the mining industry, including interstate and overseas. This expansion could also require retaining and upskilling employees to take up positions, making employees more versatile and employable and loyal to RegionalOrg.

Competitive rates and packaging

While not seeking to be a price leader, many participants noted that RegionalOrg's wage/salary rates were comparable or better than its competitors. One example was the statement: '*I've never had a guy say our rates are bad. So, I think our rates are competitive*'. Competitor labour-hire firms had lower overheads (as a result of less engagement with employees), and some were prepared to take lower margins just to win work. Price mattered, given the competitive nature of the field. Some participants noted how the boom/bust cycle affected the clients and could impede the attraction of good employees:

> ...where the client is restrained, which is what's happening in Mining at the moment is that they [clients] don't want to pay, which is very challenging trying to get the right people for them.
>
> Ultimately price matters. Mining companies are looking for the cheapest costs. Sometimes they don't care about quality. They don't. That's because they're restricted as a business. They have a budget.

Many manager participants believed that the higher engagement and emotional connection that RegionalOrg offered could result in employees being prepared to accept small wage adjustments and may reduce labour turnover in difficult times. A few managers said that they were honest with employees if they could not meet competitors' rates. That honesty and personalised relationships assist RegionalOrg in re-attracting employees once they finish their roles with competitors. Another manager noted that that there could be a degree of 'job hopping' in pursuit of financial rewards, as evident in the following quotes.

> …if we don't get that emotional connection with them, then I find they will just jump ship the minute they're offered an extra $5 somewhere else, no matter what we're offering, because, at the end of the day, some people don't care. They don't care about the engagement. They don't care about employee benefits. They don't care about that. They just want to earn the money.

The trade-off between salary and engagement was confirmed by some employee participants. One employee first came to RegionalOrg because they were paying their contractors more, but, once he had established a relationship, he stayed with RegionalOrg for broader reasons. Another employee thought that RegionalOrg paid more than the market rate, but importantly they were reliable in providing a regular income (such as active follow up if they didn't receive a timesheet, to make sure he got paid).

Beyond wage levels, many participants (professional employees in particular) noted the importance of the flexibility to negotiate benefit packages, regardless of whether the employee was casual or full-time. One manager noted that while they were constrained by their client's budget, they tried to offer package solutions to make it viable for employees to work in regional and remote locations. For example, they were flexible and creative in offering options such as salary sacrificing for flights, hire vehicles, or discounts on them. This was appreciated by contract employees, with one noting this as:

> … best experience I've had with any labour-hire company because they've treated me as an employee, and they've given me a few different options in terms of wages and salary packaging around sick leave and other forms of leave.

The accommodation was an often-mentioned challenge for employees and, while it was largely at the discretion of the client, RegionalOrg endeavoured to provide support as they recognised it as a drawcard and attraction strategy.

> … in [town name], we provide, or the client actually provides housing for employees, so it's a big drawcard, particularly for people that don't want to live in the camp, and you do certainly have a proportion of those people that aren't interested in going back to a little donga every night.

Availability of a skilled labour pool

A key dilemma for many regional organisations is attracting talent to regional and sometimes remote locations. Several participants noted that many applicants were not prepared to move to the regions, and instead preferred travel for work whilst living elsewhere. This may mean that employees are looking for FIFO 7–7 rosters rather than Monday to Friday work. One manager explained that approximately 80% of his team lived outside the town:

> So that then creates another issue for us around losses. Obviously we're trying to attract people to work Monday to Thursday or Monday to Friday for a lot of our roles. We've only got some roles that have some shorter-term durations. So, a lot of those people living out of Brisbane are looking for 7/7 here. Construction is on rosters where there's three weeks on and one week off. Because it's cheaper for transport.

As well as liveability issues, other participants mentioned the mining downturn and experiences of the previous decade. Many did not want to return to the mining industry following their experience of the downturn. The loss of corporate knowledge and expertise in certain types of work was identified as a consequence of the mining industry downturn. Another consequence was a small labour pool, and this limited labour pool could have an impact on wages, with the highest wages not always being paid in the mining industry, but sometimes in the construction industry. This labour shortage affected the capacity to pitch for more work, due to the uncertainty of having a workforce to deliver. Another challenge for RegionalOrg was the fact that some client organisations had established their own recruitment arm in direct competition with them.

One strategy to mitigate this skills shortage was RegionalOrg's effort to identify the skills of employees and train them for new roles (discussed later).

Diversity

RegionalOrg's corporate publications promote an inclusive workplace and workforce diversity. This ambition is not reflected in the current workforce profile as yet. In terms of age, the majority of the white-collar roles were held by mature employees. One participant noted that RegionalOrg likes to employ younger people who are just finishing their trades and draws on its experienced workers to mentor the younger workers.

> We can have someone fresh out of their apprenticeship. We can have a staff that's only just learning, and we will put him with an older scaffie so that he's learning things. ... We can have huge gaps in age. That benefits us because we've got the knowledge there and we've got them teaching our young guys that want to stay with us in the future, hopefully.

In terms of gender, several participants noted the attempts of the resource sector to attract more female employees. One noted that the industry had changed, and some clients 'actually want women ... [client] wanted a 50/50 diversity' and RegionalOrg factored that into their recruitment strategy for contractors for that organisation. Some participants – both managers and employees – suggested that recruiting for diversity would result in appointees having lesser skills and understanding of the jobs and would jeopardise lives, but this is a misunderstanding of the goals of diversity and would be a barrier to improving RegionalOrg's diversity profile. There was a significant difference to the pride in the employment of a wheelchair-bound employee and how they 'made it work' on-site, with nobody expressing concerns about the merit or skills of the employee with a disability. One participant noted that it would be good to have a female leader 'someone to look up to and work towards who isn't a male working in a male-dominated industry. That would be fantastic'.

Systems

The organisation appears to have adopted systems that support a large database of applicants (approximately 40,000). This was a good way to retain people in the RegionalOrg pool, and thereby reduce the necessity for extensive recruitment searches and advertising. RegionalOrg also used Seek, sometimes to proactively approach people who were registered in that system. Once recruited, this system could also be used to store documents, provide expiry dates for qualifications, and issue reminders when skills require updating.

One employee did note that being regionally based added to the challenge of increasing online recruitment. She did not like purely online systems which removed the direct contact that occurred when a phone call allowed people to *have a yarn* about the job requirements. In her judgement, an online application *'just seems to vanish into cyberspace'*. However, RegionalOrg was different, directly approaching her once she had expressed initial interest and maintaining contact without leaving her waiting and wondering.

Employee engagement through relationships

One theme that came through strongly in attraction and retention discussions was the emphasis that RegionalOrg placed on employee engagement and working relationships.

Participants reported that the implementation of an employee-care process that allows multiple people within the organisation to have constant interactions with employees. The initial contact is made by the recruitment specialist. Once the person is employed, an account manager (who is usually based in the head office) maintains contact with the employee at regular intervals:

> We have timeframes for how often we actually contact them to check-in and making sure how they enter the workplace okay, how did their first day go.

For instance, we do that, we check in the day before they start, the day of just to see if you have any issues or anything we can help with, generally a week after. From there, three monthly just in case, just to make that they're going okay.

For some managers with teams nearby, regular contact could be undertaken through site visits. For other managers, distance brought challenges with staying in touch with employees, but they took their duty of care seriously.

Some of the contracts were to make enquiries regarding the employee and the job. Other forms of contact included diarising important dates for training or licence expiry. This was both pastoral care and ensuring employees' continued access to work sites. Another example is provided by the Payroll team ensuring that employees submit their timesheets on time. A monthly newsletter also keeps employees connected with the organisation.

The interviews revealed that Professional staff required only limited support from managers. These managers required only a 'light touch', and they avoided 'pestering' or 'nurse-maiding' from above. The message was:

> We're here to support you, but we entrust you to working with our client. You're a professional. We don't need to hold your hand, but we're here to support you." Some people, they don't want.
>
> The people that report to us, report to us purely from a line function not from a performance function because the client normally takes that on. So they drive the performance of the business. We don't manage the performance directly because it's more the care of

Should there be an issue with an employee, the clients expect RegionalOrg to address, solve, and manage the issue. For instance:

> …one of our mature consultants went through some, I guess, more like mental hardships, lost his mother. Took some time off. Instead of the client probably feeling like had to check in all the time, we made sure that he had that regular support. He had access to our EAO program as well, and we transitioned him back into work. That's what we're all about, is bringing people back in, and he was personal, emotional support that we looked after him, as well as the client, checking in.

Employees appreciated the engagement

The strong and personalised relationships RegionalOrg has with employees make employees comfortable with raising their issues and concerns with the organisation. This trust strengthens employee well-being. Importantly, RegionalOrg executives recognised employees and knew what work they were doing, and this led employees to feel connected to the organisation and to be confident that RegionalOrg executive 'had their fingers on the pulse'. One employee stated that managers were available *to lend an ear if I ever need to talk. If the day gets a little bit too much for me.* This employee understood that *if they cannot do anything about it, I feel like they are listening to me and they are there if I need them, which is important when you're up here on your own.*

Another employee noted that RegionalOrg had always been very supportive, 'and if one supervisor cannot help you, they will direct you to somebody who can help, and you didn't have to chase up the reply or information' – in contrast to the experience in other companies. It was thought that this view of the organisation's management was widely held. While these personal relationships are important, there are risks if there is no underlying systematisation of the relationship and contact.

Employee retention

Health and safety

Workplace health and safety was a prominent theme, both in RegionalOrg publications and in interviews and focus groups.

RegionalOrg had identified driving and fatigue as one of their biggest risks. They were conscious of the factor driving time and travel into contracts and client budgets. RegionalOrg had also implemented safety management systems such as trip planning and contact checkpoints along the journey. Health and safety is often a client requirement too, with one client insisting on a journey management plan.

Transparency about future work and insecure work

Casualisation of the workforce and the lack of continuous employment opportunities are some of the challenges that the organisation faces concerning employee retention. Casualisation was a result of both the nature of some industry sectors and the type of contracts for some clients.

Some managers tried to provide some certainty where possible, such as fixed-term contracts, even if only 6 or 12 months at a time, and that had often paid off in retention terms. Another manager noted that they were prepared to accommodate employees who had a good performance, some corporate knowledge, and some knowledge of their good clients, to 'hold a space' in between jobs.

Several managers discussed the importance of honesty and transparency when discussing future work opportunities. Some managers stayed in regular contact with employees to identify potential future work opportunities or known gaps in opportunities when the employees might need to find other work. Clear communication was a strategy to engage, retain, and re-attract employees:

> They'll find other work and whilst they're busy, I'll say, "I don't have anything this week, guys. I only need four people from a core crew of 30. Go find other work if you need to, but please, we want you with RegionalOrg," and

they'll come back to me at the drop of a hat because we've built that relationship that these guys built at the start.

...letting them know what's coming up because they are travelling from a distance. They need to know how long they're going to be away from their families. That's in keeping them.

One employee noted the difficulties when the client cut short a contract, and she had to begin 'off-boarding' a large number of disappointed people. However, RegionalOrg was considering ways to arrange new work through other clients.

One male employee said the biggest challenge was the insecure nature of the work:

...we're all casual and when the work starts to dry up, you don't know when your next paycheck is coming in and that can be stressful. When you've got plenty of work on, you don't think about it, but when all of a sudden you get told "there's no work for two, three, four weeks, then you really start to get concerned. It's hard to be loyal to a company when they've got no work for you.

By way of contrast, another employee was not bothered by the insecurity and chose to be casual: '*I like it that way because I can take holidays when I want them.*'

Regional and remote location challenges

One key challenge for managers and employees could be the location of the work.

Distance from head office

Several participants were removed from the head office, residing in South East Queensland or interstate. They noted the social isolation of being so far from head office. The organisation was working its way through meeting protocols and information flows, with efforts being hampered by *flaky* technology in the regional head office. One participant mentioned:

You miss out on two things in a way. It's the intended stuff that you're supposed to be part of, and we try through telecoms and videoconferences and all sorts of things. But the technology sometimes lets you down because you sometimes lose – and always pick up through conversation, there's a bit of mumbling in the background so you miss on a few things. But there's also the unintended experience. The informal conversations around a cup of coffee or whatever that's the stuff you miss out on. ... If you're comfortable with that then you're okay. But if you're the kind of person that feels that you need to be attached and if you get a bit of anxiety from separation, it could be a challenge.

Several participants discussed the benefits of working remotely, such as not being *'caught up in the day-to-day office politics'* as well as having more flexibility in terms of the structuring of work.

Distance from clients and between clients

Many participants mentioned the challenges of distance beyond being away from home and dealing remotely with clients and teams:

a) First, there was the challenge of being remote from clients because some work required face-to-face contact with clients.
b) A second challenge was the distance between a manager/supervisor and employees, requiring frequent travel to maintain contact with the team.
c) Third, the clients themselves were located across Australia, and no matter where an employee was located there was a good chance at least some of their clients would not be close.

One manager mentioned:

> I can actually spend 8 or 9 hours driving for a 15-minute conversation. Which you can only do a certain amount of organisation and planning. So we actually have a lot of that dead time to make phone calls to a certain point and then you sort of hit the Telstra gaps and then you have two hours where you really don't actually have any productive sort of work going on, which really impacts the actual amount of time we spend in our jobs because we still have to do so much but you drive to three sites in a week, you lose 10 or 15 hours of actual productive work time. You have to fill in somewhere else which is usually early, late or at weekends.

Conversely, some of the account managers noted that expansion of the business could mean long hours for the management team. Clients often worked continuous 24/7 shifts requiring night and weekend calls. This work pattern made it difficult to trial other employees in these roles. Therefore, succession planning could be difficult.

Employees working away from home

Several participants mentioned that they attempted to provide realistic job previews and manage expectations about locations and remoteness. One supervisor emphasised to new young employees who had not previously worked in the mining industry that the high wages being paid were compensation for the distance and social and family challenges:

> it's not a job, it's a lifestyle. Because at the end of the day, you're giving up your two nights at the gym with your mates, your footie training and all of

this and your socialising on Friday nights with your next-door neighbour, to be out of town in regional areas to make better money than a town.

We get guys that have got 3-month-old babies and they're going into the Mining Industry ... I don't think they fully think through the impacts on what they do to their family unit.

Others thought that remote working was just part of the job that was required by RegionalOrg for its employees to work in the mining industry.

…don't take the job if you're not going to be prepared to do it. We're remotely based … a lot of it's up to you. You can't always blame the company if it's a decision that you've made!.'

One manager with a large number of employees who worked away from home noted that he was 'constantly dealing' with people with marriage breakdowns, mental health issues.

Several employees mentioned *the social challenges and isolation arising from their work but recognised this as a lifestyle rather than a work issue*. Some participants found it easier to find social support through their own work networks. Other participants mentioned challenges including long working hours that restricted socialising, fewer social clubs or sporting events in some towns and sites, and the lack of interaction with other women. Social interaction was focused on meals in the dining room, which was perceived to be a masculine environment that did not suit some female employees.

Good camaraderie amongst teams was evident with team members managing to have social interactions and 'good-natured ribbing' in their zoom and other meetings. Some team members who were remote from head office but near to each other in Southeast Queensland were able to meet with each other and discuss work issues on a semi-regular basis.

Retention through employee development

Given the skill shortages in the resource sector, RegionalOrg appears to invest considerable effort to retain its employees. Retention strategies for white- and blue-collar jobs are different.

Several participants identified the retention strategy of offering development and career advancement opportunities:

Because we are a diverse business, that's another great thing that we can offer them is "Hey look we've got other projects. We want to transition you, get you into maybe different industries.

We had him working on one of our services contracts in a trades position. While he was there, he got an opportunity just to fill in, let's call it a 'white collar' position. Got him some exposure, some systems experience. Because that's a big thing is having – you might have the really important equipment knowledge.

Someone's interested in doing something else, then we have the opportunity to then have a skills workshop or taking on town jobs or something like that, fabrication or repairs in the workshop or more business and get a draftsman in or something like they've talked about today.

Several employees noted the investment that RegionalOrg put into its contract employees. This strategy was identified as differentiating RegionalOrg from its competitors:

…there's a lot of effort and a lot of importance placed around training and I must say certain, since I've been here, yeah, a lot of training has come my way probably more so in the last ten years than anywhere else that I've worked in Australia. So, I'm rather pleased about that because it shows that there is a serious approach to training staff, whether they're contractors or not, which is refreshing after some of the places I've worked before.

Due to the nature of the industry, succession planning is a challenge, but wherever possible, RegionalOrg appeared to communicate with its employees on career planning and succession matters.

So if we've got a three-month engagement with an employee, what do the next nine months look like, or 18 months look like?
….we are that career advancement provider inadvertently, to be able to get people to be an engineer with us, labour hired, … knowing full well that if they prove themselves and they're a good employee, that they will get an Anglo shirt or a BHP shirt in 12 months. That's not necessarily a bad thing for us because if we're able to provide people of that calibre then that's a good reflection on us.

Retaining core employees

RegionalOrg had recognised the need to retain a core group of people and had therefore provided longer-term opportunities such as fixed-term arrangements for these key people. This was particularly important for the retention of employees in leadership and supervisory roles.

…it is hard to find good leadership particularly, and so those teams lead roles and those supervisor roles, we need to keep them engaged, and so the schedule of work's important, then also equally as important is securing them employment-wise and engagement-wise.

This strategy has helped RegionalOrg in building its reputation and enhancing its competitive advantage. For instance, for shut down operations, the organisation has a core set of specialists.

> …we fairly consistently have done their shutdowns for several years now because they like the quality of people that we provide, and it comes back to that core group that we've been able to hold onto as well.

Some participants mentioned that they remained with RegionalOrg because the organisation managed to keep them at work. One participant commented on the reliability of the work that enabled the organisation to employ people permanently.

Organisational culture

Our interviews and focus groups suggested that RegionalOrg has a very friendly positive organisational culture that genuinely cares for its employees. As some employees commented:

> I feel very looked after here, actually. It's surprising coming from a different company to then having someone actually paying attention to you.
> There's a lot of good people who work within the business, so that's another reason why I stayed. Just lots of professionals here who are experts in what they do.
> You come to work giving 110% and everyone – it's a collective team environment rather than individual, so that's what I enjoy.
> So, when I first got here, I was just like, "Whoa. Why are you asking me my opinion and why do you care?" And we're quite a small team down in [xxx], so I just run my show and we do get supported.
> …we had the interview, and it was just so professional and it was just so well-managed and communicated and everyone just looked so put together…I feel like I've got the support.

During recruitment, RegionalOrg attempts to ensure that they recruit employees who match their core values and support their organisational culture.

> …if we've got someone who has got all the right skills and all the right experience but if the attitude is not the attitude we need for our business culture, we're not going to employ that person, because ultimately it can just impact our business in the wrong way.

Conclusion

RegionalOrg has been a successful regional SME with a deliberate and successful strategy for growth and profit.

RegionalOrg has a clear company strategy, which is translated into a brand to attract clients, but also into an employer brand to attract and retain employees. Employer branding is a method of differentiating an organisation from its competitors, through a package of economic and other benefits identified with that employer (Backhaus & Tikoo, 2004). RegionalOrg has done successfully created a reputation or employer brand as more than a transactional labour-hire company.

There are several elements to RegionalOrg's employer branding. It had a reputation for competitive remuneration and benefits, not seeking to be a price leader, and also recognising that even when the price/salaries were slightly lower the employees recognised the other intangible benefits of the engagement, reliable processing of pays, flexible remuneration packages tailored to each employee's needs, as well as potential longer-term employment opportunities. RegionalOrg's value proposition also meant they kept informed of employee's skills, to be able to match them to opportunities, and also sometimes to train them for emerging opportunities. There was scope for more emphasis on diversity, which is another critical method of increasing a labour pool and meeting skills shortages.

RegionalOrg had also ensured systems to support their employer branding. A large database enabled them to advertise within a known labour market, rather than more expensive external recruitment exercises with unknown employees. They used these systems not just for their own organisational staffing needs, but also as part of their employee engagement strategy, retaining their corporate knowledge of employees, from skills held to licences needing renewal, and for general contact beyond job vacancies. Their systems included an employee care process, which enabled regular contact with employees, and was a key point of differentiation from the more instrumental approach of other firms that resembled pure labour-hire arrangements. Managers of RegionalOrg were also visible and approachable.

The final part of the employer branding strategy was a culture of care. Most participants observed a genuine leadership commitment to work health and safety, which is essential in this higher-risk sector. Further, RegionalOrg remained conscious that much of their work was remote and were both transparent about that in realistic job previews, and later supportive of employees by staying in touch and understanding the challenges of being away from home. And importantly for employees in a largely contracted sector, RegionalOrg remained aware of emerging opportunities and could advise employees about the potential work or shortage of work to allow more planning.

This case contributes to knowledge about managing attraction and retention in a remote workforce, by using sophisticated HR strategies to achieve strong employer-employee engagement in a sometimes-transient labour market.

References

Backhaus, K., & Tikoo, S. (2004). Conceptualizing and researching employer branding. *Career Development International, 9*(5), 501–517.

Houghton, K. (2019). *The future of regional jobs*, The Regional Australia Institute, Canberra. Retrieved from http://www.regionalaustralia.org.au/home/

13
THE TALE OF A FAILED SMALL BUSINESS

Robert Grose and Tasadduq Imam

Introduction

According to the Australian Bureau of Statistics (ABS), approximately 2,361,778 small businesses were operating in Australia in June 2020, 65% of which were non-employing businesses (i.e., the owner was the only person working in the business), and the rest employed between one to 19 people (ABS, 2021). Alarmingly, however, ABS data goes on to report that only 53% of small businesses that started operating in 2016 survived until 2020 (ABS, 2021). This is an alarming statistic as these business failures can have a significant adverse impact on its owners and their families, employees, suppliers, financial institutions, landlords, and customers.

Many articles have been written on small business failures and the mistakes made by the owners of these small businesses. Most of these articles however discuss the factors that led to the downfall of such businesses in very general terms. The following case study is somewhat unique in so far as it explains the circumstances that led to the collapse of a small business in regional Australia – a café that failed in the space of four years after its commencement. It's a sad tale of lost hard-earned past savings and should serve as a warning to those who might be contemplating starting a small business. For various reasons, the names of the owners, the café, the shopping centre, and its location have not been disclosed.

Business start-up

The business started when two friends decided to pool their expertise and funds to purchase an established café in a large shopping complex. The potential owners had previously run two profitable small businesses in the hospitality sector so they were reasonably confident they would be able to successfully operate and run a café.

The owners used the funds from the profits derived from the sale of their previous business ventures plus a reasonable amount of past savings to fund the purchase of the café. It was agreed that one of the partners would contribute 80% of the capital but not be involved with the café's day-to-day operations. The other partner would contribute the remaining 20% and run the café on a full-time basis. The owners did not borrow funds to purchase the business. The negotiations to purchase the café spanned a little over three months and mainly consisted of what the new owners thought at the time was a thorough due diligence assessment. This assessment consisted of visiting the café at various times during the week, sometimes unannounced, observing operations from afar and taking notes of how busy the café was on various days and at various times, how many staff were employed, and the type and quantity of supplies delivered and how they were paid. Having been convinced that this was a successful business the potential owners began negotiations in earnest, and it was not long before a purchase price and a purchase date was agreed. As was previously mentioned the café was in a large shopping complex that had a lot of foot traffic passing the shop front so the new owners were convinced that good profits could be made. While the new owners would pay a premium for a shop of this size it was determined that such a premium could be recouped because of the high volume of potential customers at their front doorstep.

It was initially agreed the new owners would take over the business in mid-December. However, because of unexpected delays that were beyond the control of the new owners, the takeover did not occur until late January. This was a significant setback as the new owners missed out on the Christmas shopping period and the summer school holidays. During these six weeks, turnover in a business of this type is normally 40–50% higher than at other times during the year. Whether or not this delay was a deliberate ploy by the current owner was a matter of conjecture, but the fact remained that the delay disadvantaged the new owners in terms of lost revenue.

In retrospect, the new owners should have either pulled out of the contract or re-negotiated a lower price to compensate for the revenue they had missed out on during the Christmas shopping period and the summer school holidays.

Commencement

The new owners eventually took over the business and the vendor was required to stay on for two weeks – one week before and one week after the purchase date, as is normal in contracts of this nature. During this time, the vendor was very helpful in pointing out the various idiosyncrasies of the business and providing tips on how things could be run more efficiently. During these two weeks, turnover was a little down compared to the same time of the previous year; however, the vendor assured the new owners that these minor fluctuations were not unexpected so no alarm bells were ringing at this stage. After six months of running the business, it became obvious that the new owners were questioning their decision to buy the café as the turnover was at least 20–30% less than what they had anticipated. Whether or not the reduction in turnover was due to a downturn in the economy (the whole shopping centre was not as busy as previous years according to other business owners in the shopping complex), poor management, or something else is unclear but the fact remained, turnover was substantially down on the previous year's figures. According to the hindsight of the owners, we shall now look at the factors that worked against the success of the business.

Factors constraining the business success
Lease agreement

Lease agreements with landlords at large shopping centres normally come with a significant premium. The landlords justify these higher annual leases on the grounds that large shopping centres attract significant numbers of potential customers, and it is up to the tenants to entice these customers into their business. While there is some merit in the landlords' argument it is also true that many people who shop at big shopping centres come to get a specific item and are not that interested in buying anything else, particularly food. It's also true that many large shopping centres charge parking fees on an hourly, sometimes on a half-hourly basis, and this creates a mindset for some shoppers that they need to get in and get out of the shopping centre as quickly as possible so that they do not have to pay any more parking fee than is necessary. These two factors combine to partially negate the arguments of the landlords that businesses have a ready supply of customers at their doorstep.

Landlords at large shopping centres are notorious for insisting that tenants pay their lease obligations on time. In fact, if a lease obligation is not paid by the due date tenants will normally be reminded by email the following day that the monthly lease payment is past due, and the lease is now in breach of their lease agreement. If leasee fails to pay their outstanding lease obligations within a short period after receiving this initial warning they will then receive a letter from the landlord solicitor's stating that they have breached their lease agreement and are now in default.

Not wanting to test the legalities of the landlords, the new owners decided to draw on their personal savings to make good the balance of the outstanding lease payments. While this kept the landlords at bay it was not good business practice and could not continue indefinitely. The owners approached the landlords to ask if the inflated lease payments could be re-negotiated down to a more realistic level given that the entire shopping centre was suffering from a drop-in customer. The landlords responded in their usual way by saying that there were plenty of potential tenants (which is questionable) who would be willing to take over the café and so the owners' requests fell on deaf ears. It was a sink or swim scenario as is normally the case when you enter a long-term lease agreement in shopping centres. So, while it may be possible to make good profits in large shopping centres, the reality is that many tenants struggle to make ends meet because of the exorbitant lease commitments and when combined with lower-than-expected turnover, it becomes a recipe for disaster. While landlords are generally forthcoming with strategies to increase profits, they are not so willing to review their rental agreement until the end of the lease period – which in many instances is too late for tenants as they eventually are forced to vacate the shop.

Signing a lease agreement has another downside that people should be aware of and consider before signing a contract. Most lease agreements in shopping centres, if not all, have a clause in the lease agreement which states current leaseholders must restore the shop back to just four bear walls (called a deficit) should they decide to vacate the shop before the lease expiry date or at the end of the lease period should they choose not to renew the lease. The deficit clause was inserted to save incoming tenants the cost of stripping the shop back to its shell. Deficits are very expensive, costing departing tenants anywhere between a few thousand dollars to tens of thousands of dollars. Obviously, this is not an ideal situation for tenants as once they either leave of their own accord or are forced to vacate the premises by the landlords, they usually do not have any spare money to pay for the deficit. This is exactly what happened to the new owners after four years of not making enough revenue to cover the expenses of running the business. The original bill for the deficit was more than $24,000 but was negotiated down to half the original amount once the landlords were informed that the invoice figure was grossly inflated compared to the time spent dismantling the shop. At any rate, the owners now had to further draw on what little savings they had left to finalise the exit from the shopping centre lease.

Another component of a lease agreement that needs further explanation is the extra costs that are normally added to the rental component of the lease. That is, in addition to the monthly rental payments, shopping centre leases normally add a raft of additional costs such as council rates, garbage disposal costs, and marketing costs to the base rent figure. While some of these costs can be justified and are transparent some are not, and tenants are often left wondering whether they are getting value for money. For example, the new owners could not see where they were getting any advantage from the marketing fees they were being charged. At no stage during the owners' time at the shopping centre did they see any local newspaper advertisement that referred to their café or encouraged the surrounding population to visit their cafe. Also, special promotions to attract shoppers were few and far between and those that did occur (usually during holiday periods) were normally related to women's fashion and probably funded by the large department store.

So, as has been illustrated in the above few paragraphs, while a lease arrangement has several advantages, the main one being that owners do not have to pay large sums of money to purchase a freehold premise, it does come with a significant number of drawbacks that potential business owners need to be aware of before signing a lease agreement. While the new owners, in this case, have said they would still be willing to enter into another lease agreement if the right opportunity arose, they also mentioned that they would be far more ruthless in negotiating the terms of the lease. They also mentioned that they would never enter into a lease agreement with a large shopping complex because such lease contracts are well above the market average and there are too many variables, additional costs, and fine print in the contract that the lessee has little or no control over.

Refurbishment

Another drawback of most lease agreements in large shopping centres is a clause that states current leaseholders are required to refurbish their shop every few years and be in line with the shopping centres poorly defined aesthetic principles. In the several conversations that the new owners had with the shopping centre's design team it seemed, there was no well-defined direction and their design requirements largely depended on the whim of the designer at the time of discussion which often did not align with those of previous in-house designers. In addition to the shopping centres' design team having input into the design process, the shopping centre insisted that owners should use an architect in the design of the shop; otherwise the changes would not be approved. In addition to the excessive costs associated with architects, the actual costs of refurbishment are expensive, costing owners anywhere from a few thousand dollars up to many thousands of dollars. Shopping centre management normally provides a list of approved (and very expensive) building contractors that can be used for refurbishments. If the shop owner wants to use their own builder to complete the refurbishment, they need to convince centre management that they have the skills and expertise to complete the work and all their statutory paperwork is up to date. These bureaucratic requirements often deter shop owners' from using their preferred shop fitters from taking on the job, thus forcing tenants to use the shopping centres approved, and often far more expensive, preferred contractors. Not only can the refurbishment prove to be very expensive, but it also means that the shop must be closed. Consequently, not only do the owners have to forego their only source of income during this period but they are still required to keep up to date with their lease obligations. Another detrimental effect of a temporary shop closure during a compulsory refurbishment is the potential for previously loyal customers to take their custom somewhere else, sometimes never to return.

Lack of capital

While the newly acquired business was purchased using the owner's personal savings, the new owners quickly came to the realisation that the shop front needed to be redesigned. Unfortunately, because the new owners had just used most of their savings to purchase the shop, they were not willing to depart with another $30,000 to $40,000 to redesign the shop front. Instead, the owners decided it would be best if they established themselves in the business before undertaking a redesign of the shop front. The idea behind the redesign was to take advantage of the shop's position in the food court as there were a significant number of people passing the shop front who were not inclined to come into the cafe and enjoy a 'sit down' meal. It was felt however that these passer-byes might be more willing to buy take-away meals had the shop front be a better design. In retrospect, if the required capital could have somehow been obtained, the redesign could have taken place very soon after taking over the shop as it most likely would have boosted revenue and promoted the shop as a new business in the food court rather than as an existing business run by new owners. The redesign never eventuated because, after just a few months of trading, the owners were already drawing on their personal savings to make good the shortage in revenues to cover the lease obligations. While it is a matter of debate whether a new shopfront would have saved the shop owners from failure, the fact that it did not occur was due to the owners not wanting to borrow the required funds.

Experience of staff

Most of the staff that came with the newly acquired café were experienced, very dedicated, and extremely relieved when they were told they could remain in their jobs. What the owners had not foreseen however was the inexperience of the barista they had inherited. While the vendor had assured the new owners that the barista was experienced and made a good coffee, this did not turn out to be the case. While the barista had been making coffee for more than a year, it was not up to scratch and consequently the new business was losing customers to other parts of the shopping centre. Whether or not the vendor left the new owners in the lurch will never be known but the fact remained that the current barista needed to be replaced as soon as possible. Finding an experienced barista in a short time frame is not an easy task and while this was achieved within the space of two weeks, the damage had been done and there was a significant drain of previously loyal customers to the other cafes in the shopping centre. If the owners weren't aware of it when they took over the café, they were aware of it now – peoples' preference for a good coffee is very fickle and critical to the success of a café and the new owners, for the time being, had failed this most important test. While the advertisements bought in two well qualified and popular baristas and some old customers returned and new customers arrived, the harsh reality was that the new owners had lost a significant number of customers which did not bode well for the survival of the café in the long term. So, if there is a lesson to be learnt from this situation, it is to make sure that all staff are adequately trained and can do the job that is related to their area of responsibility.

Another concern was the number of employees working at the café. This caused some tension between the owners as it was obvious, at least to the non-working partner, that too many staff were rostered on during non-peak hours. The non-working partner proposed cutting staff numbers by 20% which would result in savings and at least bring the café back to a break-even point. The working partner however resisted this proposal because he was hopeful that business would pick up and, in addition to this, he was reluctant to tell employees that they could no longer work at the café. This stand-off between the partners lasted for some time until it became obvious that the business could not survive at the current staffing levels. Again, while staff numbers were reduced it was too little too late and the accumulated losses were starting to take a toll on the owners' personal lives and their finances. Things were getting serious.

Poor management

While the working partner was extremely experienced in the hospitality sector it became apparent that personal issues were having a detrimental effect on the way the café was being managed. This was very concerning to the non-working partner because he had invested 80% of the capital into the business. It must be said however that the working partner managed to establish a good rapport with all employees and the customers which is important to the smooth running and viability of any small business. When it is all said and done however the fact that the working partner, who was being very well paid but did not seem to have any designated working role, apart from managing the day-to-day operations of the business, was not helpful for the cafes long-term viability.

In the end, it was agreed that the working owner would no longer work at the business and one of the very experienced current employees would take over the day-to-day management of the business. While this saved the business a significant amount of money in terms of saved wages, it put a significant amount of pressure on the remaining partner who had to take on a more hands-on role even though he was still in full-time employment away from the café. It must be said that the transition to a business manager was successful, and the business got back to a break-even point and in some weeks turned a small profit, mainly because of a reduction in staff numbers, the savings associated with not having to pay the working partner, and a pick-up in turnover due to good coffee, good fresh food, and very friendly staff.

Microeconomic factors

At the time the owners took over the café there was one medium-sized shopping centre within a radius of ten kilometres of the café and a few smaller satellite shopping centres. Within the space of two years of taking over the business one large and a few medium-sized shopping centres opened their doors. Because the shopping centre in question charged parking fees and because it was not easily accessible, shoppers began to shift their customers to these newly developed shopping centres that offered similar shops and services to those existing in the complex where the new owners' business was located.

Because of its location, the landlords did not want the centre's car parking spaces to be used by people who had no intention of stopping in the centre. To overcome this dilemma the landlords introduced parking fees to deter people from using the car park as an all-day car parking site. While this impost deterred city workers from using the shopping centre as an all-day car park, it had the detrimental effect of discouraging shoppers from visiting the shopping centre or, if they did visit it, it was for a short time. The upshot of the landlord's decision to charge for parking was that it discouraged potential shoppers from entering the shopping centre and, if they did enter the shopping centre, many were of the mindset to get in and get out as quickly as possible – all of which discouraged discretionary spending on consumables. When tenants presented the case of declining numbers to the landlords, it was dismissed as being incorrect and they supported their contention by presenting audited figures to show that the number of shoppers passing through the shopping centre was increasing. The tenants were sceptical of these so-called audited tallies as their turnover figures were dropping and queues (lining up to be served) were getting less frequent and shorter. It was apparent that the landlords were reluctant to admit customers numbers were down on previous years as, to do so, would provide the tenants with ammunition to negotiate lower lease agreements at the end of their lease cycle which would not go down well with the owners of these large shopping complexes.

In addition to the opening of new shopping centres and the dilemma associated with car parking fees, post the global financial crisis, consumers were becoming increasingly reluctant to spend their money on non-essentials. While this reduction in consumer spending was not isolated to the hospitality sector, indeed it impacted most forms of consumer spending, it was particularly harmful to tenants in large shopping centres that were impacted with declining customers numbers and rising tenancy related costs.

Macroeconomic factors

Although the Global Financial Crisis (GFC) began in 2007 it impacted retail spending in Australia for several years. The GFC was triggered when the threat of defaults by borrowers in the United States sub-prime mortgage market caused the collapse of confidence in the banking sector in the United States and most other markets around the world (RBA, n.d.). Australia was not immune, unemployment increased from 4.3% in October 2007 to 5.8% in October 2009 (ABS, 2007, 2009), and consumer confidence dropped sharply in the early part of the crisis (McDonald & Morling, 2011).

It was in this climate of economic downturn and its associated uncertainty that the new owners decided to purchase the café. In effect, they could not have timed a worse time to undertake a venture of this magnitude. The owners felt that much of the 20–30% decline in turnover could be directly attributed to the GFC. Although unfortunate and while the new owners had no control over the GFC it could be argued that they should have been aware of the adverse impact this global macroeconomic event would have on their turnover and factored it into their purchase price.

As it turned out, the impact of the GFC was felt in the business for its entire tenure and was yet another reason for its ultimate collapse.

Supplies

Consumers seem to be obsessed with purchasing coffee and soft drinks from household brand names. While there may be plenty of good, if not better, alternatives available in the marketplace it became apparent that any change to less well-known brands was fraught with danger. In fact, in the past when businesses have tried to change a soft drink brand or coffee brand to a less well-known and less expensive label there is a noticeable decline in sales. The soft drink and coffee wholesalers are aware of this brand loyalty scenario and sometimes try to take advantage of it by charging premium prices for the so-called privilege of stocking and selling their products. This represents a sort of 'catch 22' situation as the business owner must either purchase a cheaper but less well-known brand and most probably lose customers or buy a more expensive well-known brand and retain customers. It basically boils down to simple economics. Since the new owners were already concerned about declining sales, they opted to retain the popular brand name. So, even though sales of the well-known brand meant a lower mark-up percentage, it was thought that this would be offset with higher unit sales and therefore a higher gross profit figure (because of the higher sales volume) which could then be used to cover other operating costs.

Vending machines

Not long into the new lease the landlords decided to allow an outside vending machine operator to strategically place between 20 to 30 vending machines around the shopping centre on the grounds it was offering a service to the shoppers entering the shopping centre. Because these vending machines did not have any significant operating overheads the owners of the machines were able to offer popular brands at prices approximately 10–20% lower than those offered by all the food outlets (including the new owners) in the shopping centre. Even though several food outlets complained to the landlords about this unwanted competition, such complaints fell on deaf ears. The tenants could not do anything to stop the vending machine operators from selling their products. The owners of the café estimated that the introduction of these vending machines caused their turnover to drop by approximately $600 per week, which translates into an annual decline in turnover of $31,200. This annual decline in income was a significant blow to an already stressed business.

Opening of new businesses

Landlords receive their income stream from the annual lease charges imposed on tenants. Thus, it is no surprise that the landlords would allow the construction of new shops in the centre as it will increase their profits and hopefully attract more customers to the shopping centre. The trouble with this strategy is that the new shops are often in direct competition with existing loyal tenants and consequently their revenue stream will be diluted and, in some instances, lead to them becoming unviable.

Within the first six months of the owners purchasing the business, three new food outlets opened at the shopping centre – one directly in front of the new owner's shop that sold products that were in direct competition with the products sold by the café. Also, because all the available space on the inside walls of the shopping centre were exhausted, the landlords allowed these new food outlets to build their new shops in the middle spaces of the shopping centre that had high exposure to passing shoppers. Again, existing tenants complained to the landlords and again these complaints fell on deaf ears. Centre management tried to justify the introduction of these new establishments with the now well-worn out phase that they were offering an additional service to shoppers and a novel new justification, that it would add to the ambience of the shopping centre. The truth is that the landlords (rightly or wrongly) were mainly interested in an additional revenue stream and, it would seem, they were not interested in the detrimental impact the introduction of these new shops would have on the viability of existing tenants.

Taxation

Food outlets in Australia are normally taxed in two ways. First, they are taxed on the net taxable income disclosed in the financial year at a rate 27.5% and second, they must pay taxes at a rate of 10% on their GST liability, which can be either paid on a monthly or quarterly basis. This second arm of Australia's taxation system is referred to as the Goods and Services Tax (i.e., GST). While the owners understood that they would need to pay a 10% GST they assumed that the café would earn enough income to easily cover both categories of taxation expenses. Unfortunately, and as has been well documented above, the café was not making profits before tax and consequently they often were unable to pay their GST liability out of operating income. The owners argued that this scenario represents a major flaw in the GST legislation as the government makes no adjustments in those instances where a business is not making profits. The situation was made even worse in the current owner's situation because, although the café was not making a profit, both their revenues and corresponding expenses were quite high and consequently their GST liability was significant for a business that was in a loss situation.

Other reason why small businesses fail

In addition to the specific issues that led to the failure of the above-mentioned café, it might be helpful to document some other common reasons why small businesses fail. The following list, although not exhaustive, are just some of the common reasons why small businesses tend to fail.

Lack of planning

To give the business the best chance of succeeding it is important to map out both a short-term and long-term plan. The plan should consist of every step, beginning with the decision to undertake the business venture to an exit strategy should that be relevant. Essentially your business plan should document where you want your business to be in the next few months to several years down the track. A good plan normally entails a specific to-do list with dates and deadlines.

No differentiation

Although it has already been suggested that one of the reasons why the café failed was because it didn't differentiate itself enough from other cafes in the shopping centre, it is important to emphasise this factor a little more. While the café was renowned for good fresh food, excellent coffee, and good customer service, more could have been done to entice customers to the shop. As has already been suggested above, the owners regretted not spending an additional $30,000 to $40,000 in the first few months of operation to update the front counter to attract more take-away customers. The shop always had a lot of foot traffic passing by and the owners were of the view that a modern takeaway display unit serving both hot and cold food could have increased turnover by approximately 20% per annum. The fact that this refurbishment did not occur in the first few months of operation will always be a regret of the owners as it had the potential to save the shop from its eventual closure. By not updating the shop front the café was just another café in the shopping centre that couldn't be differentiated from other cafes.

Ignoring customer needs

As the saying goes – 'Customers Come First'. Once you attract customers you have to fight hard to keep them. For food retailers like cafés, this can be a tricky juggling act. In this specific case, the café attracted a very conservative group of loyal customers who turned up at regular times during the week and consequently the owners were not willing to upset these customers by becoming too creative with the menu. The café didn't fail because of the lack of customers; it mainly failed because of the exorbitant lease payments and the decline in people visiting the shopping centre. In this specific instance, the owners believed they had successfully catered for the needs of its customer base – they were not being ignored. While the café could have offered a broader menu choice it was deemed that this would have been economically unviable. That having been said, the café did cater for changing customer trends by offering weekly specials, which in some instances because of their popularity became permanent fixtures on the specials board.

In a more general sense however, it is critical not to ignore customer needs. Businesses that do not cater to the needs of their customers by failing to listen to their preferences, failing to keep a track of trending customer values or failing to respond to negative reviews is courting disaster.

Premature scaling

Growth is good provided it is carried out in a systematic and controlled manner. Uncontrolled growth, if not handled correctly, can cause a business to fail very quickly. Uncontrolled growth can mean too much money is spent of marketing, too many people are hired before they are needed or too many inventory items are purchased before, they are required. If there isn't a corresponding increase in sales things can get out of control very quickly and the creditors will come in asking for their debts to be repaid.

Successful growth requires proper planning, an experienced management team, and strong systems and controls.

Lack of entrepreneurial skills

Deciding to start a small business is a big step. Although a good idea, dedication, and hard work are important, but it may not be enough to ensure success. Lack of entrepreneurial skills, particularly in the first phase of a new business venture, can cause a business to fail. Small business ventures can face many unforeseen obstacles and variables during its very early stages. And if the new owners do not possess the entrepreneurial skills to navigate their way through these issues the new venture has a very real chance of failure.

The impact of COVID-19 on retailers in large shopping complexes

If retailer's thought that surviving in a large shopping complex was difficult enough, the advent of the COVID-19 pandemic during 2020 and 2021 escalated things to a whole new level of pain. As a result of the five lockdowns experienced by Melbournians during 2020 and 2021, many retailers were forced to either close their doors or offer reduced trading hours. With these closures, the income stream of many retailers vanished overnight. While some retailers were able to secure a semblance of their previous income stream, many couldn't because of the nature of their business model.

Faced with substantially reduced income streams, retailers were hoping that landlords would be sympathetic to their plight. While some landlord offered rent relief to retailers most didn't, and where rent relief was offered it was often too little too late and as a consequence many retailers were forced out of business and in many instances lost their life savings overnight. In fact, some have argued (Knight, 2020) that landlords were using the coronavirus as a means to squeeze the more vulnerable small retailers. While corporate landlords deny this is occurring there are many retailers who would argue otherwise.

So, the message remains very clear – if you are ever contemplating setting up a small business in a large shopping complex, do your homework and be aware of the pitfalls associated with a long-term lease agreement.

There is another angle to consider. COVID-19 has presented a situation where public health restrictions like lockdowns and social distancing have hampered normal business operations. A significant number of restaurants permanently closed during the COVID-19, especially from the decreasing dining rate and the consequent impacts on revenues (McCarthy, 2020). However, many restaurants and cafes can overcome the impacts of COVID-19 by being innovative in marketing and product and service offerings. Thus, just following the crowd (i.e. other business owners) may not be the answer when planning for your new business in the post-COVID-19 context. Think of your planned business context. What can you do differently from your competitors? How well prepared are you to adapt your business model if normal business operations cannot continue? Do you have a backup plan? Furthermore, do you have enough capital to cover such emergencies?

Conclusion

The decision to start a small business is one of the most important business decisions a person can make in their lifetime. The small business venture described in this case study explains the circumstances that led to the collapse of a small business in regional Australia – a café that failed in the space of four years after its commencement. The owners did many things right in this business venture but ultimately failed because they didn't sufficiently factor in the exorbitantly high lease payments and a decline in customers numbers which could be largely attributed to macroeconomic issues linked to the global financial crisis. The facts of the case study should serve as a reminder that the decision to start a small business venture is not a decision that should be taken lightly as it can cause the loss of many thousands of dollars in hard-earned money.

References

ABS. (2007, November 8). *6202.0—Labour Force, Australia, Oct 2007*. Australian Bureau of Statistics; c=AU; o=Commonwealth of Australia; ou=Australian Bureau of Statistics. www.abs.gov.au/AUSSTATS/abs@.nsf/Lookup/6202.0Main+Features1Oct%20 2007?OpenDocument=

ABS. (2009, November 12). *6202.0—Labour Force, Australia, Oct 2009*. Australian Bureau of Statistics; c=AU; o=Commonwealth of Australia; ou=Australian Bureau of Statistics. www.abs.gov.au/AUSSTATS/abs@.nsf/allprimarymainfeatures/75DD254CA9FEC2C ECA257687001D2FAB?opendocument

ABS. (2021, February 23). *Counts of Australian Businesses, Including Entries and Exits, July 2016–June 2020*. www.abs.gov.au/statistics/economy/business-indicators/counts-australian-businesses-including-entries-and-exits/latest-release

Knight, B. (2020, July 17). "Going to be a Bloodbath": Landlords to Send Small Retailers to the Wall. *ABC News*. www.abc.net.au/news/2020-07-18/coronavirus-small-business-struggling-rent-melbourne/12465454

McCarthy, K. (2020, July 25). Nearly 16,000 Restaurants Have Closed Permanently Due to the Pandemic, Yelp Data Shows. *ABC News*. https://abcnews.go.com/Business/16000-restaurants-closed-permanently-due-pandemic-yelp-data/story?id=71943970

McDonald, S. and Morling, S. (2011). The Australian Economy and the Global Downturn, Part 2: The Key Quarters. *Economic Roundup*. The Treasury, Australian Government, Issue 2, pp. 33–60.

Reserve Bank of Australia (RBA, n.d.). *The Global Financial Crisis* (Explainers). The Reserve Bank of Australia. www.rba.gov.au/education/resources/explainers/pdf/the-global-financial-crisis.pdf

14
CONCLUSION

Quamrul Alam and Robert Grose

This book has used case studies to help students understand the evolving nature of small to medium-sized enterprises (SMEs) in Australia. Case studies were chosen as they provided a critical analytical framework to examine the various issues faced by the owners and managers of SMEs. The case study approach could be viewed as an exercise in learning by doing, as this mode of learning provides the reader with detailed contextual information about the changes and opportunities for different industries and companies in different settings. The case study approach provides students with the ability to improve their analytical skills and expose them to the real situations faced by company managers in the performance of their strategic responsibilities.

SMEs play an increasingly important role in the development of the Australian economy. According to the Australian Bureau of Statistics (ABS, 2021), there were approximately 2,422,404 businesses in Australia at the end of June 2020. Using employment as a measure to classify businesses (Table 14.1), 97.5% of these businesses would be classified as small, 2.3% would be classified as medium, while the remaining 0.2% would be classified as large businesses. As of 30 June 2018, according to ABS data and ASBFEO calculations, there were 4.94 million people employed by small businesses, representing 44.2% of Australia's total workforce, 2.69 million people employed by medium-sized businesses, and 3.54 million people employed by large businesses. Many of these small to medium-sized businesses are in regional towns across Australia.

Further classification (Table 14.2) shows that the majority of all Australian businesses (63.9%) are sole traders with no employees. Micro businesses (i.e., those employing between 1 and 4 people) represent 24.8% of all Australian businesses, while 8.8% would be classified as small businesses (i.e., those employing between 5 and 19 people). Medium-sized businesses (i.e., those employing between 20 and

TABLE 14.1 Business size measured by employment

Business size	Number	Percentage
Small (0–19 employees)	2,361,778	97.5
Medium (20–199 employees)	56,257	2.3
Large (200 + employees)	4,367	0.2
Total	**2,422,404**	**100.0**

Source: Australian Bureau of Statistics (ABS, 2021). *Counts of Australian Businesses, including Entries and Exits, July 2016–June 2020* (Table 13a).

TABLE 14.2 Businesses by annualised size range

Business size	Number	Percentage
Non-employing	1,546,865	63.9
Employing		
1–4 (micro)	601,687	24.8
5–19 (small)	213,226	8.8
20–199 (medium)	56,257	2.3
200 + (large)	4,367	0.2
Total Employing	875,539	36.1
Total	**2,422,404**	**100.0**

Source: ABS. (2021). *Counts of Australian Businesses, including Entries and Exits, July 2016–June 2020.* Australian Bureau of Statistics (Table 13a).

199 people) account for 2.3% of all Australian businesses while the remaining 0.2% (i.e., those employing more than 200 people) are classified as large businesses.

Structural change can be explained as the constant evolution of the economy as some industries grow and others decline. Over time, this results in changes to the industrial composition or 'structure' of the economy. For the most part, structural change is a necessary and beneficial aspect of a functioning market economy. However, it is a mistake to argue structural changes are unambiguously good or bad for a particular region because change imposes costs on people and businesses. The impact on any individual region can be either positive or negative, depending on whether a change in that area is driven by industry growth or decline or a combination of the two (Australian Government, 2015).

Understanding historical and prospective trends in structural change is a priority for formulating policy. Structural change influences labour market outcomes (including skills demand and educational requirements), infrastructure demand, and trade policy. It also has implications for spatial policy. Of particular importance here is that industries that tend to cluster in specific locations or regions will have an impact on the industrial growth (or decline), the employment of people, and the development of infrastructures in that geographic location (Australian Government, 2015). The structure of the Australian economy has changed significantly since the mid-1970s. There has been a shift away from agriculture, forestry and fishing, retail trade and manufacturing towards business services, health care services, social assistance services, and the mining sector. These national trends are amplified in regional Australia where the mining boom has had a strong employment impact in regional and remote areas. Declines in agricultural employment are also concentrated in regional and remote areas (Cassells et al., 2018).

As mentioned above, the small to medium-sized business services sector has become an increasingly important part of the Australian economy, both in terms of its output share and in its integration in the production of other sectors' goods and services. The shift towards services is a common feature of developed countries like Australia where economies become wealthier, and people tend to spend more on services than they had previously. The rising importance of business services has also affected the labour market and the types of skills required.

Australia has been moving towards a service economy and away from agriculture and manufacturing for some time. In the ten years to 2016, Australia lost around 270,000 manufacturing jobs and gained almost 400,000 jobs in the health sector. The share of workers employed in the manufacturing sector has halved in the last 30 years from 15.4% to 7.2%. Employment growth in the Health Care and Social Assistance sector averaged 4.5% annually between 2008 and 2018 – almost three times the pace of employment growth across all other sectors (Cassells et al., 2018).

In another structural change, more people are moving from the formal employment sector to independent employment or contract work during the middle of their working lives. This move reflects the new opportunities that are on offer in technology-related sectors. Bankwest Curtin Economics Centre estimates show that 11.6% of the Australian workforce are independent contractors, which is equivalent to around 1,270,000 workers. Women and younger workers are more likely to hold multiple jobs. Software development, incorporating programming, web design and data science is the largest category of online freelancing services in Australia, with listings rising from 26% to 37% of all services between 2016 and 2018. In an ever-changing work landscape, approximately 1 in 5 employed persons work regularly from home, with relatively no change over time, although the COVID-19 pandemic would have increased the ratio of those working from home even further. In 2016, 41.2% of managers and 38.2% of professionals regularly worked at home (Cassells et al., 2018).

The agricultural sector is particularly interesting in terms of structural change. The sector is crucial to the success of Australia's economy and the COVID-19 pandemic has made it harder for farmers to find the workers they need to fill their labour shortages. Temporary visa holders can help fill some of these shortages to ensure harvest work continues and agriculture can continue to play an important role in securing Australia's prosperity. The Government has recently introduced several temporary visa measures to address labour shortages in the agricultural sector and assist temporary visa holders to continue to work in agriculture, thereby increasing the number of visa holders available to employers (Working in Agriculture, 2021).

By any measure small to medium-sized enterprises (SMEs) play an important role that is critical to the stability, strength, and viability of the Australian economy. The major reason why SMEs are important to the health of the Australian economy rests with the fact that they provide a major source of employment for the Australian population. According to the Reserve Bank of Australia (RBA), SMEs employ nearly 68% (43% employed by small businesses and the remaining 25% employed by medium-sized businesses) of Australia's total labour force. It should also be noted that many of those people working in SMEs are unskilled workers and consequently this helps decrease the unemployment rate to acceptable levels which have the flow on the advantage of decreasing the number of people on welfare payments, helps lower crime rates, and helps improve the living standards for Australians.

SMEs also represent, and as has been amply demonstrated in many of the case studies in this book, a major source of innovation and entrepreneurship. SMEs are not weighed down by many of the bureaucratic roadblocks that are commonplace in most large organisations. To survive, SMEs need to be nimble and be able to change quickly with new trends and not get bogged down in endless and time-consuming board room discussions that seem to be commonplace in a large organisation's

Many of the chapters in this book have highlighted the innovative practices of SMEs in regional Australia. For example, the chapter that reviewed the human resources practices in a regionally owned organisation in Far North Queensland highlighted several innovative human resource management practices designed to train and retain highly skilled and incentivised employees. The strategy proved so successful that the regional organisation is now widely known for its value proposition, and its reputation has supported a growth strategy to expand beyond mining into commercial ports and infrastructure sectors, which has proved critical to buffer against the cycles synonymous with the resources sector.

Chapter 10 looked at the Macadamia industry and the innovative practices that helped make it a world leader in its field. For example, the National Macadamia Breeding and Evaluation Program, in collaboration with the University of Queensland, plus the Australian Macadamia Society-funded research and development programs to help improve the cultivation, productivity and marketing of macadamias. Another entrepreneurial endeavour was based on the recognition that macadamia have become very popular snack food for health-conscious consumers. For example, macadamias are increasingly being used in the bakery industry to bake bread, cookies, and to make healthy drinks. The use of the macadamia nut in confectionery and snacks globally has increased by 20% in the last few years (Charleston, 2020) and the industry continues to find new uses for this versatile nut.

In another case study, the demise of the regional newspaper seemed an inevitability because of the huge costs associated with each print run and reduced circulations due to a decline in readership and competition from social media platforms. Economies of scale were not possible, and the readership base was not of sufficient size to cover all the costs associated with publishing a regional newspaper. Innovation came to the rescue in the form of inkjet printers that were more economical and cost-effective with smaller print runs because of the minimal set-up costs associated with inkjet printers. Other innovative practices, designed to widen the readership base and reduce costs, included splitting what was originally one single daily title into three: the *Daily Journal* (Warwick), a free weekly (*The Country Journal*) and a twice-weekly for the *Daily Journal*, the *Stanthorpe Record*. As a result of these innovative practices, circulation rose on the days the new group of titles were published. Advertising revenue also rose, because advertisers gained the additional impact from the increased circulation of the paid editions and the addition of the free home-delivered edition. The net impact of the loss of circulation income from the loss of four paid editions a week was more than offset by the reduction in costs. With the heavy losses addressed, the new operation has become sustainable and continues to employ more journalists working in the region than any other news media operation with a presence in the circulation area.

In Australia, the last twelve months have been unprecedented in the scale and the speed of changes impacting businesses, from the 2019–2020 Australian bushfire season starting in late-2019, through to the COVID-19 pandemic impacting Australia from March 2020. These events have impacted businesses in different ways; some industries have been heavily restricted (e.g., the tourism industry resulting from bushfire evacuations and border closures due to COVID-19), while others have been marked with strong growth.

As the COVID-19 pandemic wears on, its impact will continue to be felt across regional Australia. However, while the effects of the pandemic have the potential to adversely affect every part of our lives, there are winners. For example, there has been an explosion in the number of online business transactions, the acceleration of home-based work practices has reshaped human resource management practices, the rise of home delivery services, options to purchase online using 'click and collect' e-platform have resulted in a huge boost to those businesses that have quickly adapted to this brave new world. According to a 2021 Australia Post (2021) – online shopping growth for the 12 months to 30 June 2021 was up 31.8%, which was in line with the previous financial year increase of 33.2%.

When the COVID-19 lockdowns forced consumers to remain at home, e-commerce experienced huge growth in the volume of online sales. Businesses in some sectors were quick to adopt innovative practices to cater for the increased demand. COVID-19 has changed how businesses work today. Businesses have moved rapidly to deploy digital and automated technologies. Many organisations are conducting their businesses from remote locations. Shopping, entertainment, and even medicine went online, and businesses everywhere scrambled to deploy digital systems to accommodate the shift. Changes in consumer behaviour and business models will persist in metropolitan and regional areas after the pandemic becomes a thing of the past. The pandemic has reshaped the future of work, consumer behaviour, and business management practices. It is obvious that the next normal is going to be different. It will not mean going back to the conditions that prevailed in 2020 or before. Indeed, just as the terms 'pre-war' and 'post-war' are commonly used to describe the 20th century, generations to come will likely discuss the pre-COVID-19 and post-COVID-19 eras (Kevin Sneader and Shubham Singhal, 2021).

This book will assist students and researchers in understanding the processes of industrial localisation. The case book includes business cases to highlight the background, innovation, local resource leverage, social and entrepreneurial skills, knowledge of local and international markets used by these businesses. The analysis of the success stories will assist readers in theorising how locational advantages can be used by businesses to withstand competitive pressure and achieve growth in an innovative and sustained manner. The COVID-19 pandemic has forced organisations around the world to re-evaluate many aspects of management and work practices, workforce composition, and workplace layout to avoid risks and avail opportunities.

There is no doubt that SMEs play an important role in helping to maintain and enhance Australia's economic prosperity. As was indicated at the beginning of this chapter, SMEs make up most businesses currently operating in the Australian landscape and their role in sustaining high employment levels, innovative practices and wealth creation cannot be under-estimated. In a nutshell, SMEs are the foundation of a strong and thriving Australian economy. It is incumbent of the Australian government to look after SMEs, for without them Australia's economic prosperity would be severely damaged.

References

ABS. (2021, February 23). *Counts of Australian Businesses, Including Entries and Exits, July 2016–June 2020*. Available at: www.abs.gov.au/statistics/economy/business-indicators/counts-australian-businesses-including-entries-and-exits/latest-release

Australia Post (2021). *Inside Australian Online Shopping – eCommerce Update 2021*. Available at: https://auspost.com.au/content/dam/auspost_corp/media/documents/inside-australian-online-shopping-update-july-2021.pdf

Australian Government (2015). *State of Regional Australia: Progress in Australian Regions*. Available at: www.regional.gov.au/regional/publications/sora/files/State-of-Regional-Australia-2015.pdf

Cassells R, Duncan A, Mavisakalyan A, Phillimore J, Seymour R and Tarverdi Y (2018), 'Future of Work in Australia: Preparing for Tomorrow's World', Bankwest Curtin Economics Centre, Focus on the States Series, Issue #6, April 2018.

Charleston, L J (2020). Our Thriving Macadamia Industry. Aus Biz Media. https://ausbizmedia.com/macadamia-industry/

Kevin Sneader and Shubham Singhal (2021) The next normal arrives: Trends that will define 2021—and beyond, Mckinsey @ Company, January 4.

Working in Agriculture. (2021) Support Farmers, Support Australia. Available at: https://immi.homeaffairs.gov.au/visas/working-in-australia/regional-migration/working-in-agriculture/visa-options

BIOGRAPHY OF CONTRIBUTORS

Quamrul Alam is a Professor of International Business and Strategy in the School of Business and Law at Central Queensland University (CQUniversity), Melbourne, Australia. Before joining CQUniversity Alam worked at Monash University, La Trobe University, Victoria University, the University of Dhaka. He did his PhD in Development Economics from Flinders University and an MA in Economics from Manchester University. He has published over 60 journal articles, 19 book chapters, and 4 books. His articles have been published in the *Thunderbird Journal of Business Review*, *European Journal of Management*, *Administration and Society*, *Public Administration and Development*, *Public Management Review*, *International Review of Administrative Sciences*, *Australian Journal of Public Administration*, *International Journal of Public Administration*, *South Asian Journal of Management History*. He has supervised 20 PhD students. Recently Alam and his colleagues edited two books which were published by Routledge Taylor and Francis Group: *Managing Change for Better Public Service Delivery*, and *Economic Development of Bangladesh in the Asian Century: Prospects and Perspectives*. His research interest areas are international business, public governance, regulation and governance, and social business.

Robert Grose is a Lecturer in Accounting at the CQUniversity's School of Business and Law. Robert is a very experienced teacher who has taught in a variety of educational settings across multiple campuses to large numbers of domestic and international students both in Australia and at overseas universities. Before joining CQUniversity, Robert acted as Program Manager in RMIT's Bachelor of Business Studies Program run out of Malaysia and Singapore. Robert is an active researcher whose research interests lie in the areas of accounting education, the use of technology in accounting education, financial accounting and auditing. In addition to publishing several academic journal articles and academic conference papers, Robert has also authored several accounting, auditing and accounting software textbooks published through Pearson Australia.

Biography of contributors 185

Elena Konovalov completed her PhD project focused on Community Well-Being and Tourism at James Cook University. After completion of her PhD, Konovalov worked as a lecturer in Marketing and Management at the School of Business and Law, CQUniversity and taught undergraduate and postgraduate students in Marketing, Management, Business, and HR disciplines as well as continuing and expanding her tourism marketing and entrepreneurship research. Currently, Konovalov continues her research in an Adjunct Research Fellow capacity and her research interests include tourism and tourism impacts, community well-being, social innovation and entrepreneurship, sustainable tourism development, indexes and indicators of social progress, student success, and social and social media marketing.

Rumana Parveen is a graduate research student in the School of Business and Law at Central Queensland University, Melbourne, Australia. Being an Assistant Professor of Management in the top state university of Bangladesh, the University of Dhaka, she moved to Australia for higher studies. She completed Master's in Management (with thesis) from Monash University, Melbourne in 2018 with an Endeavour Scholarship (by Govt. of Australia). Previously, she acquired a prestigious MBA (Strategic & International Management) from the University of Dhaka and then served as a lecturer of Management at Daffodil International University and East-West University in Bangladesh during 2005–2008. She had been actively working with Yunus Center since 2010 as an expert in social business. Currently, Ms Parveen is a Casual Faculty at Central Queensland University and Federation University, Melbourne, Australia. Her research interest areas are Strategic Management, Corporate Sustainability, Social Business, Social Entrepreneurship, Indigenous Entrepreneurship, Hospitality Management, and Organisational Behaviour. Ms Parveen produced thought-provoking articles based on original research works and attended several academic conferences at home and abroad. She also works as an active volunteer at Beyond Blue, Australia, Cancer Council Victoria, and the City of Melbourne.

Sardana Islam Khan is a Lecturer at CQUniversity, Australia. She has earned a PhD in Management from La Trobe University, Australia. She has published 12 journal articles in international journals such as *Personnel Review* among others and four book chapters with Routledge and other reputed publishers. She has co-edited two volumes of the 'East West Journal of Business and Social Studies'. Sardana is also a member of the editorial board of the *Journal for Service Quality Enhancement* (JSQE). She served as the Associate Professor and Deputy Executive Director of East West University Center for Research and Training. She has successfully managed a World Bank-funded 'Higher Education Quality Enhancement Program (HEQEP)' sub-project on capacity building and knowledge sharing (2014–2016). She earned several best paper awards in international conferences, ANZAM Best Reviewer Award (2019), AusAID Australian Leadership Award (2009), and La Trobe Gold Leadership Award (2012) for academic and community contributions. She is currently supervising ten PhD and research students at CQUniversity.

Ho Yin Wong is a Senior Lecturer in the Department of Marketing at Deakin Business School. His research interests include international marketing, strategic marketing, and branding. He has published in *International Marketing Review*, *Journal of Strategic Marketing*, *Journal of Business & Industrial Marketing*, *Journal of Brand Management*, *Managing Service Quality (Journal of Service Theory and Practice)*, *Journal of Cleaner Production*, and the *Asia Pacific Journal of Marketing and Logistics*, among others. He has won excellence and highly commended paper awards from the Emerald Literati Network.

Tasmiha Tarafder is an academic at the School of Management, RMIT University, Melbourne, Australia. She received the master's (by research) degree from the University of Canberra, Australia. Her research papers are published in journals, including *Food Quality and Preference* and *Australasian Journal of Regional Studies*. She has published several book chapters with renowned publishers, including Edward Elgar and Emerald, and a few papers in refereed proceedings. Tasmiha received the Best Paper Award 2013 and the Highly Commended Award 2012 from the ANZSRAI conferences. She also published one research monograph (book) and one children's storybook. Her research interests include entrepreneurship, management, occupational health and safety, women at the workplace, health beliefs, and attitudes.

Parves Sultan is a multi-disciplinary academic and researcher. He has a solid background in research methodologies and data analytics with a focus on behavioural sciences. His research interests include firm performance and internationalisation, CSR, consumer behaviour, marketing, sustainable education, quality and performance measurement and branding of the profit and non-profit sectors, SDGs relating to health and the environment. He was awarded the research excellence award from the Emerald Literati Network in 2013. Parvez's research articles are published in many top-ranked scholarly journals, including the *Journal of Cleaner Production*, *Food Quality and Preference*, *Journal of Brand Management*, *Managing Service Quality (Journal of Service Theory and Practice)*, *Journal of Business and Industrial Marketing*, *Asia Pacific Journal of Marketing and Logistics*, *International Journal of Bank Marketing*, *Journal of Food Products Marketing*, *Quality Assurance in Education*, *International Journal of Quality and Service Sciences*, *Accountability in Research*, *International Journal on Disability and Human Development*, and *Australasian Journal of Regional Studies*. He can be contacted at: parvessultan@yahoo.com.

Lisa A. Caffery is a social researcher based in Emerald, Central Queensland and has completed a PhD thesis looking at health inequity, rural and regional communities, and social impact. Her research interests are driven by innate curiosity and by the ambition to make a connection between research and practice. She is particularly interested in understanding what the trade-offs are between living in a rural and remote community and having limited access to local health care services. The results from Lisa's PhD research have informed the development of several new health equity assessment tools for small rural towns. With a professional background in community engagement and social impact sshe has worked as a consultant in social impact. Lisa also holds director positions for numerous not-for-profit rural charities and a statutory health board.

Biography of contributors

Olav T. Muurlink is a social and health psychologist who attained a PhD from Griffith University and serving at the School of Business and Law of Central Queensland University. He is a member of the Australian Psychological Society, Working Time Society and College of Reviewers, Higher Educational Research and Development. He is also a member of Appleton Institute and Centre for Regional Economies and Supply Chains of CQUniversity. He is the chair of the management committee/head of the country of one of the largest educational charities in Bangladesh, 'Co-operation in Development'. As a psychologist, he has worked as a consultant on projects for the British, New Zealand and Queensland governments. His research interests are overwork/workaholism, working hour research, counter attitudinal behaviour, public health issues, climate impacts on health and welfare, and demographics. He published a number of research works in the areas of health, mental health, education, gender studies, health management, public health issues at high-ranking journals, books, and conference proceedings.

Michael Segon is an Associate Professor and Director of the MBA at CQUniversity, Melbourne, Australia. He has specialised in business ethics and corporate social responsibility, at both the academic and corporate levels, and the applied nature of this discipline within leadership and management. He's been an avid skier for over 40 years and has recently researched the economic and employment benefits of the Alpine industry both in Australia and Japan.

Andrew W. Taylor-Robinson is an infectious disease immunologist specialising in mosquito-borne pathogens working as Professor of Immunology & Haematology at the School of Health, Medical and Applied Sciences, Central Queensland University, Brisbane, Australia. He has over 30 years of research experience in malaria, dengue, and other tropical diseases that pose a major global public health threat. In Australia, he works on several projects on human health and well-being in rural and remote communities. These include investigating the transmission cycles and reservoir hosts of potentially pathogenic arboviruses that are unique to the country. Through translational research on bacterial infections of the upper respiratory tract, contributing to otitis media in young children, his interests have expanded to consider broader aspects of diseases of poverty. This encompasses the consideration of social innovation as a tool to address healthcare responses in underprivileged populations. Andrew holds appointments at Vin University (Vietnam), University of Pennsylvania (USA), Central Queensland University, and Charles Darwin University (Australia). He has published more than 300 peer-reviewed journal articles and book chapters.

Linda Colley is a graduate of Public Sector Management who attained PhD from *Griffith* University. She has been serving at the School of Business and Law of Central Queensland University since 2010. She is a member of Appleton Institute of CQUniversity, a multidisciplinary research institute with a focus on health and well-being at work, rest, and play. Her research interests and expertise include career service employment, merit and tenure, job security, redundancy and downsizing, as well as gender at work. She published many research works relevant to public administration, public policy, gender studies, industrial relations, and political science in high-ranking journals, books, and conference proceedings.

Malcolm Johnson is an Associate Professor in the College of Business, School of Business and Law, CQUniversity, Australia. Leading a team of academics in management and innovation, Malcolm adds a commercial insight with a background in business planning, strategy, turnarounds, and start-ups. He completed his MBA with a thesis on corporate strategy while working for Shell Australia. He completed his doctorate in behavioural finance leading to an Australian Innovation Patent. He applied these insights to build and sell two sizeable businesses in the wealth management sector. He is committed to building organisational capability through current research and practice.

Upamali Amarakoon has been a university faculty more than 13 years in universities in both Sri Lanka and Australia. She attained PhD in Human Resource Management from the University of Queensland in 2014 (with Dean's Award for Outstanding Research Higher Degree Thesis). Her research interest is in the areas of Strategic HRM and HRM innovation, regional staffing challenges, and volunteer management. She published a number of research works on Human Resource Management in several journals, books and conference proceedings.

Tasadduq Imam is a multidisciplinary academic with research and teaching track records in business management and information technology. He has published research articles in diverse areas, including small and medium enterprises, financial management, data mining, and business analytics. He has received multiple research grants, successfully supervised multiple research projects, and is a member of multiple professional societies, including the Statistical Society of Australia, Accounting and Finance Association of Australia and New Zealand, and Australian Computer Society. He has received multiple teaching awards and is regularly commended institutionally and by his students for his teaching style. He also has led multiple committees and holds a professional interest in entrepreneurship and business development.

INDEX

Note: Page numbers in **bold** indicate tables; those in *italics* indicate figures.

account managers 150, 154–155
advertising: Harvey Norman 137–139, 144; newspaper 72, 73, 74, 77, 182; resources sector 154, 162
age factors: resources sector 153; structural changes in the economy 180
agency theory 55
agricultural sector 180
AgriFutures Australian Rural Woman of the Year award 14, 22
Airbnb 20
Alibaba 3
Alpine industry 79–81, 89; climate change 79, 83, 85–87, 89; comparison of resort areas 81–83, **82**; COVID-19 pandemic 87–89; economic benefit to Victoria 83–84, **84**; investment 86, 87, **88**; visitation 80, 83, **84**, 84, 87–89
Alpine Resorts Act 81
Alpine Resorts Management Act 81
Amankwah-Amoah, J. 44
Amazon 30, 34
American Marketing Association 14
Apple iPhone 20
architectural innovation 20
artificial snowmaking 83, 86, 87, 89
Asahi Holdings (Australia) Pty Ltd 27
Asia: Bundaberg Brewed Drinks 32–33; business context 2; macadamia industry 122, 126; trade 2
asset sales 56

Association of Southeast Asian Nations (ASEAN) 5, 6
Australia Post 92–93, 109–110; business competencies 104–107; competitors 93, **94**, 97, 98; COVID-19 pandemic 95, 100, 106, 108–109, 110; economic conditions 94–96, *95*, *96*; environment and sustainability 99–100; five-year trend (2016–2020) **101**; globalisation 93–94; legislation and regulations 97; market position 100–101; performance against targets **108**; political environment 96; societal values 97–98; successes 107–108; supply chain *106*; technology and internet 92, 98–103, 106–108; value networks 102–104
Australia Postal Corporation 92
Australian Air Express 105
Australian Broadcasting Corporation (ABC) 12
Australian Bureau of Statistics (ABS): government assistance for small businesses 57; Household Survey 35; small business failures 164
Australian Community Media (ACM) 75
Australian Competition and Consumer Commission (ACCC) 96
Australian Macadamia Handlers Association (AMHA) 121
Australian Macadamia Society Ltd (AMS) 118–119, 124–131, 181

Australian Newsroom Mapping Project 74, 75
Australian Nut Industry Council (ANIC) 130
Australian Postal Commission 92
Australian Postal Corporation Act 92
Australian Securities and Investment Commission (ASIC) 41
Australian Tax Office (ATO): Central Highlands Healthcare 61; small businesses 41, **43–44**, 57
Australian Telecommunication Commission 92
aviation industry 114–117

Baier, S. L. 5
banana products 11–15, 17, 19, 22
Bangladesh 3
bankruptcy of declining small businesses 54
Banksia Food for Sustainable Thought Award 13–14
Barcellos, M. D. de 20
Beaulieu, M. 139
beauty products 15, 22
Belgium 72
Bergstrand, J. H. 5
Best, A. 60
Bossle, M. B. 20
Boydell, Andy 88
Brazil: GDP growth 3; newspaper publishers 70
broccoli powder 15, 22
Brunei 32, 33
BSR Australia Ltd 136
Bundaberg Brewed Drinks (BBD) 25–26, 38; Asian expansion potential 32–33; challenges 34–37; future strategic focus 33–34; non-alcoholic drink industry 27–28; product profile 26–27; sustainability practices 28–28; UK market opportunity 29–32
Burnett, Jolyon 124, 125, 126, 129
bushfires 6–7, 182; Alpine industry 87; Australia Post 108; Harvey Norman 145; Natural Evolution Foods 21, 23; tourism industry 182
business context 2
business plan, lack of, and small business failure 174
business services sector 180
business size, classification of 178–179, **179**

café, failed 164, 176; capital, lack of 168–169; commencement 165–166; differentiation, lack of 174; lease agreement 166–168; macroeconomic factors 171; management, poor 170; microeconomic factors 170–171; opening of new businesses 172–173; refurbishment 168; staff experience 169–170; start-up 164–165; supplies 172; taxation 173; vending machines 172
California 118
Campbell, S. 76
Canada 19
Canstar Blue 36
carbon offsetting 29
case study approach 178
casual work 156–157
Central Highlands Development Corporation (CHDC) 65
Central Highlands Healthcare (CHH) 66–67; innovation 64–66; overview 60–61, **61**; products and services 61–63; social enterprise attributes **62**; strategies 63–64
Central Highlands Regional Council (CHRC) 65
Central Queensland University 30
change, resistance to 21–22
China: Bundaberg Brewed Drinks 25, 32–33; GDP growth 3; geo-political tensions 115; large companies 2; macadamia industry 122–123, 125, 126, 128, 130; manufacturing hub 6; newspaper publishers 70; tourists from 113–114
China–Australia Free Trade Agreement (ChAFTA) 126
China Post 105, 107
China Southern Airlines 113–114
Chowdhury, S. D. 45
circular economy 11, 17, 23
Clarke, Jason 21
climate and weather events: Natural Evolution Foods 21, 23; *see also* climate change
climate change: Natural Evolution Foods 23; winter sports industry 79, 83, 85–87, 89
CO2 Australia 29
Coca-Cola 25, 27, 29, 31, 36, 37
Coles 109
collaboration: Bundaberg Brewed Drinks 36–37; macadamia industry 121, 126–129, 130; Natural Evolution Foods 18–19, 22; *see also* joint ventures; partnerships; strategic alliances

Colonial Leisure Group 115
Colonial Sugar Refiners (CSR) 119
Commercialisation Australia 13
Community Service Obligations (CSO) 96
comparative advantage 5
competitive advantage: Australia Post 106; aviation industry 115; cooperative and networking behaviour 19; FTAs 2; macadamia industry 120, 124; Mount Buller 81–83, 89; Natural Evolution Foods 16; resources sector 161; tourism 115
computer retailing industry **134**, 135–136
core competencies: Australia Post 104, 106; Harvey Norman 139
corporate social responsibility 38
CorProcure 102, 103
Country Journal, The 74, 182
COVID-19 pandemic 7–8, 182–183; agricultural sector 180; Australia Post 95, 100, 106, 108–109, 110; as Black Swan event 113; computer and software retailing industry 136; entrepreneurship 116; Experience Co 114; Harvey Norman 135, 136, 145–146; macadamia industry 126, 129–130, 131; mergers and acquisitions 114; Morris's portfolio 117; newspaper publishers 74–76; shopping centres 175–176; soft drinks 28, 34–35, 36, 37; tourism industry 115, 182; winter sports industry 84, 87–89; working from home 180
Croatia 133, 144
customer needs, ignored, and small business failure 174–175
Cuthbert, R. 19
cyclones 21, 23

Daily Journal 73, 74, 76, 182
Daintree Ecolodge 115
David Jones 140
declining small businesses *see* revival of declining small businesses
deficit clause, lease agreements 167
design thinking 64, 66
Deutsche Post 93
developing countries *see* emerging economies
DHL 93, 101, 105
differentiation: Harvey Norman 137, 139–140, **140**; lack of, and small business failure 174
disabilities, people with: blindness 105; employees 154

disposable income, and soft drinks industry 35
disruptive innovation 20
diversification: Australia Post 93, 98, 102; Natural Evolution Foods 17–18, 22; nut industry 130; revival of declining small businesses 51; risk 116
diversity: Australia Post 103; resources sector 153–154, 162
Domayne 133
domestic appliance industry **134**, 136
down scoping 44, 52, 56
Dubai 3

eBay 97
eco-innovations 20–21
e-commerce 182; Australia Post 100, 109, 110; COVID-19 pandemic 7; Harvey Norman 142
Edison Award 14
electric vehicles 100
email: Australia Post's e-Letter service 107–108; as postal industry competitor 98
Emerald Medical Clinic *see* Central Highlands Healthcare
emerging economies: business context 2; FTAs 5; GDP growth 2–3; R&D 4; tax avoidance practices 6; technology 4
employees: agricultural sector 180; attraction strategy 150–151; Australia Post 95, **100**, 100, 103–104, 107, 109, 110; Bundaberg Brewed Drinks 35; business size measured by 178, **179**; competitive rates and packaging 151–152; core 160–161; COVID-19 assistance measures 37; development 159–160; diversity **100**, 100, 154, 162; engagement 149, 151–152, 154–156, 160–163; failed café case study 169–170; Harvey Norman 137, 143, 145; human resource management innovation 148–163, 181; macadamia industry 119; Mount Buller 81, 84; newspaper publishers 74; resources sector 148–163; retention 156–161; revival of declining small businesses 52; skilled labour pool, availability of 153–154; SMEs 164, 181; structural changes in the economy 179–180; UK soft drinks industry 29
Emyria *see* Central Highlands Healthcare
endowment factors 26
entrepreneurship 181; Central Highlands Healthcare 65; founder factor 116–117; Harvey Norman 142–143; lack of skills,

and small business failure 175; Natural Evolution Foods 11–13, 15–16, 22–23; newspaper publishers 75, 76; revival of declining small businesses 45, 50, 54–58; technological development 3
environmental responsibility: Australia Post 99–100, 109; Mount Buller 86; Natural Evolution Foods 17
Ernst & Young Victorian Alpine Resorts Economic Contribution Study 83
ethical issues: Bundaberg Brewed Drinks 33; tax avoidance 6
Europe: macadamia industry 123, 128, 130; obesity 23
European Free Trade Association (EFTA) 5
European Union (EU): FTAs 5; Harvey Norman 144; postal industry 97; soft drinks 31
Evolution Industries 15–16
Experience Co (EXP) 114, 115; financial status **114**, 114
exports 59; Australia Post 107; Bundaberg Brewed Drinks 25, 27, 29–34, 36; macadamia nuts 118, **120**, 120, *121*, 123, 124, 128–131
Express Courier International 107

Facebook 3; news 73
factor endowment 5
failed small businesses 164, 176; café case study 164–173; COVID-19 pandemic 175–176; customer needs, ignored 174–185; differentiation, lack of 174; entrepreneurial skills, lack of 175; planning, lack of 174; scaling, premature 175
Fairfax 69, 75
fast-moving consumer goods (FMCG) 37
FedEx 93, 97
Fentimans 30, 31
Fever-Tree 30, 38
Finasucre Group 130
fires *see* bush fires foreign direct investment (FDI): business context 2; COVID-19 pandemic 7; FTAs 5; R&D 3–4
Forests Act 81
Four'n Twenty 37
fragmentation 6
France: newspaper publishers 72–73; Sugar Tax 27
franchising: Australia Post 104; Harvey Norman 133–134, 137, **138**, *138*, 139–143, 145–146

free trade agreement (FTAs) 2, 5–6; macadamia industry 126, 128
freelancers 180
Friedman, Thomas 94
Fujifilm Holdings Australasia Pty Ltd 93
furniture retailing industry 134–135, **134**

G20 6
GBR Helicopters 114, 115
gender factors: Australia Post 100; resources sector 154, 159; revival of declining small businesses 56; structural changes in the economy 180
Gerber, Norm 119
Germany: Bundaberg Brewed Drinks 25; macadamia industry 123
ginger beer 25–34, 38
Global Financial Crisis (GFC): aftermath 2, 171; failed café case study 171, 176
Global Macadamias 130
global trading systems 2
global value chain 7
global warming *see* climate change
globalisation 1, 2; Australia Post 93–94; Bundaberg Brewed Drinks 26; FTAs 5
Good Guys 140
Goods and Services Tax (GST): failed café case study 173; Harvey Norman 144
governance, Central Highlands Healthcare 65, 66
government: Australia Post 92–110; Central Highlands Healthcare 61, 65; COVID-19 assistance measures 37, 145; COVID-19 restrictions 87; eco-innovations 20; franchisee support 145; 'Go Local, Grow Local' campaign 16–17; Goods and Services Tax 144, 173; GP Super Clinics Infrastructure Program 61; Greenhouse Challenge 99; Harvey Norman 145, 146; labour shortages in agricultural sector 180; macadamia industry 121, 124, 128, 130; Natural Evolution Foods 16, 18; newspaper publishers 72, 73, 76–77; Regional and Small Publishers Innovation Package 77; revival of declining small businesses 52, 57; SMEs 183; tourism 115
Great Barrier Reef: macadamia industry 124; tourism 114, 115
Grollo 81
Gross Domestic Product (GDP) growth 2–3
growth, premature, and small business failure 175

Hackworth, Colin 83, 88
Halley, A. 139
Hamel, G. 139
Hamlin, R. 19
Hantel, M. 85
Hardner, Craig 124
Harris, R. M. B. 85
Harvey, Gerry 139, 142–144
Harvey Norman (HN) 133–134; business model 136–138, **138**, *138*; core competencies 139; COVID-19 pandemic 135, 136, 145–146; future challenges 144–145; repositioning strategies 139–142, **140**, *141*, *142*; retail industry 134–136, **134**; strategic group map *141*; strategic leadership role of Gerry Harvey 142–144
Harvey Norman Holdings Ltd 133, 137
Hawaii 118, 119, 124
health and safety, resources sector 156, 162
health issues: macadamia industry 126, 129, 131, 181; social innovation in health response 59–67; soft drinks 27, 31, 32, 35
Henneberg, S. 19
Herbert, C. 60
Hill, Walter 119
Holgate, Christine 109
home working *see* working from home
Hong Kong 32, 33
Hong Kong Post 105
Horticulture Innovation Australia (HIA) 124, 128
Hsinchu, Taiwan 3
Hubbard, G. 137
human resources *see* employees
human rights 1

imports, as challenge for Harvey Norman 144
inclusivity, resources sector 153–154
India: GDP growth 3; macadamia industry 126; newspaper publishers 69
Indigenous Australians: Australia Post 100; government support 17; health needs 59; macadamia nuts 119
Indonesia 33
information technology (IT): Harvey Norman 139, 141; newspapers 70, 73
innovation 4, 181; Australia Post 98, 104; categories 20; eco-innovations 20–21; human resource management 148–163, 181; macadamia industry 121, 124, 126, 127, 181; Natural Evolution Foods 11–16, 19–23; newspaper publishers 70–72, 76, 182; restaurants and cafés 176; revival of declining small businesses 50; social, in health response 59–67; strategy 20
Innovation in Sustainable Technologies Award 13
insecure work 156–157
internal analysis, Australia Post 101
international division of labour 4
international knowledge sourcing 3–4
internet: Australia Post 98, 100, 103; Central Highlands Healthcare 66; computer and software retailing industry 136; disruption 3; Harvey Norman 139, 144
investment 1; Australia Post 95, 98, 105, 106, 109; COVID-19 pandemic 7; failed café case study 165, 168–169, 170, 174; FTAs 5–6; Harvey Norman 137, 138; macadamia industry 119, 120, 124, 127, 128; Mount Buller 86, 87, **88**; Natural Evolution Foods 13, 16; newspaper publishers 73; tax avoidance practices 6
iPhone 20
Ireland 133

Japan: FTAs 5; macadamia industry 122, 123, 128, 130; Natural Evolution Foods 15; newspaper publishers 70; tourists from 113
Japan Post 105
JB Hi-Fi 136, 140, 144
Jetstar 105
job creation: Australia Post 100; Bundaberg Brewed Drinks 29, 34
job losses, newspaper publishers 69, 74
joint ventures 105
Jonsson, E. 44
Joyce Mayne 133
JR Haulage 105

Kaplan, R. 143
Kerraoul, Jean-Pierre Vittu de 72
Kirkpatrick, R. 75
Kirks 36
Knight, J. 19
Koch, A. 137
Kodak 20
Komisar, R. 137
Korea *see* South Korea
Korea Post 105
Krones 34

labour laws 1
Lacy, P. 17, 22

landlords, shopping centres 166–167, 170–173, 175
Latin America 2
leadership: Central Highlands Healthcare 66; Harvey Norman 142–144; for turnaround 50
lease agreements, shopping centres 166–168, 176
legislation: Australia Post 95, 97; failed café case study 173; Goods and Services Tax 173; macadamia industry 124
life cycle stage: domestic appliance industry 136; furniture retailing industry 134–135; macadamia industry 120, 125; revival of declining small businesses 51–52
liquidation of declining small businesses 54
local focus: Bundaberg Brewed Drinks 25, 35, 36–37; Natural Evolution Foods 16–17
Lohrke, F.T. 55

Macadamia Conservation Trust (MCT) 128–129
Macadamia Farm Management (MFM) 127
macadamia industry 118–119, 130–131; collaboration 126–129; COVID-19 pandemic 126, 129–130, 131; evolution 119; innovation 181; opportunities and threats 126; product and supply chain 121–123; production and exports 118, **120**, 120, *121*, 123, 124, 128–131; strengths 125–126; structure 119–121; sustainability 123–125
Macadamia Marketing International 130
Macadamia Processing Company 130
Macadamias Direct 130
Maine, John 69
Malaysia: Bundaberg Brewed Drinks 32, 33; Harvey Norman 133
Malta 32
management: cognition of declining small businesses 48–49, 54–55; failed café case study 170; turnaround capabilities 49–50, 55–56; *see also* top management team
marketing: Australia Post 103, 109; Harvey Norman 137, 139; lease agreements 167; macadamia industry 123, 127–128, 129, 130, 181; restaurants and cafés 176; revival of declining small businesses 54
Marquis Macadamias 130
Maxwell, Ross 26, 28–29
McLean, John 25, 26–27, 32, 34, 36, 37
ME Engineering 35
Melbourne Age 76

Mercosur 5
mergers and acquisitions (M&As): aviation industry 115; computer and software retailing industry 135; COVID-19 pandemic 114–115; domestic appliance industry 136; macadamia industry 130
Messenger 3
Meuller, Ferdinand Von 119
Mexico 27
micro-newspapers and micro-presses 71–74, 182
Microsoft Teams 3
Middle East 2
migration 97
mining industry 148–163; employment impact 180
mobile phones 3; as postal industry competitor 98
Montgomery, C. A. 18, 144
Morning Bulletin 74
Morris, Chris 114, 116–117
Morris Aviation 115, 116
Morris Group 115
motivation for turnaround 49, 54–55
Mount Buller 79, 89; climate change 85–87; competitive advantage 81–83, **82**; competitor resorts **82**; COVID-19 pandemic 87–89; economic benefit to Victoria 83–84, **84**; history and background 80; investment 86, 87, **88**; resort management 80–81; visitation 80, 83, **84**, 84, 87–89
Mount Buller and Mount Sterling Alpine Resort Management Board (RMB) 80–81, 84, 86–87
Mount Buller Ski Lifts (BSL) 81, 86, 87, 88
Mount Mulligan Lodge 115
Mullins, J. 137
multinational enterprises (MNEs) 2; tax avoidance 6
Mumbai 3
Murdock, A. 62
MY Flying Fish 115
Myer 140

Nachman, S. 142
National Broadband Network (NBN) 66
National Macadamia Breeding and Evaluation Program 124, 181
natural disasters: Harvey Norman 145; Natural Evolution Foods 21; *see also* bushfires
Natural Evolution Foods 11–12, 22–23; challenges 21–22; growth potential

13–15; history 12–13; products/services 15–16; strategies 16–21
Naudé, P. 19
Nautilus Aviation 115
networking 18–19; revival of declining small businesses 51
New Zealand: Bundaberg Brewed Drinks 25, 36, 37; Experience Co 114; farming networks 19; Harvey Norman 133; postal industry 97
News Corp 69, 71, 73–76
News Ltd 75
newspaper publishers 69–70, 75–77, 181–182; COVID-19 pandemic 74–76; micro-newspapers and micro-presses 71–74; technological innovation in print 70–71
Nicholls, A. 62
Nine 75
Nock, Catherine 124
non-alcoholic drinks 25–38
non-tariff barriers 5
Norman, Ian 143
North American Free Trade Agreement (NAFTA) 5
Northern Ireland 133
Norton, D. 143
nut industry 130; *see also* macadamia industry
NutroLock technology 11, 13, 14, 15–16, 18, 22

O'Brien, Terry 25–26
offshoring 4
Old Jamaica 30, 31
omni-channel strategy, Harvey Norman 140–142, *142*
online recruitment 154
online shopping 7, 182; computer and software retailing industry 135–136; domestic appliance industry 136; Harvey Norman 144; postal industry 95, 97, 100, 108, 110
organisational culture, resources sector 161
Orpheus Island Lodge 115
outsourcing 2; R&D 4

Pacific Gold Macadamias 130
packaging: Australia Post 99, 100; Bundaberg Brewed Drinks 26, 29, 30, 32, 36
parenting advantage 116
partnerships: Australia Post 97, 99, 102, 105, 107, 109; Bundaberg Brewed Drinks 31, 32, 33, 34; Central Highlands Healthcare 63, 64–65; macadamia industry 127; Mount Buller 87; Natural Evolution Foods 15, 18–19, 22; revival of declining small businesses 54; *see also* collaboration
Pearce, J. A. 45
PepsiCo 25–26, 27, 29, 31, 34, 36
Peter Kenny Medal 14
Pharmacy Guild of Australia 109
Pisano, G. P. 20
planning, lack of, and small business failure 174
Plantation Brew Co 15
Polaroid 20
population growth, urban 2
Porter's Five Forces model 100–101
portfolio investment analysis 115
Post Logistics 105
postal industry *see* Australia Post
post-global financial crisis 2, 171
Postmaster General's Department (PMG) 92
Prahalad, C. 139
preferential trade agreements 5
production networks 6
protectionism 6

Qantas 99, 105
QML 63
Queensland Premier's Exporter of the Year award 27
Queensland Times 74

radical innovation 20
refurbishment clause, lease agreements 168
regulations: Australia Post 97; aviation 115; Great Barrier Reef 115; macadamia industry 121
remote working: employee retention 157–158, 159; *see also* working from home
Research and Development (R&D): Bundaberg Brewed Drinks 28–29; international knowledge sourcing 3–4; macadamia industry 123, 124, 127, 128–129, 181; Natural Evolution Foods 13, 16, 19–21, 22
Reserve Bank of Australia (RBA) 181
resistance to change 21–22
resources sector 148–163, 181; employment impact 180
retirement 50
retrenchments 44, 56

revival of declining small businesses 41, 57–58; concession policies 41, **43–44**; external factors **46**, 52–53; implications for entrepreneurs and policymakers 57; influencing factors 45, **46–48**, 54–55; managerial factors **46**, **47–48**, 48–50, 55–56; organisational factors **46**, 50–52; pattern of turnaround response and outcomes 56; process 44; profiles **42–43**; turnaround responses 53–54, *53*
Robbins, K. 45
Rosella 37
routine innovation 20
Rural Woman of the Year award 14, 22
Rutqvist, J. 17, 22

Safferstone, T. 143
Sai Cheng Logistics International 107
salaries *see* wages
Salmat Holdings 93
Santa Catarina, Brazil 3
Santora, J. 145
Sarros, J. 145
Sauvée, L. 20
scaling, premature, and small business failure 175
Schweppes 25, 36
seasonal factors: macadamia industry 123; soft drink consumption 31; winter sports industry 80, 81, 83, 85–89
Seek 154
self-efficacy for turnaround 49, 55
service economy 180
Shanghai 3
Shepherd, Andrew 34
Sheppard, J. P. 45
Shrivastava, P. 142
Signet 29
Singapore: Bundaberg Brewed Drinks 32, 33; Harvey Norman 133
Ski Club of Victoria (SCV) 80
ski industry 79–81, 89; climate change 79, 83, 85–87, 89; comparison of resort areas 81–83, **82**; COVID-19 pandemic 87–89; economic benefit to Victoria 83–84, **84**; investment 86, 87, **88**; visitation 80, 83, **84**, 84, 87–89
skincare products 15, 22
Slovenia 133, 144
small businesses: failures 164–176; revival of declining 41–58
Small Newspaper Company (SNC) 73–74
snowmaking 83, 86, 87, 89
social media 3; Bundaberg Brewed Drinks 32, 34; news 73; as postal industry competitor 97, 98

soft drinks 25–38
software development 180
software retailing industry **134**, 135–136
Sogémedia 72
Solent Southampton University 30
South Africa 118, 120–121, 130
South Korea: Bundaberg Brewed Drinks 25, 33; FTAs 5; macadamia industry 122, 128, 130
South–South trade 2
Southern Free Times 72
Spirit International Prestige Awards 27
Sports Trade 88
stakeholders: Australia Post 107–108; revival of declining small businesses 51–52
Stanthorpe Record 74, 182
Star Trak 99
StarTrack Express 105
start-ups: Central Highlands Healthcare 66; concession policies 41; small businesses 164; technological development 3
State Warehousing & Distribution Services (SWADS) 105
Steiger, R. 89
Stoney Ginger Beer 29
strategic alliances 104–105
Strategic Press Development Fund, France 72
structural changes in the economy 179–180
succession planning: resources sector 158, 160; revival of declining small businesses 50, 51
Sugar Tax 27, 32
Sunshine Coast Daily 74
supply chains: Australia Post *106*, 107; Bundaberg Brewed Drinks 36; FTAs 6; Harvey Norman 139; macadamia industry 119, 121–123
sustainability practices: Australia Post 99–100, 109; Bundaberg Brewed Drinks 28–29; Central Highlands Healthcare 65; macadamia industry 124–125, 127, 128; Mount Buller 81
sustainable development: eco-innovations 20; Natural Evolution Foods 17
Sustainable Development Goals (SDGs) 99
sweet potato products 15, 22
SWOT analysis 101
Sydney Morning Herald 76

Taiwan: GDP growth 3; macadamia industry 122, 123, 128
Taleb, N. N. 113
tariffs 5–6; Chinese imports of Australian wine 37; macadamia industry 126, 129

tax avoidance 6
taxation: Australia Post 92; failed café case study 173; imports 144; small businesses 41, **43–44**, 57
technological determinism 70, 76
technology: Australia Post 92, 98–103, 106–108; Bundaberg Brewed Drinks 34, 35, 36; business context 2; Central Highlands Healthcare 62–63, 66; COVID-19 pandemic 7, 182; disruption 3; emerging economies 4; Harvey Norman 144, 146; macadamia industry 127; Natural Evolution Foods 11, 13–16, 18, 22–23; newspaper publishers 70–71, 72, 76; R&D 3; remote working 157; structural changes in the economy 180; *see also* information technology
Telecom Australia 92
telehealth 62–63, 66
Telstra 92, 98
Tesco 30
Thornton, S. 19
Tianjin, China 3
TNT 93, 101
top management team (TMT): Harvey Norman 139, 144–145; human resource management innovation 149, 150; revival of declining small businesses 45, 50–51, 55
tourism 113–114, 115–116; *see also* Mount Buller
trade liberalisation 6
Trahms, C. A. 45, 49
Transatlantic Trade and Investment Partnership (TTIP) 5
Trans-Pacific Partnership (TPP) 5
transparency 33, 156–157, 162, 167
Tropical North Queensland Innovation Award 14
Tru Blu Beverages Pty Ltd 27
Turkey 32
turnaround responses *see* revival of declining small businesses

Uber 3
United Arab Emirates 3
United Kingdom (UK): Bundaberg Brewed Drinks 25, 29–32; ginger beer **28**, 28, 29–32; Harvey Norman 133; newspaper publishers 69, 72; postal industry 97; Sugar Tax 27, 32
United Nations Sustainable Development Goals 99
United States of America (USA): Bundaberg Brewed Drinks 25, 26, 27, 34; Global Financial Crisis 171; macadamia industry 118, 119, 123, 124, 126, 128; newspaper publishers 69; Sugar Tax 27
University of Queensland 124, 181
UPS 93, 97, 101
urban population growth 2
US Postal Service 105

value networks, Australia Post 102–104
Van Buren, M. 143
Veblen, Thorstein 76
vegemite 37
Victorian Alpine Resorts Economic Contribution Study 83
Vieira, L. M. 20
visas 180

wages: COVID-19 assistance packages 145; failed café case study 170; Harvey Norman 145; postal industry 95, *96*; resources sector 151–152, 153, 158–159, 162
Waitrose 30
Warwick Daily News 73, 182
waste: circular economy 17; Natural Evolution Foods 11–12, 14–17, 19, 22–23
Watkins, Robert (Rob) and Krista 11–16, 19, 21–23
weather events *see* climate and weather events
WeChat 3
Weitzel, W. 44
WhatsApp 3
Whittaker's 37
winter sports industry 79–81, 89; climate change 79, 83, 85–87, 89; comparison of resort areas 81–83, **82**; COVID-19 pandemic 87–89; economic benefit to Victoria 83–84, **84**; investment 86, 87, **88**; visitation 80, 83, **84**, 84, 87–89
Woolworths 15, 105, 109
working from home 180, 182; Australia Post 108, 109; Harvey Norman 145, 146; *see also* remote working
World Trade Organization (WTO) 5

Young Farmer of the Year award 12, 22

Ziehlke, Lynne 125
Zoom 3, 36, 159

Taylor & Francis eBooks

www.taylorfrancis.com

A single destination for eBooks from Taylor & Francis with increased functionality and an improved user experience to meet the needs of our customers.

90,000+ eBooks of award-winning academic content in Humanities, Social Science, Science, Technology, Engineering, and Medical written by a global network of editors and authors.

TAYLOR & FRANCIS EBOOKS OFFERS:

- A streamlined experience for our library customers
- A single point of discovery for all of our eBook content
- Improved search and discovery of content at both book and chapter level

REQUEST A FREE TRIAL
support@taylorfrancis.com